SOCIAL IDENTITY

SECOND EDITION

Richard Jenkins

Routledge
Taylor & Francis Group

LONDON AND NEW YORK

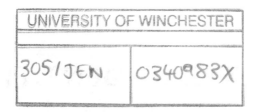
First published 2004
by Routledge
2 Park Square, Milton Park, Abingdon, Oxon, OX14 4RN

Simultaneously published in the USA and Canada
by Routledge
270 Madison Ave, New York, NY 10016

Reprinted 2005 (twice), 2006 (twice)

Routledge is an imprint of the Taylor & Francis Group, an informa business

© 2004 Richard Jenkins

Typeset in Garamond and Scala by
Keystroke, Jacaranda Lodge, Wolverhampton
Printed and bound in Great Britain by
TJ International Ltd, Padstow, Cornwall

British Library Cataloguing in Publication Data
A catalogue record for this book is available from the British Library

Library of Congress Cataloging in Publication Data
A catalog record for this book has been requested

ISBN10: 0–415–34096–9 (hbk)
ISBN10: 0–415–34097–7 (pbk)

ISBN13: 978–0–415–34096–0 (hbk)
ISBN13: 978–0–415–34097–7 (pbk)

No man is an Island, entire of it self; every man is a piece of the Continent, a part of the main; . . . any man's death diminishes me, because I am involved in Mankind; And therefore never send to know for whom the bell tolls; It tolls for thee.

John Donne

It is not the consciousness of men that determines their existence, but their social existence that determines their consciousness.

Karl Marx

CONTENTS

ACKNOWLEDGEMENTS

The first edition of this book (1996) was a long time in the making. Its intellectual thread began with my PhD, about the transition to adulthood in Belfast, continued through the subsequent research into racism in the West Midlands labour market, moved on to work in South Wales about the transition to adulthood in different contexts, made a useful detour to sniff around informal economic activity, and eventually turned into an interest in national identity in Denmark. Although the consistency of that thread was not necessarily obvious to others, I don't think I ever lost hold of it, no matter how gloomy or intimidating the maze.

As a result it is more difficult than usual – and it's *never* easy – adequately to acknowledge my debts. In one way or another all those with whom I have worked, whether as direct collaborators or interested colleagues, have influenced my thinking about the ideas that I present and explore in this book. My students have been particularly important, especially those on the 'Social Identity' course at Sheffield. Of my teachers and mentors, two in particular share most of the credit that is due. The late Milan Stuchlik started the ball rolling in the Department of Social Anthropology at Queen's, Belfast, and I have been trying to catch up with it ever since. John Rex, from the sidelines, has egged me on.

More directly, a particular text demands specific acknowledgements. Chris Rojek's initial encouragement was important. Since 1992 the intellectual support and inspiration supplied during regular visits to the anthropology departments at the Universities of Aarhus and Copenhagen, Denmark has been vital. Over the years, the Department of Sociology and Anthropology at the University of Wales Swansea and the Department of Sociological Studies at the University of Sheffield offered teaching contexts in which my disregard for the boundary between anthropology and sociology could survive. Sheffield has also, from time to time, given me the space necessary to think and write, for which I am most grateful.

At Swansea John Parker deserves a broader acknowledgement than his mentions in the footnotes. Conversations with Jess Madge were helpful in orienting me to the post-Piagetian model of infant socialisation. Similarly, Pia Christensen's contribution to my thinking about embodiment was important. All or part of versions of the first edition of the book were read and commented on by Stephanie Adams, Steve Ford, Janne Bleeg Jensen, Melanie Jones, Sharon Macdonald, and two anonymous referees. For this second edition, I owe a particular debt in this respect to Miles Hewstone and Allison James. They *all* deserve my gratitude. However, the usual disclaimer applies: I cannot take all the credit for the book's virtues, but its failings are my own. Finally, and as usual, Jenny Owen deserves acknowledgements of too many different kinds to list.

Richard Jenkins
Sheffield, October 2003

1

KNOWING WHO'S WHO

It is a cold Friday night, rainy and windy. You are dressed for dancing, not the weather. Finally you reach the head of the queue outside the club. The bouncer – or, as he prefers to be known, the doorman – raises his arm and admits your friend. He takes one look at you and demands proof of your age. All you have is money. That isn't enough (or, rather, you don't have enough).

You telephone the order line of a clothing catalogue to buy a new jacket. The young man who answers asks for your name, address, credit card number and expiry date, your customer reference number if you have one, establishing your status as someone to whom, in the absence of a face-to-face encounter, goods can be dispatched in confidence. And also, of course, putting you on the mailing list if you're not already there.

On a train, the stranger in the opposite seat smiles and excuses herself: she has noticed you reading last week's newspaper from a small town several hundred miles to the east. You explain that your mother posts it to you, so that you can keep up with the news from home. She recognised the newspaper because her husband is from your home town. You, it turns out, were at school with her sister-in-law. Before leaving the train she gives you her telephone number.

You hand your passport to the immigration officer behind her glass screen. She looks at your nationality, at where you were born. Your name. She checks your visa. These declare your legitimacy as a traveller, your desirability as an entrant. She looks at the photograph, she looks at you. She asks you the purpose of your visit. She stamps the passport and wishes you a pleasant stay. Already she is looking over your shoulder at the person behind you.

In everyday situations such as these, one's identity is called into question and established (or not). But identification is not always so routine or so trivial. It can shake the foundations of our lives.

You hand your passport to the immigration officer behind her glass screen. She looks at your nationality, at where you were born. Your name. She checks your visa. She looks at the photograph, she looks at you. She types something into her computer terminal. She asks you the purpose of your visit. During the conversation she checks again the screen beside her and presses a button under her desk, to alert airport security. Abruptly you find yourself being removed from the queue of incoming passengers by two male officers and led away to an interview room. Already she is dealing with the person behind you in the queue.

The annual company dinner. You have always gone alone, and always left alone, early. This year, however, you have someone to bring. What will your colleagues, the MD especially, think of her? There is a promotion coming up in February, and you know what they're like about that kind of thing. You take a deep breath, push open the glass door, and walk into the bar of the Thai restaurant. Your boss, smarmy Mark, comes across, hand out, glass of red in his hand: 'Susie, lovely to see you.' He turns slightly, there is a question in his eyes . . . Big deep breath: 'Mark, this is my partner, Alison.'

Belfast, 1973. The buses are off. Finding a public phone box that works you try for a taxi. Your usual number has nothing available: a bomb scare's tying up the traffic. Do you walk home? No, it's too far and it wouldn't be safe. You find what's left of the phone book and start dialling other taxi companies. Eventually you get one. Ten minutes later it comes and you settle in for the ride home. It doesn't take you long to realise that instead of heading up Divis Street to the Falls Road you're driving over the bridge into protestant East Belfast. The next afternoon, when you come round in hospital, a voice that you don't recognise is telling someone else that you were lucky to get off with a shot through the kneecap, some burns, and a bad beating.

The morning of your sixty-fifth birthday. As well as birthday cards and presents, it brings retirement, a pension instead of a salary, a concessionary public transport pass, and special rates every Tuesday at the hairdresser's. Beyond that, free medical prescriptions and invitations to the Senior

Citizens Club at something called 'the Day Centre' are intimations of dependence and disability. Death. It may be the same face you see in the bathroom mirror but you will no longer be *quite* the person that you were yesterday. Nor can you ever be again.

Who we are, or who are seen to be, matters enormously. Identification is not just a matter of the encounters and thresholds of individual lives, however. Although it always has implications, at the very least, for individual biographies, something else – collectivity and history – may also be at stake.

Gay or lesbian identity, for example, is not reducible to individuals in or out of the closet. Mass public occasions such as the Sydney Mardi Gras, or Gay Pride in London, are public affirmations that being gay or being lesbian can be collective identifications. For participants these occasions may – or, indeed, may not – affirm their individual sexual identities, but they are collective rituals, celebrations of identification and political mobilisation, before they are anything else.

Imagine a contested border region. It might be anywhere in the world. There are a range of ways to settle the issue: violence, a referendum, international arbitration. Whatever the means adopted, or imposed, the outcome will have consequences for people on both sides, depending on who they are. While some will accept it, some may not. Populations may move, towns and regions may be 'cleansed', genealogies may be rewritten. The boundaries of collectivity may be redrawn.

SIMILARITY AND DIFFERENCE

The scenarios above may be imagined but they are not imaginary: each is an illustration of how identity affects real human experience. It is the most mundane of things and it can be the most extraordinary. But what does it mean, to say that these situations all involve 'identity'? What do they have in common? How do we know who we are, and how do others identify us? How does our sense of ourselves as unique individuals square with the realisation that, always and everywhere, we share aspects of our identity with many others? How can we reconcile our sense of ourselves as consistently 'who we are' with the knowledge that we can be different things to different people and in different circumstances? To what extent is it possible to become someone, or something, other than who we now are? And is it possible to 'just be myself'?

This book sets out a sociological framework for thinking about identity and addressing questions such as these. The topic is particularly seductive because it brings the sociological imagination to bear on the mundane dramas, dreams and perplexities of everyday life. It is the best device that I know for bringing together C. Wright Mills's 'public issues' and 'private troubles' and making sense of each in terms of the other. To put this another way, 'identity', as a meta-concept that makes as much sense individually as collectively, is strategically significant for the structure–action debate in social theory.

The notion of identity applies to the entire universe of creatures, things and substances, as well as to humans, and its general meanings are worth considering. *The Oxford English Dictionary* offers a Latin root – *identitas*, from *idem*, 'the same' – and two basic meanings:

- the sameness of objects, as in A1 is identical to A2 but not to B1; and
- the consistency or continuity over time that is the basis for establishing and grasping the definiteness and distinctiveness of something.

From either angle, the notion of identity involves two criteria of comparison between persons or things: *similarity* and *difference*. Exploring further, the verb 'to identify' is a necessary accompaniment of identity. There is something active about identity that cannot be ignored: it isn't 'just there', it's not a 'thing', it must *always* be established. This adds two further items to our starter pack:

- to classify things or persons; and
- to associate oneself with, or attach oneself to, something or someone else (such as a friend, a sports team, or an ideology).

Each of these locates identity in practice: they are both things that people do. The latter also implies a degree of reflexivity.

We are now back in the realm of *social* identity. While this second edition retains the book's original title – marketing considerations will have their say – I prefer now, wherever possible, simply to talk about 'identity'. If my argument in this book is correct, all human identities are by definition *social* identities. Identifying ourselves or others is a matter of meaning, and meaning always involves interaction: agreement and disagreement, convention and innovation, communication and negotiation. To add the 'social' in this context is therefore somewhat redundant. In addition, since I have argued elsewhere that it's unhelpful to distinguish analytically between the 'social' and the 'cultural' (Jenkins 2002: 39–62), sticking with plain 'identity' prevents me from being seen to do so. So this book is about 'cultural identity', too.

Too much contemporary writing about identity treats it as some*thing* that simply *is*. This pays insufficient attention to how identity 'works' or 'is worked', to process and reflexivity, to the social construction of identity in interaction and institutionally. Understanding these processes is central to understanding identity. Indeed, identity can *only* be understood as process, as 'being' or 'becoming'. One's identity – one's identities, indeed, for who we are is always singular *and* plural – is never a final or settled matter. Not even death freezes the picture: identity or reputation can be reassessed, and some identities – sainthood or martyrdom, for example – can only be achieved beyond the grave.

As social scientists, therefore, keen to avoid reification, we should probably only ever talk about 'identification'. High-mindedness of that kind, however, might make talking to the rest of the world more difficult. It wouldn't be very elegant style either. 'Identity' contines to have its uses, therefore, as long as we remember that it always implies 'identification'. 'It' is *not* a 'thing'.

Fine, but what is it? For sociological purposes identification can be defined minimally as the ways in which individuals and collectivities are distinguished in their social relations with other individuals and collectivities. Identity is a matter of knowing who's who (without which we can't know what's what). It is the systematic establishment and signification, between individuals, between collectivities, and between individuals and collectivities, of relationships of similarity and difference. Taken – as they can only be – together, similarity and difference are the dynamic principles of identification, the heart of social life:

> the practical significance of men for one another . . . is determined by both similarities and differences among them. Similarity as fact or tendency is no less important than difference. In the most varied forms, both are the great principles of all internal and external development. In fact the cultural history of mankind can be conceived as the history of the struggles and conciliatory attempts between the two.
>
> (Simmel 1950: 30)

Identification is a game of 'playing the *vis-à-vis*' (Boon 1982: 26). Identity is our understanding of who we are and of who other people are, and, reciprocally, other people's understanding of themselves and of others (which includes us). The outcome of agreement and disagreement, at least in principle always negotiable, identity is not fixed.

This definition is somewhat at odds with much contemporary social theory that distinguishes sharply between identity and difference, the former meaning either similarity or identification *with* someone or something (e.g. Anthias 1998; Benhabib 1996; Taylor 1998; Woodward 1997). Writing about personhood, Harré's distinction between identity and individuality invokes a broadly similar distinction (1998; 2000: 284–6). There are, however, good reasons to question this approach. Leaving aside the established meanings of the word 'identity' discussed earlier – for meanings are always contestible – it misses the utter dependence, in formal logic and in everyday practice, of similarity and difference. Neither makes sense without the other and identity involves both. In addition, sociologically at least, this approach has tended to privilege difference as what *really* matters, underplaying in the process collectivity, community and solidarity (all of which deserve better).

WHO'S WHO (AND WHAT'S WHAT)

The human world is unimaginable without some means of knowing who others are and some sense of who we are. Since, unlike other primates, we don't rely on smell or non-verbals – although these aren't insignificant in identification during encounters – one of the first things that we do on meeting a stranger is attempt to identify them, to locate them on our 'mindscapes' (Zerubavel 1997). The information we rely upon includes embodiment, clothing, language, answers to questions, incidental or accidental disclosures of information, and information from third parties. We are not always successful, either: 'mistaken identity' is a common enough experience to be a staple of folktales and literature. Equally familiar is the theme of 'lost' or 'confused' identity: people who can't prove who they are, who appear not to know 'who they are', who are one thing one moment and something else the next, who are in the throes of 'identity crises'.

Situations such as these give, and have given, all humans occasional cause to reflect upon identity. We try to work out who strangers are even when merely observing them. We work at presenting ourselves so that others will work out who we are along the lines that we wish them to. We wonder whether so-and-so is doing *that* because of 'their identity'. And we talk. We talk about whether people are born gay or become gay because of their upbringing. About what it means to be 'grown up'. About the differences between the English and the Scots (or the Welsh, or the Irish). About the family who have just moved in round the corner: we shake our heads, what can you expect, they're from the wrong part of town? About 'Arabs', 'Muslims', 'rag heads' and 'terrorists'. We talk about identity all the time (although we may not always use the word itself).

Change, or its prospect, is particularly likely to provoke concerns about identity. The transformation of everyday life in the affluent west during the 1950s and 1960s, for example, occurred amid argument and conflict about gender, sexuality, generation, race, class, imperialism and patriotism. All of which speak very directly to the topic here. More recently in the United Kingdom, monetary union in Europe – and, indeed, every other aspect of the European Union, from decision-making in the Council of Ministers to the regulations governing sausage manufacture – conjures up the ghosts of centuries of strife with our continental neighbours and is interpreted as another attempt to undermine British national identity.

Levels of concern about identity may wax and wane, but, whether individually or collectively, we can't live routine lives as humans without identification, without knowing – and sometimes puzzling about – who we are and who others are. This is true no matter where we are, or what the local way of life or language. Without repertoires of identification we would not be able to relate to each other meaningfully or consistently. We would not have that vital sense of who's who and what's what. Without identity there could be no human world.

Which suggests the fundamental importance to sociology of understanding identity and its workings. Knowing who's who and what's what is as fundamental to the sociological enterprise as it is to everyday life. Apropos that enterprise, this book doesn't pretend to cover the complete spectrum of debate about identity. That would involve knowing much more than I do, and for that reason, if no other, some areas are absent. Literary criticism and theory, studies of sexuality, and lesbian and gay studies are only the most obvious. My word limit has also set some boundaries: I have not, for example, tried to present the rich historical and local diversity that characterises the everyday detail of human individual and collective identification. Finally, I have sidestepped much of the literature on postmodernism, and not only because it is gradually receding into obscurity. Most commentators on postmodernism are on a historicist mission by any other name, substituting a meta-narrative of fragmentation for the old story of progress. In the pursuit of such grand themes, the mundane is likely to be overlooked. My focus is firmly on the mundane: on how identification *works*, on the interactional constitution of identity.

The intellectual scope of this discussion is, therefore, unapologetically limited. My academic working life has been spent on the borders of social anthropology and sociology. These disciplines, with social psychology, provide the broadly sociological framework[1] of the argument that follows. Other disciplines will be raided on occasions, but this is essentially a sociological text.

2

A SIGN OF THE TIMES?

'Identity' became one of the unifying themes of social science during the 1990s, and shows no signs of going away. Everybody has *something* to say: anthropologists, geographers, historians, philosophers, political scientists, psychologists, sociologists. From debates about the modernity of self-identity to the postmodern and postcolonial fascination with difference, from feminist deconstructions of gendered social conventions to urgent attempts to understand the apparent resurgence of nationalism and ethnic politics, the field is crowded. Identity, it seems, is bound up with everything from political asylum to credit card theft. And the talk is about change, too: about new identities, the return of old ones, the transformation of existing ones. About shape-shifting, on the one hand, and the deep foundations of selfhood, on the other. About new politics of identity. In the words of Brubaker and Cooper:

> the term 'identity' is made to do a great deal of work. It is used to highlight non-instrumental modes of action; to designate same-ness across persons or sameness over time; to capture allegedly core, foundational aspects of selfhood; to deny that such core, foundational aspects exist; to highlight the processual, interactive development of solidarity and collective self-understanding; and to stress the fragmented quality of the contemporary experience of 'self', a self unstably patched together through shards of discourse and contingently 'activated' in differing contexts.
>
> (Brubaker and Cooper 2000: 8)

While I agree with much of their diagnosis, and sympathise with their impatience, I can't embrace Brubaker and Cooper's suggested cure, to discard the notion of 'identity' for social analytical purposes. If only because the genie is well and truly out of the bottle – 'identity' is already an established part of the sociological tool kit – this isn't going to work. More important, for reasons that I began to outline in Chapter 1, 'identity' and 'identification' are still essential concepts if we are to understand the human world. Let's explore that proposition further.

IMAGE AND POLITICS

One reason why 'identity' is here to stay in the medium term – because nothing in social science is eternal, after all – is that social scientists and other intellectuals have no monopoly on the notion. The advertising industry, for example, has long understood how to sell people more, and more expensive, stuff by selling them an identity: a 'new look', a 'make-over', a 'new me'. The diversity of identification has become part of the self-conscious stock in trade of advertising and marketing, in the identification of niche markets and categories of consumer and the careful negotiation of the myriad possibilities for consumer alienation and offence (Costa and Bamossy 1995). On the other hand, the appropriation of brand names and mass products for assertive and very specific identity projects is increasingly well documented (e.g. Molnár and Lamont 2002), as is the more general significance of consumption patterns for identification (Bourdieu 1984; Lamont and Fournier 1992). While anthropology suggests that identification, consumption and display have always been connected, what *may* be new – although I'm not wholly convinced – is our disenchanted awareness of what we're doing and self-conscious collusion with the sirens of the global market (even after we've read *No Logo*).

Moreover, the market in identities doesn't just involve buying new accessories. Some people seek their 'new me' in different marketplaces, in psychotherapy or spirituality. For others, the pilgrim's way leads to the beaches of Goa or the bright lights of the big city. For many of us, however, the pursuit of new or alternative identities never gets beyond our day-dreams. The routine stability and constancy of ordinary lives is something important that is often lost sight of amid all the talk about identity.

In international politics, to take another example, identity seems to have become a symbolic public good, the defence of which asserts a legitimacy that is beyond criticism or opposition. Reified into a sacred and holy apotheosis, 'identity' is something to which everyone has a *right*. It allows the pursuit of narrowly sectional interests to pass – covered by at least a fig leaf of sincerity – as a defence of the ineffable. It is a difficult card to trump (although, as ever, a different kind of common sense – *realpolitik*, power and business interests – still determines foreign policies).

Issues of identity have, what's more, infiltrated national political mainstreams. In an increasingly globalised world, politicians far from the extreme right seem to feel perfectly comfortable wrapped in the flag. On the actual left – such as it is at the moment – political parties in the capitalist social democracies spent the 1980s and beyond embracing 'identity politics', attempting to appeal to disadvantaged constituencies based on identities other than class. Gender is important in this respect and is also a basis for politics in its own right. For decades women all over the world have been questioning and confronting their established identities and striving to establish more equal and self-determined ways of being women. Indigenous peoples, too, have begun to identify themselves as political actors, distancing themselves from the metropolis, establishing new relations of difference and similarity within which to challenge unchecked tourism and the expropriation of environmental resources. Their national governments, in turn, are discovering that although the well-shod tourist's fascination with the downtrodden of the earth may be as shallow as their lifestyle holiday – the contemporary equivalent of the nineteenth-century European grand tour – it is precisely that which encourages them to spend their hard currency. Elsewhere, in the former state socialist countries of Eastern Europe, the politics of local identity continue to mushroom in the rubble of bureaucratic centralism. Identity, it seems, is the touchstone of the times.

MODERNITY AND IDENTITY

Much of the recent social science of identity resembles closely what the politicians and marketing people are saying. The urgency of some of the issues at stake means, for example, that *what* identity is – or, indeed, *that* it is and that it *matters* – is often taken for granted in analysing the local specifics of messy situations. Less excusable theoretically is the celebration of collective or individual *self*-identification and difference, or the presumption that what we buy is *necessarily* an expression of who we are.

The argument that discourses about identity are relatively new – perhaps even diagnostic of post- or late modernity – does, however, seem to be a speciality of social theorists (e.g. Benhabib 1996; Hall 1992; 1996; Seidman 1997). Relatively untroubled by the discipline imposed by systematic inquiry into the observable realities of the human world, this position isn't convincing. It's true that *how* we talk about 'who's who and what's what' is historically and culturally specific. It's true that the *volume* of discourse about identity has reached new magnitudes, if only because global noise and chatter about *everything* has increased with the population and the sophistication of communication technologies. But reflections upon identity are not a historical novelty.

An established sociological and psychological literature about identity goes back to the turn of the twentieth century and before: James, Cooley, Mead, Simmel come to mind immediately. In the present (post)modern hubbub this body of work has been somewhat neglected, but it remains fundamental to social theory and the sociology of identity. Going back further, Locke's *Essay Concerning Human Understanding*, for example, published in 1690, includes a chapter on 'Identity and Diversity'. Six hundred years before that, the same themes were important to Indian philosophers (Harré 2000: 64–6). And to pick an obvious literary source, when Shakespeare wrote 'All the world's a stage', in *As You Like It*, among other things he anticipated Goffman by three centuries. We sacrifice historical perspective if we neglect the variety of intellectual traditions that have reflected on identity: there is nothing intrinsically new about these issues (see also Williams 2000: 13–30).

Which is not to deny modern concerns about identity and identity-related issues, or *their* modernity. They reflect the uncertainty produced by dramatic changes: reorientations of work and family, class and status mobility, migration, medical and technological innovation, the redrawing of political borders. Our cognitive maps no longer fit the social landscape around us. We encounter people whose identities and natures are not clear to us. We may no longer even be sure about ourselves. The future no longer appears as predictable as it seems to have been for earlier generations.

But change – the confrontation of languages, traditions and ways of life; the transformation of divisions of labour; demographic flux; catastrophe and calamity; progress and social improvement – is not in any sense modern. It is arguably the norm in human experience. It isn't anachronistic, for example, to recognise 'crises of identity' in early modern witch-hunting or in the medieval persecution of heretics, Jews, lepers and homosexuals, or to contextualise these in contemporary change and upheaval (Moore 1987). Or in the almost perpetual motion of a city such as Wroclaw, in today's Poland – also known, between the eleventh and twentieth centuries, as Wrotizla, Vretslav, Presslaw and Breslau, and ruled by Poles, Czechs, Germans, Bohemians, Austrians, Prussians and then Germans again – to see struggles about identification: about who's who and what's what in that particular corner of central Europe (Davies and Moorhouse 2002).

The privacies of the person occupy a particular and important place in contemporary social science discourses about identity. 'Reflexive self-identity' is among the phenomena hailed as peculiarly and diagnostically modern by some social theorists, most notably Anthony Giddens. *Modernity and Self-Identity* (1991) expands upon his earlier critique of the notion of postmodernity (Giddens 1990) to take in the intimacies of selfhood and their apparent transformations at the end of the twentieth century. Giddens is concerned with the politicisation of the personal, the private and the intimate. He argues that self-identity is a distinctively modern project within which individuals can reflexively construct a personal narrative for themselves which allows them to understand themselves as in control of their lives and futures. Apparently, 'life politics' have emerged in the capitalist democracies to fill the vacuum left by the decline of the politics of class, and therapy and counselling are now among the characteristic – perhaps even the most distinctive – discourses of modernity (Giddens 1991: 33). An expression with its origins in the women's movement of the 1960s, 'the personal is the political' provides the subtext to Giddens's argument about our contemporary concern with identity.

That argument, predicated as it is upon definitions of rationality, reflexivity and self-identity that tie them to the modern era post-Weber and post-Freud (thus effectively finishing any argument before it begins), is *at least* an overstatement, revealing more about the conceits of western modernity, and its intellectual elite, than anything else. Where, for example, does it leave the many millions of people, in Europe and the United States, never mind anywhere else, who, for whatever reasons, do not spend much, or even any, time agonising over 'life narratives' and 'personal growth'? Who have other things – not better, please note, just *other* – to fret about? Are they outside the loop of the 'late modern age', stranded in a historical cul-de-sac?

Nor is it straining interpretive licence to see in religions of personal redemption thoughtful, *reflexive* responses to 'ontological insecurity' (Giddens 1991: 53). Salvation is as much a project of the self – although that word begs as many questions as it answers – as 'personal growth' or 'psychological integration' (or whatever). Ideologies of spiritual salvation seek to understand and identify the essentials and the meaning of individual conscious existence no less than ideologies of personal growth. Both offer a raft to cling to in the storms of life; in both the relationship between self-deception and self-knowledge is intimate. Saint Augustine's *Confessions*, for example, written about 1,600 years ago, is a testament to the possibilities for reforging the self – personal growth – offered as an example to others. Similarly, going back nearly another thousand years, one can understand Buddhism as a project for the reformation of selfhood (Carrithers 1985).

Our concerns about identity at the beginning of the twenty-first century are, of course, to a considerable extent specific to their moment, as are their contexts and the media in and through which they are expressed. There is something distinctive about where we are now, as there is something distinctive about every time and place. It would, for example, be foolish to suggest that the women's movement has not been a major historical development, and modern to boot. But there is nothing to gain from annexing notions such as selfhood, identity and reflexivity as definitively modern – didn't people know who they were, or think about it, before the twentieth century? – and some claims are simply too ponderous to carry their own weight. There is, for example, the well-known argument that the individual 'subject', having first appeared as a definitive and unique product of the European Enlightenment, has disappeared under conditions of postmodernity (e.g. Jameson 1991). At best, this rests upon a notion of subjectivity and agency that is too narrow, too trivial indeed, for sociological use. At worst, it takes the presumptions of modernity too much at their own, self-serving face value. In both of its major claims – at the dawn and the supposed dusk of modernity – it can and should be challenged empirically.

The facts of the matter aside, there are grounds for concern about the implications for social theory of these discourses about (post)modern identity. Brubaker and Cooper's disquiet has already been registered: identity 'is too ambiguous, too torn between "hard" and "soft" meanings, essentialist connotations and constructivist qualifiers' to be of any further use to sociology (2000: 2). Going further, it has been suggested that the ways in which identity is understood by Giddens and others[1] – a fundamental essence of individual selfhood: vital to personal well-being, on the one hand, evanescent, utterly constructed and situationally contingent, on the other – combine to produce incoherence and theoretical incapacity (Bendle 2002). Although both these critiques go too far, they are necessary and important antitheses to a self-sustaining body of argument whose authors have forgotten the fundamental importance to theory of systematic inquiry into the observable realities of the human world, increasingly (mis)taken the proper subject of social theory to be social theorists, and, one suspects, (mis)understood their own existential crises to be universal problems of the age.

So it is nothing new to be self-conscious about identity: about what it means to be human, what it means to be a particular kind of human, what it means to be an individual and a person, whether people are who and what they appear to be, and so on. It is nothing new to be uncertain about it from time to time, or to think that it matters. To suggest otherwise risks assigning most of human experience to a historical anteroom, waiting for modernity to turn the lights on, and reinvents ethnocentrism and historicism under the reassuring sign of postmodernism's break with both. What we need instead is a generic framework for understanding how identification works that will accommodate its roots in human nature as well as its construction and contingency, allowing us to get on with the sociological business of approaching all human experience on its own terms in order better to understand it. The rest of this book offers just such a framework.

3

UNDERSTANDING IDENTIFICATION

One of the assumptions that much social science has in common with the 'everyday thinking' of 'common sense' or 'common knowledge' is a radical distinction between the individual and the collective.[1] This means that *collective* identity and *individual* identity are typically understood as different kinds of phenomena, and the relationships between unique individuality and shared collectivity tend to be unexamined or treated as axiomatic. Much otherwise sophisticated sociological argument, for example, offers a 'black box' where there should be an attempt to understand identification processes. Even social psychology – such as 'social identity theory' (e.g. Hogg and Abrams 1988; Robinson 1996) or 'discourse theory' (e.g. Antaki and Widdicombe 1998; Potter 1996; Potter and Wetherell 1987) – which *does* look at process, typically focuses on individuals, treats 'personal' identification and 'social' identification as different psychological conditions or constructs, and understands groups in a coarse-grained and reified fashion. Something important is still taken for granted, something important still missed.

In this book I adopt another approach. This perspective, which is not dramatically new, argues that:

- with respect to identification, the individually unique and the collectively shared can be understood as similar in important respects;
- the individual and the collective are routinely entangled with each other;

- individual and collective identification only come into being within interaction;
- the processes by which each is produced and reproduced are analogous; and
- the theorisation of identification must therefore accommodate the individual and the collective in equal measure.

The most significant contrast between individual and collective identification in this model may be that the former emphasises difference and the latter similarity. This is only a matter of their respective *emphases*, however: each emerges out of the interplay of similarity and difference.

The differentiation of individual and collective identity is often underpinned by a further ontological assumption: that either individuals or collectivities are the more substantial or 'real'. Common sense and psychology – even at its most 'social' – both tend to privilege the individual. Sociologists (and social anthropologists) tend to the reverse. While some espouse methodological individualism – the view that the only acceptable *data* are statements about individuals and aggregates of individuals – and a few advocate ethnomethodology or rational actor theory at its most extreme, sociologists are unlikely to embrace the radical theoretical individualism of psychology (or economics).

This is not to say, however, that sociology is definitively collectivist while common knowledge is individualistic. Neither proposition is, in any straightforward sense, true. In the first place it depends on how one defines sociology. C. Wright Mills offers a view which still commands considerable support:

> The sociological imagination enables its possessor to understand the larger historical scene in terms of its meaning for the inner life and the external career of a variety of individuals . . . to grasp history and biography and the relations between the two within society . . . Perhaps the most fruitful distinction with which the sociological imagination works is between 'the personal troubles of milieu' and 'the public issues of social structure'.
>
> (Mills 1960: 5, 6, 8)

There is nothing collectivist about this: the individual is, in fact, placed at the heart of the enterprise (although not more so than the collective). What Mills calls 'society' – and I call the 'human world' (Jenkins 2002: 3–5) – is the field upon which the individual and the collective meet and meld. This view is an important foundation for the understanding of identity offered in this book.

Characterising common sense, or common knowledge, as individualistic raises different issues. Primarily, we must ask *whose* common sense or knowledge? Staying close to home, within 'western common sense' or 'western European common sense' there is enormous diversity: even within national borders – the United Kingdom or France, for example – the differences in everyday thinking are as remarkable as the similarities. Individualism, for example, is a broader and more heterodox church than suggested by the dominant western political ontology of liberalism. How, for example, should we characterise the distinctively Scandinavian attachment to corporatist social democracy *and* individualist egalitarianism? What about the core platform of Christianity, combining as it does communion and congregation with the pursuit of individual salvation? On the other side of the balance sheet, let's not forget that socialism is originally a distinctly European ideology. Expanding our horizons, and even more striking, a coarse-grained view ignores variation in time and space of understandings of the collective and the individual: what about the almost infinite plurality of 'non-western' common knowledges?

We may move closer to the intersubjective[2] realities of everyday life – and, indeed, everyday thinking – if we view the individualist viewpoint as a pragmatic interpretive framework which permits actors to construct a first line of sense and defence in a human world which, whatever else, is peopled by embodied individuals, of which we are each one, and with whom we each have to deal. We are all to some extent – and of necessity – pragmatic individualists in our dealings with others. As suggested by the quotation from Mills, above, *pragmatic individualism* is a prerequisite for the exercise of the sociological imagination rather than a barrier to it. It is also the only possible foundation for understanding identity.

The pragmatic individualism of this book is grounded in an understanding of the human world that I have developed elsewhere (Jenkins 1997: 56–8; 2002: 68–76). Leaning heavily on Erving Goffman and, to some extent, Anthony Giddens, I suggest that the world as constructed and experienced by humans can be best understood as three distinct 'orders':

- *the individual order* is the human world as made up of embodied individuals, and what-goes-on-in-their-heads;
- *the interaction order* is the human world as constituted in relationships between individuals, in what-goes-on-between-people; and
- *the institutional order* is the human world of pattern and organisation, of established-ways-of-doing-things.

This is a way of looking at a complex but unified phenomenon, the human world, and viewing the same observable realities – humans and their works – from different points of view, paying attention to different stuff: embodied individuals, interaction, and institutions, respectively. The three orders are simultaneous and occupy the same space, intersubjectively and physically. As may become apparent below, it is almost impossible to talk about one without at least implying the others. The notion of the 'order' both emphasises that the human world is ordered if not always orderly, and reminds us that this is a classificatory scheme, intended to further our understanding of the human world, and nothing more.

The proper sociological place for the concept of 'identity' is at the heart of our thinking about the relationships between concrete individual behaviour and the necessary abstraction of collectivity. As I have already suggested, this isn't a radical proposition and the model of identification that stems from it is, in most important respects, not new. The ideas of George Herbert Mead, Erving Goffman and Fredrik Barth have been particularly influential in shaping it: the line of intellectual kinship connecting them is the genealogy of this book. The work of many other authors has been significant – among others Karl Marx, Georg Simmel, Gilbert Ryle, Howard Becker, Peter Berger and Thomas Luckmann, Henri Tajfel, Anthony Cohen, Pierre Bourdieu, Anthony Giddens and Ian Hacking – but Mead, Goffman and Barth remain my inspirations.

THE INDIVIDUAL ORDER

If identification is a necessary prerequisite for human life as we understand it, the reverse is also true. Individual identity – embodied in selfhood – is not a meaningful proposition in isolation from the human world of other people. Individuals are unique and variable, but selfhood is thoroughly socially constructed: in the processes of primary and subsequent social-isation, and in the ongoing interaction during which individuals define and redefine themselves and others throughout their lives. This view derives from American pragmatism, via the seminal contributions of Cooley (1962; 1964) and Mead (1934). From their work, an understanding emerges of selfhood as an ongoing and, in practice simultaneous, synthesis of (internal) self-definition and the (external) definitions of oneself offered by others. This offers a template for the basic model, which informs my whole argument, of the *internal–external dialectic of identification* as the process whereby all identities – individual and collective – are constituted.

Mead distinguished the 'I' (the ongoing moment of unique individuality) from the 'me' (the internalised attitudes of significant others). Although this formulation requires considerable modification – and gets it in Chapter 5 – the general idea does not: while I argue for a unitary model of selfhood, that unity is a dialectical synthesis of internal and external definitions. Mead further insisted that self-consciousness, indeed cognition itself, can only be achieved by taking on or assuming the position of the other, in his terms a collective 'generalised other'. This is another idea which cannot be swallowed whole. However, and drawing also upon Ryle's philosophy, the view that 'mind' is processual, interactional – rather than radically and individually autonomous – and reciprocally implicated in identification, is central to the model which I outline here. In everyday terms, Mead suggests that we can't see ourselves at all without also seeing ourselves as other people see us. For him the collective reality of 'society' is no more than an extension of this basic theorem of identification.

Mead is equally clear that mind and selfhood are attributes of *embodied* individuals. The embodiment of identity is another thread in my argument. That human beings have bodies is among the most obvious things about us, as are the extensive communicative and non-utilitarian uses to which we put them. The human body is simultaneously a referent of individual continuity, an index of collective similarity and differentiation, and a canvas upon which identification can play. Identification in isolation from embodiment is unimaginable.

Individual identity formation has its roots in our earliest processes of socialisation. Recent post-Piagetian understandings of learning in infancy and childhood and the 'new' sociology and anthropology of childhood allow the development of cognition and the development of identification to be located side by side in primary socialisation. This further suggests that identities which are established early in life – selfhood, human-ness, gender and, under some circumstances, kinship and ethnicity – are *primary identities*, more robust and resilient to change in later life than other identities. Although change and mutability are fundamental to identification, some identities are more changeable and mutable than others. The primary identifications of selfhood, human-ness and gender, in addition to their deep-rooting in infancy and early childhood, are definitively embodied (as local understandings of kinship and ethnicity may be too). Where locally registered embodiment is a criterion of any identity, be it individual or collective, fluidity may be the exception rather than the rule.

THE INTERACTION ORDER

To return to the internal–external dialectic, what people think about us is no less significant than what we think about ourselves. It is not enough to assert an identity. That identity must also be validated (or not) by those with whom we have dealings. *Identity is never unilateral*. Hence the importance of what Goffman (1969) famously described as 'the presentation of self' during interaction. Although people have (some) control over the signals about themselves which they send to others, we are all at a disadvantage in that we cannot ensure either their 'correct' reception or interpretation, or know with certainty how they are received or interpreted. Hence the importance, too, of what Goffman calls 'impression management strategies' in the construction of identity. These dramatise the interface between *self-image* and *public image*. Impression management draws to our attention the performative aspects of identity and the fact that identification is a routine aspect of everyday life.

An important assumption made by Goffman (and, indeed, by Barth, about whom more below) is that individuals consciously pursue goals and interests. They seek to 'be' – and to be 'seen to be' – 'something' or 'somebody', to successfully assume particular identities. This raises two important questions. First, does a self-conscious decision-making model encourage a better understanding of human behaviour? Second, is this kind of choice-making with respect to identity peculiar to modern, industrialised societies? My answers, which underpin the entire argument, are a qualified 'yes' to the first question and an emphatic 'no' to the second.

Bourdieu (1977; 1990), another anthropologist heavily influenced by Goffman, offers a helpful perspective on these questions when he emphasises the improvisational quality of interaction. Improvisation is facilitated and encouraged by 'habitus', the domain of habit, which, in the presentation of self, operates neither consciously nor unconsciously, neither deliberately nor automatically. Although the notion of habitus may in some respects be problematic (Jenkins 2003: 74–84), it resonates loudly with my perspective on identity: habitus is simultaneously collective and individual, and definitively embodied.

Not only do we identify ourselves in the internal–external dialectic between self-image and public image, but we identify others and are identified by them in turn. One unfairly neglected account of this dialectic is offered by the labelling perspective in the sociology of deviance (e.g. Becker 1963; Matza 1969). It describes the interaction between (internal) self-definition and definition by others (externally) as a process of internalisation. Internalisation may occur if an individual is authoritatively labelled within an appropriate institutional setting. This model of internalisation isn't, however, sufficient. The capacity of authoritatively applied identification to constitute or influence individual *experience* affects whether or not individuals internalise the label(s) concerned. This is a matter of whose definition of the situation *counts* (put crudely, power). Identification by others has *consequences*. It is the capacity to generate those consequences and make them stick which matters. Labelling may also, of course, evoke resistance (which, no less than internalisation, is an 'identity effect' produced by labelling). Although the labelling perspective emerged from the study of deviance and control, the model works in other contexts – education and the labour market, for example – and for positive as well as negative labels.

THE INSTITUTIONAL ORDER

Moving on to more collective identities, Karl Marx distinguished between a 'class in itself' and 'a class for itself'. The first is unified only in the eye of the beholder, in that its members are believed to have something significant in common (in this case their relationship to the means of production). In the second, those individuals realise that they share a similar situation and define themselves accordingly as members of a collectivity. Appropriating the methodological distinction between groups and categories, a distinction can be made between a collectivity which identifies and defines itself (a group *for* itself) and a collectivity which is identified and defined by others (a category *in* itself).

To avoid reifying the 'reality' of collectivities, it makes sense to insist on the centrality of process: *group identification* and *categorisation*. Revisiting the internal–external dialectic further makes the point: group identification and categorisation can feed back upon each other, and are very likely to do so. Problematising the group–category distinction also underlines again the centrality of power, and therefore politics, in identity maintenance and change. Asserting, defending, imposing or resisting collective identification are all definitively political. In general, one of my core arguments is that the external or categorical dimensions of identity are not only indispensible but have been insufficiently recognised in social science accounts of identity.

Tajfel's social psychological work in the 1970s, as developed into 'social identity theory' and 'self categorisation theory' (Hogg and Abrams 1988; Robinson 1996), suggests that group identification and categorisation are generic processes – and real for individuals – in the human world, with collective identifications emerging in the context of 'external' *inter*group relations. This is also a reminder that distinctions between the individual, interaction and institutional orders are only heuristic: here we are, under the rubric of 'the institutional order', folding the argument back into individualist social psychology.

A model of collective identification that is similar to Tajfel's in many respects can be traced in the slightly earlier anthropological theories of

Barth (1969; 1981). Owing an explicit debt to Goffman, Barth offers a model of ethnic and other identities as somewhat fluid, situationally contingent, and the perpetual subject and object of negotiation. One of his key propositions is that it isn't enough to send a message about identity: that message must be accepted by significant others before an identity can be said to be 'taken on'. As a consequence, identifications are to be found and negotiated at their *boundaries*, in the encounter between internal and external. Staying with Barth, but drawing also upon Anthony Cohen's discussion of the symbolic construction of community (1985), group identification is characteristically constructed across the group boundary, in interaction with others. Boundaries are permeable, persisting despite the flow of personnel across them, and identity is constructed in transactions at and across the boundary. During these transactions a balance is struck between (internal) group identification and (external) categorisation by others.

Barth's distinction (1969) between 'boundary' and 'content' – the 'cultural stuff' which is supposed to characterise an ethnic group, for example – allows a wider distinction to be drawn between *nominal identity* and *virtual identity*: between the *name* and the *experience* of an identity. It is possible for individuals to share the same nominal identity and for that to mean very different things to them in practice, to have different consequences for their lives, or for them to 'do' or 'be' it differently. Nominal–virtual may be related to the group–category distinction but it isn't coterminous with it (not least because it can be applied to individual identification as well). It also reaffirms the importance of the consequences of identification, as in the discussion of labelling above.

The nominal–virtual distinction is important. The name can stay the same – 'X' – while what it means in everyday life to be an 'X' can change dramatically. Similarly, the experience may stay relatively stable while the name changes. Both can change. *Either* group identification or categorisation, or both at the same time, can contribute to the array of possibilities. Power and politics are unavoidable, again. To return to Marx, the transformation of a category into a group is a political process of mobilisation, which may be influenced from within and/or without. It is a change of virtual identity that may also become a nominal change. Nominally, the categorisation of people, by state agencies for example, may be subject to change and it may be resisted. It may also be part of a virtual change in their conditions of existence and quality of life. While the nominal and the virtual are analytically distinct, in the real human world they are everywhere chronically implicated in each other.

Institutions are among the more important contexts within which identification becomes consequential. Institutions are established patterns of practice, recognised as such by actors, which have force as 'the way things are done'. Institutionalised identities are distinctive due to their particular combination of the individual and the collective. Particularly relevant are those institutions which the sociological literature recognises as *organisations*. Organisations are organised and task-oriented collectivities: they are groups. They are also constituted as networks of differentiated membership positions which bestow specific individual identities upon their incumbents.

In addition, identity is bound up with *classification*. In order for persons to be classified, however, a classificatory lexicon must exist: positions and categories, for example. Since organisations – whether formal or informal – are made up, among other things, of positions and procedures for recruiting individuals to them, they are important vehicles of classification. The constitution and distribution of positions is the outcome of political relationships and struggles, within and without organisations. Institutional recruitment procedures, in allocating persons to those positions, authoritatively allocate particular kinds of identities to individuals, drawing upon wider typifications of identity to do so. This is one of the ways in which nominal and virtual identification are implicated in each other: the allocation of positions (names) is also the allocation of resources and penalties (consequences). Consistency in recruitment practices between organisations – in the labour market, for example – may contribute to the formation, maintenance and transformation of consistent collectivities, classes of persons characterised by similar life-chances and experiences.

Thus individual and collective identities are systematically produced, reproduced and implicated in each other. Following Foucault, Hacking (1990) argues that the classification of individuals is at the heart of modern, bureaucratically rational strategies of government and control (which is not a back-door admission of the distinctive modernity of discourses of identity, or reflexive identity itself). Identities exist and are acquired, claimed and allocated within power relations. Identification is something *over* which struggles take place and *with* which strategems are advanced – it is means and end in politics – and at stake is the classification of populations as well the classification of individuals.

THE INDIVIDUAL AND THE COLLECTIVE

So far, two basic threads run through my argument. First, identity is a practical accomplishment, a process. Second, individual and collective identities can be understood using a unified model of the dialectical interplay of processes of internal and external definition. To return to the model of the three 'orders', there is more at stake here, however, than a better understanding of identification. Perhaps the most persistent issue in social theory is the structure–action problem, most recently incarnated as the debate about 'structuration' (Parker 2000). From Marx to Weber to Parsons to Berger and Luckmann to Giddens to Bourdieu, broadly similar questions have been asked:

- How to bring together analytically the active lives and consciousnesses of individuals, the abstract impersonality of the institutional order, and the ebb and flow of historical time?
- How to bring public issues and personal troubles into the same frame?

As one of the rare concepts that make as much sense individually as collectively, identity is a strategic concept in broaching these questions:

- Although identities are necessarily attributes of embodied individuals, they are equally necessarily collectively constituted, sometimes at a high level of abstraction. In identification, the *collective* and the *individual* occupy the same space.
- If identity is conceptualised in terms of process, as identification at work and at play in the interaction order, the distinction between *structure* and *action* may be avoided.
- If those processes are conceptualised as a perpetual dialectic of two analytically (but only analytically) distinct moments – the internal and the external – then the opposition between the *objective* and the *subjective* may also be sidestepped.
- Since identity is bound up with shared repertoires of intentionality (such as morality) *and* interactional networks of constraint and possibility, it is an important concept in our understanding of action and its outcomes, both *intended* and *unintended*.
- The *institutional order* is, at least in part, a network of identities (positions) and of routinised practices for allocating positions (identities) to individuals.
- There is a direct relationship between the distribution of *resources and penalties* and identification: identity is both a criterion for distribution and is constituted in terms of patterns of distribution (means and end again).
- In the internal and external moments of identification a necessary connection is made between *domination and resistance* and identification.
- The *classification* of populations as a practice of state and other agencies is powerfully constitutive both of institutions and of the interactional experience of individuals.

This list is not offered as an exhaustive catalogue. It has the virtue, however, of moving the debate from the stratosphere of grand theory to the more oxygenated altitudes of what Merton (1957: 5–10) calls 'theories of the middle range'. The basic question becomes: how can we relate individuals and collectivities to each other so that neither is privileged, neither is reified or caricatured, and, above all, we are enabled to understand better the real human world?

THE INTERNAL AND THE EXTERNAL

At which point more needs to be said about the external–internal distinction. As with Mead's choice of 'I' and 'me' – one of the contexts in which the distinction first appeared, and first appeared to be problematic – this usage is unfortunate in some senses. There is a danger of reifying or objectifying a distinction that, in the interests of explanation and illustration, commits necessary violence to the complexities and subtleties of being. It should be understand metaphorically, and does not imply necessary sequence: first one, then the other. The expression 'moments of identification' is intended to suggest that in principle and in practice the 'external' and 'internal' may be simultaneous (and simultaneity is *very* difficult to write about, since sequence is one of the things that makes language make sense). In this dialectic the focus is firmly upon the synthesis.

Nor is it my intention to suggest a difference of kind. Your external definition of me is an inexorable part of my internal definition of myself – even if I only reject or resist it – and *vice versa*. Both processes are routine everyday practices, and neither is more significant than the other. At most, I am indicating different modes of mutual identification which proceed, not side by side, but in the same interactional space. While it may, for example, be possible and analytically necessary to distinguish different kinds of collectivities – groups and categories – in terms of the relative significance to each of internal or external moments of identification, this is only a matter of emphasis.

That identity is, so to speak, both interior and exterior is one reason why it's significant for the integration of the individual and the collective within social theory. So, too, is the centrality of *time* and *space* to identification, as already implied with respect to sequence and simultaneity (see also Jenkins 2001). The three dimensions of space, and their material coalescence into a 'sense of place', are implied by the interior–exterior metaphor. Identification is always from a point of *view*. For individuals this point of view is, in the first instance, the body. Individual identification is always embodied, albeit sometimes imaginatively, as in fiction or myth, or

Internet chat rooms. Collective identities are usually located within territories or regions, and these too can be imagined, as in diasporic myths of return or charts of organisational structure. In that bodies always occupy space, the individual and the collective are to some extent superimposed.

Philosophers have long understood that time is bound up with space in one's experience of self and others (Campbell 1994): space makes no sense outside of time. Apart from the inexorable *passage of time* during interaction, a sense of time is inherent within identification because of the *continuity* which, even if only logically, is entailed in a claim to, or an attribution of, identity. Continuity posits a meaningful past and a possible future, and, particularly with respect to identification, is part of the sense of order and predictability upon which the human world depends. We are back to knowing who's who and what's what. The past is a particularly important resource upon which to draw in interpreting the here and now and forecasting the future. Individually, 'the past' is memory; collectively, it is history (although individuals do have histories and it isn't absurd to talk about collective memory, even if it might be a potential reification). Neither, however, is necessarily 'real': both are human constructs and both are massively implicated in identification.[3] That they are imagined does not, however, mean that they are imaginary.

The argument summarised in this chapter relies heavily on the work of others and is not dramatically innovative. It combines perspectives – particularly from social anthropology, social psychology and sociology – which, as will occasionally become clear, sometimes frustrate me in their apparent mutual ignorance of each other. The goal is a synthesis that is greater than the sum of its parts, a theoretical space within which 'self' and 'society' can be understood as different abstractions from the same phenomenon, human behaviour and experience. I shall begin with the 'self'.

4

SELFHOOD AND MIND

What do we mean when we talk about 'the self'? *The Oxford English Dictionary* charts the word's known pedigree back more than a thousand years to Germanic roots. Four basic meanings emerge from several pages of usages and examples:

- the first indicates uniformity, as in the 'self-same', for example;
- the second, and most common, refers to individuality or the essence of a person or thing – herself, yourself, myself, itself, self-interest – simultaneously evoking consistency or 'internal' similarity over time and difference from external others;
- the third takes in introspection or reflexive action, as in 'self-doubt', 'self-confidence' and 'self-consciousness'; and
- finally there is a sense of independence and autonomous agency, as in 'self-improvement', 'self-propulsion' and 'she did it herself'.

Thus the meanings of the word 'self' parallel the general meanings of 'identity' discussed earlier: there are the core features of *similarity*, *difference*, *reflexivity* and *process*. This is no coincidence. It leads me to propose a definition of the self as an individual's reflexive sense of her or his own particular identity, constituted *vis-à-vis* others in terms of similarity and difference, without which she or he wouldn't know who they are and hence wouldn't be able to act.

SELFHOOD (AND PERSONHOOD)

The literature about the self[1] is so vast, and so varied, that I cannot pretend to survey it comprehensively. A theme which runs through much of it is the distinction between the *self* and the *person*. A long-standing conventional understanding of these notions distinguishes the private, internal self from the public, external person (e.g. Harré 1983; Mauss 1985). The self is the individual's private experience of herself or himself; the person is what appears publicly in and to the outside world.

Some distinction between the internal and the external is unavoidable. Not everything going on in our heads and hearts is obvious to others, nor is there always harmony between how we see ourselves and how others see us (or how we imagine they do). Since this is fundamental to the view of identity I am offering, we need some way of talking about it. However, an absolute distinction between 'inside' and 'outside' obscures that view. Against the well-established conventional distinction between 'self' and 'person', I want to insist that selfhood and personhood are completely and utterly implicated in each other.

Finding a metaphor for this simultaneity is difficult: 'different sides of the same coin' might catch it, describing them as eddies in the same stream is better. Selfhood/personhood are aspects of individual identification, and in each the internal and the external cohabit in an ongoing process of identification. The notion of the internal–external dialectic of identification attempts to communicate this. The internal and external aspects of this process can be regarded as simultaneous moments, implying temporality, process and materiality, but not necessarily sequence. One should not be seen as following the other (which isn't to say it can never happen). The word 'moment' is another metaphor, derived from applied mathematics: *moment* expresses the forces around a central point as combined functions of mass and distance. The central point is, if you like, the identity at issue, the synthesis of the external and internal. Mass and distance suggest the interactional factors which determine the strength of the identification process, whether internal or external.

It's also important to recognise that we often don't differentiate self and person in everyday speech. If I speak *personally* to you, for example, my claim to authenticity relies upon my implied selfhood. In general terms, in fact, the difference between selfhood and personality is not clear, a confusion which exists as much in psychology as in common sense. This might, as Mauss suggested (1985: 20), reflect a historical convergence of meanings in this respect in European culture: the public persona has increasingly been defined in terms of the psychological characteristics of the self.

However, an equally plausible reason why selfhood and personhood are difficult to distinguish might be that the 'internal' and the 'external' are, for each of us, inextricably entangled.

European intellectual traditions recognise two polar models of humanity, the 'autonomous' and the 'plastic' (Hollis 1977), each with its implicit model of the self. The autonomous self evokes reflexivity and independence. The emphasis is on the internal. Although this may be how we would prefer to see ourselves in the mirror, it is also an image of anxiety and uncertainty, of an existential world in which individual moral judgements derive from personal preference or feeling, rather than from external authority or the responsibilities of position. Resembling the fragmentation which Marx called alienation, and even more closely Durkheim's *anomie*, this has been characterised by Alasdair MacIntyre (1985: 31ff.) as the 'emotive self'.

At the other end of the spectrum, the plastic self is an epiphenomenon of collectivity, determined rather than determining. Here the emphasis is on the external. Structural–functionalism and structuralism, each drawing on Durkheim, are conventionally regarded as sociological exemplars of this theme (although Parsons or Lévi-Strauss read in their own words reveal more moderation in this respect than textbook summaries often suggest). This model of the self reaches its logical end in Althusser's argument – of which there are loud echoes in Foucault – that the 'autonomous subject' is an ideological notion which fools individuals into misunderstanding their own domination as self-willed. Therefore they 'freely' accept it: 'There are no subjects except by and for their subjection' (Althusser 1971: 182).

Images of autonomy and plasticity each contain more than a grain of truth. Each, just as obviously, is inadequate. There are as many good reasons for rejecting a model of selfhood defined in terms of individual interiority, autonomy and reflexivity, as for refusing to accept a view of the self as externally determined. The first suggests an essential self that is, at least in part, untouched by upbringing, knowing its own mind but little else. The second denies the reality of a 'creative' or 'authorial' self (Cohen 1994: 21–54), able to make up its own mind and to act. To borrow Dennis Wrong's famous expression (1961), where one is undersocialised, the other is oversocialised. Both are manifestly out of kilter with the observable realities of the human world and our own experience of our*selves*.

With respect to these themes, and before discussing them further, it should be pointed out that my account of selfhood – in this book's first edition – has been criticised for denying the interior subjectivity upon which individual authenticity depends. Craib, making a stark distinction between consistent 'personal identity' and contingent 'social identity', suggests that I ignore 'half the picture, that half which goes on "inside" the bearer of identity or identities, and the process of internal negotiation which this involves' (1998: 4). Vogler goes further: 'he [i.e. Jenkins] emphasises the external social dimension to a much greater extent than the individual dimension and omits the unconscious and emotional dimensions of identity entirely' (2000: 21–2).

I plead guilty to neglecting the unconscious. As I've argued elsewhere (2002: 78), the problem with 'the unconscious' is that it cannot be shown to exist. Although conscious rationality isn't the sum total of human 'mind' – we dream, we forget and remember stuff, our decision-making can be intuitive and elusive, we improvise as we go along, our emotions are powerful, control of what we are doing isn't always possible, and so on – the existence of a mental territory called '*the* unconscious' is epistemologically and ontologically problematic. It cannot simply be assumed. As a rhetorical device of psychotherapy 'the unconscious' may have its uses, but it isn't a usable sociological concept rooted in the observable realities of the human world.

Moving on to emotion, it didn't have an index entry in the first edition, but it wasn't omitted either. It's there, among other places, in the discussions of the affective power of primary identification (see Chapters 5 and 6, following) and ritual and symbolisation (Chapter 13). With respect to the interiority of individual selfhood, the entire point of the model of the internal–external dialectic of identification underpinning my understanding of identification is to avoid privileging either side of that relationship. I leave it to the reader to decide whether I manage that balancing act in what follows.

MINDS AND OTHER MINDS

That neither autonomy nor plasticity are convincing images of the exercise of rationality by thinking actors who share knowledge, meaning and morality with others suggests that, in order to come to terms with the self, we need to understand *mind* – consciousness and thinking – as well. Given that the mind is more *and* less than the brain, what is it? A sociological approach to this question suggests an answer that doesn't collapse into physiology, psychoanalysis or metaphysics, thus: the mind is the sum of our organised processes of consciousness, communication and decision-making. A model of this combination of perception, information handling, and intentionality – which, apropos Craib and Vogler, all involve emotion – is a prerequisite if we are to understand human agency, including identification.

For many people, mind and self are axiomatically synonymous. This appears to be reasonable: a self without a mind is unimaginable, and *vice versa*. However, such an equivalence of self and mind is deeply problematic. Does a damaged mind mean a damaged self? Do differing grades of intellectual competence have implications for selfhood? These are awkward questions to ask, let alone answer. They are at the heart of debates about the treatment of impaired foetuses or neonates, or the legal and personal status of people with learning difficulties. The issues they raise are ambiguous, delicate and profound. For the moment, suffice it to say that although mind and selfhood are difficult to contemplate in isolation of each other, they're not the same phenomenon.

Another pertinent difficulty is familiar to philosophers as the 'other minds' problem (Wisdom 1952): how can we know what is going on in someone else's mind, since we cannot observe or hear it? Hence, how can we understand someone else's selfhood? This is a mundane question, of a type which confronts us in everyday life, but it's also fundamental to social science epistemology. According to one answer, the only mental processes to which we can ever have access are our own. Reflecting upon these, all we can do is to assume that those of other humans are similar in their workings if not in their content. This view often entails a second presumption that there *is* something special upon which to reflect, which differs from – and is causally prior to – overt behaviour. Anthony Cohen – much as Craib and Vogler – adopts both positions, arguing for 'the primacy of the self'. Whether it be soul, spirit or mind, in this view every individual has, or is, a cloistered essence of selfhood: 'Selfhood rests on the essential privacy of meaning; in what else might it consist?' (Cohen 1994: 142).

Before attempting to answer Cohen's question, his argument, like those of Craib and Vogler, raises epistemological issues. For example, he describes his scepticism about the 'reasonable' assumption that uniformity of behaviour within a group indicates uniformity of thought, as 'purely intuitive' (1994: 89). The issue is not whether he's wrong: I'm in fact sure that he's right. Nor is it that he seems to have missed Wallace's convincing logical argument that 'cognitive non-sharing' is, in fact, a 'functional prerequisite' of collective organisation (1970: 24–38). No, the problem is that in *presupposing* the existence of a private self which has causal 'primacy' as a core of individual being, Cohen is led into metaphysical assertion rather than defensible argument. His position, which closely resembles Craib's, is inscrutable, and thus can be neither wrong nor right. The same is true, arguably to an even greater degree, of Vogler's assumption that 'the unconscious' exists.

Why are there epistemological difficulties with respect to the self and, by extension, the mind? Well, first, the 'other minds' problem is real. We cannot 'read' other people's minds. But this doesn't demand that we accept an interior–exterior model which identifies a domain of selfhood that is accessible only privately and uniquely to each individual, about which others can only intuit, at best. If that was true, everyday life would be very difficult indeed. How would we come to know other people at all, let alone get to know them well? Life is full of surprises, but it would be impossibly unpredictable if we couldn't know something – enough to be going on with – about the minds of others. And much sociological research would be in vain. So, perhaps the wisest thing to do where possible is to avoid, as incapable of resolution, ontological arguments about the nature of selfhood. Instead, making a simplifying assumption that there *is* a self – as defined at the beginning of this chapter[2] – I will ask, what can we know about it?

NETWORKS AND INTERACTIONS

Gilbert Ryle, in his robust critique of the Cartesian dualism of the mental and the physical, argues that an individual's understanding of herself is no different in kind from her understanding of others:

> The sorts of things that I can find out about myself are the same as the sorts of things that I can find out about other people, and the methods of finding them out are much the same. A residual difference in the supplies of the requisite data makes some differences in degree between what I can know about myself and what I can know about you, but these differences are not all in favour of self knowledge.
>
> (Ryle 1963: 149)

The data Ryle has in mind are visible behaviour, talk (whether silent to oneself, vocal to oneself, or vocal to others), and other communicative practices – such as writing – and their products. 'Unstudied talk', which is 'spontaneous, frank, and unprepared' (ibid.: 173), is particularly important. Our methods for deciding what we are about, and what others are about, Ryle describes as *observation* and *retrospection*.

For Ryle, introspection is implausible, requiring a capacity to do something and to think about doing it – thus to do two things – simultaneously. He uses this very particular definition of introspection to argue that actors possess no privileged way of knowing themselves, compared to their ways of knowing others. But he overstates the case about doing two things at once. The point is literally true. Just as no two physical 'things' can occupy the same space at the same time, no two words – whether uttered or thought – can issue from the same speaker simultaneously. But I can, for example, engage in a conversation while, during the same performative flow of time, reflecting on the conversation and the behaviour of all the parties to it (including myself). Although this is, strictly, *retro*spection, it can be understood as a species of introspection: my reflections will always be at least a micro-second behind the action, but interactionally they are contemporaneous with, and part of, their object. By this argument, retrospection isn't possible until the business of interaction is actually finished. If this is correct, introspection doesn't require privileged access: it is observing oneself rather than observing others.

Reflexivity, therefore, involves observation and retrospection, and is similar whether I am considering myself or others. Potentially I have different data available in each case. I may have more information about myself, including recollections of my talk with myself, and biographical data only I know. On the other hand, I cannot observe myself in *quite* the way that I can observe others. Ryle is correct: self-knowledge is not necessarily more accurate than our knowledge of others, and self-awareness does not entail 'privileged access' to the mind. Accepting this, we can begin to account for the common realisation that our understanding of ourselves is at *least* as imperfect as our understanding of others (something which Cohen, for example, doesn't sufficiently acknowledge).

A further possibility that Ryle doesn't consider is *projection*. To know what we are doing and who we are, we must have some idea of what we are going to or might do. Intentionality is thus an important aspect of mind (and therefore selfhood). But more than intentions are involved: planning involves drawing on direct and indirect experience, on theoretical reasoning and on the hunches of implicit practical logic, in the attempt to make the future more predictable. However, projection is concerned with more than reducing uncertainty. It is a human characteristic to look beyond the here and now, to locate oneself as the link between a past and a future (Clark 1992; Jenkins 2001). Thus it makes sense to include projection with retrospection and observation in the repertoire of reflexivity.

For Ryle, minds are not occult or secret: 'Overt intelligent performances are not clues to the workings of minds; they are those workings' (1963: 57). If the mind is conceived of as mental *processes*, then these are to be found 'out there' as much as 'in here'. This doesn't uncouple individual minds from embodied individuals: that would be absurd (and, anyway, individual persons are also 'out there'). But it does suggest that minds work as much *between* bodies as *within* them. Ryle's is a model of 'mind' – as well as '*the* mind' – which offers the prospect of a theoretical framework bringing together individuals and the collective human world without either being seen to determine the other.[3]

While this view doesn't sit easily with the presumptions of common sense, other writers agree with its basics. Bateson's 'ecology of mind' (1972) pictures the relationship between individual organism and environment as a cybernetic network within which information flows backwards and forwards: 'mind obviously does not stop with the skin' (Bateson 1991: 165). Bourdieu's notion of 'habitus' (1977: 72–95; 1990: 52–65) is also suggestive, and in the same way. Habitus is a corpus of dispositions, embodied in the individual, generative of practices in ongoing and improvisatory interactions in, and encounters with, 'social fields' of one kind or another. The key point is that individual habitus only 'works' in the context of a social field, which itself is a kind of collective habitus: the one seems to flow into and out of the other. Which is not *too* dissimilar to Wittgenstein's argument (1974) that for humans the 'outside world', rather than existing in the eye of the beholder or in objective reality, is a contingent product of our negotiated language games.

Drawing upon Wittgenstein, Harré and Gillett's notion of the 'discursive mind' is perhaps more straightforward. Rooted in what Harré (1979) calls the ethogenic revision of social psychology, with its emphasis on meaning and agency – and drawing, too, upon recent critiques of behaviourism's model of mental process as a 'black box', unavailable for inspection – Harré and Gillett understand 'mental life as a dynamic activity, engaged in by people, who are located in a range of interacting discourses and at certain positions in those discourses' (1994: 180). Mental processes are thus *always* interactional. Even more thoroughgoing is the mutualist perspective, rooted in the ideas of James, Dewey and Vygotsky, that argues that to talk about 'interrelations' is insufficient (Still and Good 1991).[4] Through the use of metaphors such as 'steeped and dyed in' – drawn from William James – and dialectical models of process, mutualism emphasises the utter perceptual and cognitive interdependence of human beings.

MIND, SELF AND G. H. MEAD

William James and John Dewey belong to the heterogeneous, largely American, pragmatist philosophical tradition. Pragmatism emphasises the purposive dimension of human behaviour, and derives meaning and criteria of judgement from behaviour's practical outcomes: 'the proof of the pudding is in the eating'. Sociologically, the key pragmatists are Cooley and Mead, and the direct sociological descendent of their arguments about mind and self is symbolic interactionism. Charles Horton Cooley uses the metaphor of an orchestra to emphasise that mind, the 'social mind', is an organic whole, though not necessarily one that is either 'made up' or in agreement. It is a system of which individuals are active parts: 'everything that I say or think is influenced by what others have said or thought, and, in one way or another, sends out an influence of its own in turn' (Cooley 1962: 4).

Writing in 1909, Cooley doesn't mention Durkheim. It would have been perfectly appropriate of him to do so. Each in their fashion flirts with metaphysical notions of the 'group mind' (Parsons 1968: 64), and each tends towards a consensual view of the human world. However, the difference between Cooley's 'social mind', and Durkheim's *conscience collective*, systematically discussed in 1893 in *De la division du travail social*, is each's starting point. Durkheim begins with the collective, Cooley with the individual. For Cooley, 'society really has no existence except in the individual's mind' (Mead 1934: 224fn.).

Although critical of Cooley, George Herbert Mead acknowledges his influence.[5] Describing his own position as 'social behaviorism', Mead begins with two related assumptions: that 'no sharp line can be drawn between individual psychology and social psychology' (1934: 1), and that interaction produces consciousness, not the other way around:

> the whole (society) is prior to the part (the individual), not the part to the whole; and the part is explained in terms of the whole, not the whole in terms of the part or parts . . . from the outside to the inside instead of from the inside to the outside, so to speak.
>
> (Mead 1934: 7, 8)

Mead argues that our perception of an environment of objects – the consciousness which creates meaning – depends upon being able to see *ourselves* as objects (a proposition which resonates psychoanalytically with Winnicott's theory of object-relations [1965] and Lacan's notion of the 'mirror stage' in human development [1977: 1–7]). The perceptual basis of cognition is an internal–external dialectic between mind and environment. Interactionally, consciousness emerges within the pre-linguistic 'conversation of gestures' with others, and in the basic other-oriented behaviour of taking up attitudes (which doesn't here mean 'values' or 'views') towards others.

However, the development of language, the symbolisation of that conversation of gestures, is the crucial step. Speech, says Mead, 'can react upon the speaking individual as it reacts upon the other . . . the individual can hear what he says and in hearing what he says is tending to respond as the other person responds' (1934: 69, 70). Thus an individual can adopt the attitude *of* the other as well as adopting an attitude *toward* the other.

The point made earlier, that I cannot observe myself as I can another, indicates the limitations of gesture and attitude without language. Mead argues that with language one can *hear* oneself in the same 'objective' way that one can hear another, and the situation is transformed: 'Out of language emerges the field of mind' (ibid.: 133). In language, reflexivity, which is for Mead the principle uniting 'mind, self and society', comes into its own:

> It is by means of reflexiveness – the turning-back of the experience upon himself – that the whole social process is thus brought into the experience of the individuals involved in it; it is by such means, which enable the individual to take the attitude of the other toward himself, that the individual is able consciously to adjust himself to that process, and to modify the resultant of that process in any given social act in terms of his adjustment to it. Reflexiveness, then, is the essential condition, within the social process, for the development of mind.
>
> (Mead 1934: 134)

Reflexive interaction doesn't just introduce the wider human world into the individual's interior world. Without language there is no distinctively human interior world. Without the stimulus of interaction with others there would be nothing to talk about or think. (The) mind is thus simultaneously 'internal' and 'external'.

Collins argues persuasively (1989: 15) that, although Mead's great contribution is to demonstrate the *possibility* of a sociology of mind, his theory is underdeveloped; that he overemphasises the impact of the collective on the individual, and like Durkheim (or, indeed, Cooley) 'slides into the assumption that society is unified'. Be that as it may, it is less easy to agree with Collins that Mead reduces consciousness to mere behaviour or reflex. In fact, Mead's insistence that mind emerges out of cooperative interaction is more reminiscent of Marx than Durkheim: 'language, like consciousness, only arises from the need, the necessity, of intercourse with other men' (Marx and Engels 1974: 51).[6] Mead offers us the prospect of placing the thinking of individuals at the centre of the human world without lapsing into either precious subjectivity or mechanical objectivity. Mental processes become neither wholly interior nor wholly exterior.

Cognition and consciousness may seem to be some distance from identity. An interactional view of (the) mind is, however, vital for an understanding of identification. The self is unimaginable without mental processes, and *vice versa*. Identity without selfhood is similarly implausible. Both mind and selfhood must be understood as embodied within the routine interaction of the human world, neither strictly individual nor strictly collective. To make safe the foundations of the account of identity offered here, mind and selfhood must be understandable within the internal–external dialectical model. The arguments of Ryle and Mead have provided perspectives that allow us to do that. Some of their further implications will be explored in the next chapter.

5

EMBODIED SELVES

Ian Burkitt calls 'the idea that there is a basic division between society and the individual . . . a nonsense' (1991: 189). If he's right – and on balance, depending on what he means by 'division', I think he is – why is it such plausible and popular nonsense, as attractive to social theorists as to more mundane folk-in-the-street? Are the concepts and issues involved in thinking about individuality and collectivity so obscure, and so *difficult*, that gross simplification is the only way to deal with them them? Perhaps. Leaving 'collectivity' to one side for discussion elsewhere, the previous chapter has left unresolved some important matters to do with individuality and selfhood.

THE PROBLEM OF 'I'

Gilbert Ryle describes 'I' as an 'index word', that locates what is being referred to with respect to the speaker. Like 'here' or 'now', it is always uttered from a point of view, and those points of view are always changing: spatially, over time, from individual to individual. There cannot be *an* 'I'; only my 'I', your 'I', her 'I', etc.

In everyday life, according to Ryle, people find this 'I' – selfhood – perplexing and 'systematically elusive' (1963: 178). Yesterday's self seems to be substantial and easy enough to account for and explain, but the self of the ongoing moment is fugitive, harder to pin down. This is his argument about introspection again: he argues that the one item of my behaviour about which any commentary of mine must necessarily be silent is itself (ibid.: 186). Self-reflexivity, for Ryle, is always *retro*spective: the 'I' that does something has to wait until later before it can be considered. 'I' cannot look at itself: 'I' can look at 'her' or 'you', but not at 'I'.

Ryle may be logically correct, but interactionally he is wrong. Whatever people do they do within or over *periods* of time – even if very short periods – not in successive nano-seconds. I can approach myself, look at myself and comment on myself in the present, which is a relatively stable time zone of the here-and-now (Jenkins 2001). I can, for example, tell someone over the phone that 'I'm sitting in the garden enjoying the sun'. I can stop in the middle of a very busy day and take stock of what I'm doing. I can say that 'I'm pissed off', and explain why. And so on: the present-tense first-person singular, 'I am', makes very straightforward sense.

Giddens, too, argues that 'I' – in his case when compared to 'me' – is specially problematic (1984: 43), and he is no more convincing. It is not clear why 'I' should be more elusive than other index words: you, here, there, now, then, etc. For all the perplexity which Giddens and Ryle accuse it of producing, 'I' is a much-spoken word that is relatively unproblematic in use: when I use it I know who I am referring to and so do you (as do I when you use it, and so on). It is testament to the ordinariness of 'I' that individual difficulty with the word's use may be taken to indicate cognitive or emotional disorder (Erikson 1968: 217).

So, what *is* the problem here? In rejecting the dualism of mind and body, Ryle argues that Mind and Matter are different, non-comparable *kinds* of things. While this allowed him to restructure the philosophy of mind, it prevented him from recognising the embodiment of mind and selfhood. He simply ruled the body out of court. Since the point of view of index words is *always* that of a speaker existing in time and space, and hence embodied, we may begin to appreciate why 'I' seemed so elusive to Ryle.

This centrality to selfhood of an embodied point of view (Burkitt 1994) is probably the major reason for the plausibility of the categorical distinction between the individual and the collective. Embodied individuals exist in common sense and experience in a way that collectivities do not (Jenkins 2002: 63–84). Hence the 'pragmatic individualism' discussed in Chapter 3: embodied individuals are the space–time coordinates of minds and selves and are thoroughly and reciprocally implicated in, and constitutive of, human relationships and the human world.

Cooley, writing in the first decade of the twentieth century, talks about the 'empirical self' (1964: 168): actual people who acknowledge their presence and their actions in the world. For Cooley, that empirical self always implies the presence of others. It is always an *interactional* self, similar to and different from others. Part of this is summed up in his image of the 'looking-glass self':

A self-idea of this sort seems to have three principal elements: the imagination of our appearance to the other person; the imagination of his judgment of that appearance, and some sort of self-feeling, such as pride or mortification . . . The thing that moves us to pride or shame is . . . the imagined effect of this reflection upon another's mind.

(Cooley 1964: 184)

To Cooley, this dimension of selfhood is fundamental to collective life: to the adjustment of self to others, the internalisation of collective norms, and the production of an ordered and orderly human world. It is particularly important, he suggested, in the early socialisation of children.

THE 'I' AND THE 'ME'

Cooley draws heavily on William James, and in turn he provides part of the inspiration for Mead's more systematic model of selfhood. However, Mead's interest in actual, embodied people – for him 'society' is objectively something more than an idea in the consciousness of individuals – leads him to criticise Cooley's models of selfhood and mind (Joas 1985: 111–12). Mead wants to establish a cognitive foundation for selfhood in the 'inter-nalized conversation of gestures . . . the origin and foundations of the self, like those of thinking, are social' (Mead 1934: 173). For Mead the self is more than 'the bare organization of social attitudes'; he characterises it as a *relationship* between 'I' and 'me' (concepts also derived from William James). Mead appears to be talking about 'selves' or a 'plural self' rather than 'the self':

The 'I' reacts to the self which arises through the taking of the attitudes of others. Through taking those attitudes we have introduced the 'me' and we react to it as an 'I' . . . The 'I' is the response of the organism to others: the 'me' is the organized set of attitudes of others which one himself assumes.

(Mead 1934: 174, 175)

The 'I' is the acting self: the 'ego' that moves 'into the future', the individual's often unpredictable answer to others, the custodian of initiative (ibid.: 177). The 'me' is the other side of the argument: it is what 'I' react against, the voice in part of others, the foil which gives form and substance to the 'I' (ibid.: 209). It might catch the spirit of the 'me' to call it the 'what me?'. Although it represents external control, Mead's 'me' is not a Freudian censor: the 'I' is capable of winning the argument. The 'me' exercises a moral, not a mechanical, imperative over the 'I'. Mead's self is not determined by the internalised voice of others to the same extent as Cooley's looking-glass self. Reflexivity, which is of the essence for Mead, involves a conversation with *oneself* (Blumer 1986: 62–4; Burkitt 1991: 38).

Mead and Ryle have something in common.[1] Mead's 'I' cannot be apprehended in the here and now, either: 'I cannot turn round quick enough to catch myself' (1934: 174). As soon as someone remembers her 'I' of a minute ago, it has become a 'me', something with which 'I' can only enter into dialogue. The 'I' is not directly available in experience. Here Mead is trying to reconcile the cumulative, organised, learned resources of common sense and common knowledge, which we draw upon in the ongoing production of our lives, with the evanescent immediacy of being in the world, which is perpetually in the present tense: 'the "me" is the individual as an object of consciousness, while the "I" is the individual as having consciousness' (Joas 1985: 83). Mead doesn't mean, however, to imply a 'split personality':

> The 'I' both calls out the 'me' and responds to it. Taken together they constitute a personality as it appears in social experience. The self is essentially a social process going on with these two distinguishable phases. If it did not have these two phases there would not be conscious responsibility, and there would be nothing novel in experience.
>
> (Mead 1934: 178)

Even so, the two are not on an equal footing: ideally, the 'me' is more in charge than the 'I'. It is the source of an integrated personality.

At this point, Mead hypothesises the existence of a 'generalized other', representing the organised community to which an individual belongs and against which she is poised and defined. Simply taking the attitude(s) of specific individual others – a looking-glass self – might produce a series of 'me's, rendering the self inherently unstable over time (the 'me' would thus be similar to the 'I'). A degree of personal consistency in the self can, therefore, only be assured by taking on consistent attitudes. Hence the 'me' also adopts the internalised voice of a generalised other. This differs from Durkheim's *conscience collective* or Cooley's 'social mind' in that it is the product of ongoing encounters between individuals within group relationships. Every person will, in principle, have their own generalised other; but every group member will, also in principle, have much in common with every other. Without the generalised other, the Meadian self is incomplete:

only in so far as he takes the attitudes of the organized social group to which he belongs toward the organized, co-operative social activity or set of such activities in which that group as such is engaged, does he develop a complete self . . . only by taking the attitude of the generalized other toward himself, in one or another of these ways, can he think at all; for only thus can thinking – or the internalised conversation of gestures which constitutes thinking – occur.

(Mead 1934: 155, 156)

Here we return to the origins of cognition in interaction. The generalised other is acquired early in childhood, it is the parent of mind and self (and its 'voice' is often literally a parent's). Although Mead doesn't say that 'society' is 'all in the mind', he insists that without the generalised other 'organized human society' (ibid.: 155) is impossible. Unless collectivity is *also* in the minds of its members – *as well* as 'out there' in actual people and their behaviour – there can be no universe of discourse, no meaningful human relationships, no human world. Since for Mead 'mind' is as much 'out there' as it is anywhere, it adds up to the same thing, from whichever direction you look at it.

In Mead's social theory, 'mind, self and society' are not different *kinds* of thing. 'Society' is relationships between individuals, and individual humans cannot exist outside those relationships. Without relationships human mind and selfhood would not exist. For Mead, selfhood is intrinsically interactional, emerging out of the reciprocal relationship between the individual dialogue in the mind between 'I' and 'me', on the one hand, and the individual's dialogue with others during interaction, on the other. 'Society' is a conversation between people; the mind is the internalisation of that conversation; the self lies within and between the two.

THE UNITY OF SELFHOOD

Giddens's remark, that 'the "I" appears in Mead's writings as the given core of agency, and its origins hence always remain obscure' (1984: 43), is representative of a standard criticism of Mead, to which there are several, related answers. To start with, questions about origins are of doubtful value: it isn't clear how one could ever answer fully a question of this kind. Rooting the self in cognition, Mead simply argues that human physiology entails the capacity for/of mind (1934: 226n). Given that capacity, mind and selfhood emerge from the conversation of gestures, from interaction. The 'I' is thus part of the response of our species-specific capacity for intelligence – 'the physiological mechanism of the human individual's central nervous

system' (ibid.: 255) – to the stimuli provided by other humans
by this token, an aspect of 'human nature': Mead nowhere sugg
mind and self are *only* constructs (Honneth and Joas 1988: 59–70
to meet Giddens's comment head on, the 'I' isn't the 'core of agency': the
dynamo of agency in Mead's model is the *relationship* between 'I' and 'me'.

Giddens's comments do, however, suggest that the the terms 'I' and
'me' – implying as they do a plural or multiplex self – are not straightforward. Despite these problems, to which I return below, Mead's account
of selfhood offers a basis for a general sociological theory of identification.
In particular, it encourages us to understand intimate processes of mind and
selfhood as an internal–external dialectic. Despite its discussion of 'society',
however, it isn't the basis for an adequate theory of the human world in
all of its collectivity. This point can be made in two ways. First, in a manner
which recalls Cooley, Mead sees 'society' as essentially consensual and
relatively simple: power and domination aren't recognised. In particular,
the 'generalized other' makes little allowance for institutionalised conflicts
or variations in common knowledge (Burkitt 1991: 52). 'Being able to see
the other person's view' held out to Mead the prospect of a defensible
collective rationality (or rational collectivity). Conflict, in this view, is
largely the product of poor communication.[2]

Which leads on to the second point. Meadian selfhood, rooted in
cognition, is cerebral and pragmatic. Mead dismisses Freudian psychoanalysis, for example, for focusing on 'the sexual life and self-assertion in
its violent form', which is outside 'the normal situation' (1934: 211).
Compared to Durkheim, for example, 'Mead has a flat, unidimensional
world. Utilitarian actions of individuals are primary; social interaction
enters merely as means to these ends' (Collins 1989: 14). Collins further
suggests that Mead overlooks the human drive to sociability. If we relate
to each other it is because it is in our natures to do so, we cannot do otherwise: 'sociality' is an adaptive feature of *homo sapiens sapiens* (Carrithers
1992). This criticism isn't wholly fair. As we have already seen, it's clear
that Mead understands the intersubjectivity on which his theory depends
to be part of the basic human repertoire: human nature. But it's also true
that there is little room for emotion, frivolity, passion, doubt or conflict in
Mead's world.

Mentioning emotion suggests a need to explore further the genesis in
interaction of intimate psychology and personality (Burkitt 1991; Giddens
1984: 41–109; Harré 1986). That is beyond the reach of this book. There
is, however, one related matter requiring attention: the apparent resemblance between Mead's 'I' and 'me', and Freud's 'ego' and 'superego' (Freud
1984: 351–401).[3] In particular, the superego, as the internalised parent(s)

and the internalised voice of external control, looks *very* like the 'me' and the 'generalized other'. And even when transactional analysis reconstituted psychoanalytic selfhood as a trio of ego states – parent, adult and child – the internalised parental voice remained (Berne 1968: 23–32). Freud, Mead and Berne, in their different ways, agree that selfhood is interactionally constructed within what I have called an internal–external dialectic of identification. They all attempt to integrate the internal regulation of autonomy and the external constraint of plasticity. However, they also share a serious shortcoming – touched upon during the discussion of 'the unconscious' in Chapter 4 – in their characterisation of selfhood as a system of different 'bits': in Freud modelled as zones or territories (which have frontiers), in Mead and Berne as entities (who have identities and hold conversations).

This is problematic because most of the time most people don't seem to experience themselves as an assembly of different bits, and particularly not as a plurality of entities. Perhaps the most important source of this consistency – in the eyes of ourselves and others – is, as Burkitt argues (1994), the embodiment of selfhood. Although over time and across situations we recognise conflicts and different possibilities within ourselves, these don't constitute a committee or a cast of characters. Consider, for example, the notion of the internal conversation (which is something very like Craib's internal negotiation, discussed in the previous chapter). Is it really a conversation? Probably not. I recognise the experience of 'talking to myself' and I don't confuse it with a conversation with some*body* else. Giddens is right to say (1984: 7–8) that talking about the self as if it's peopled by 'mini-actors' is unhelpful and unnecessary: talking about 'moral conscience' is, for example, a straightforward substitute for 'superego' (or the 'me' and the 'generalised other').

Dividing the self up into 'bits' loses sight of the fact that most humans most of the time live their lives as more-or-less unitary selves. Not everyone, however: when unity appears to be threatened or fragmented, serious personal disorder may be diagnosed by medical, religious or other specialists. If we are to acknowledge a continuum of differentiation between those who experience such states and 'most people most of the time' who do not,[4] we need a model of the self as routinely more-or-less unitary. A similar point can be simply made: although we can talk about someone 'being in two minds', there is no equivalent sensible remark about 'being in two selves'. To have two selves transgresses one of the roots of selfhood, a degree of individual consistency over time.

Perhaps the most fundamental objection to 'bits models' is that they are actually much too *simple*. To acknowledge the many facets of selfhood would require the proliferation of bits into potentially infinitely complex, and infinitely unmanageable and implausible, models: the committee of three would become a very unruly assembly indeed. By contrast, adopting a unitary model allows us to recognise selfhood as simultaneously cognitive and emotional, a rich amalgam of knowledge and feelings, both individual and collective, and thoroughly interconnected and interdependent (it probably wouldn't 'work' otherwise). *Inter alia* this mixture includes:

- a sense of embodied being in the spatial world;
- emotions;
- sensual memory (tactile, visual, olefactory, etc.);
- creativity and imagination;
- tacit embodied competences; and
- retrievable information.

Some of this is easily reviewed and recalled, some not; some is in contradiction, some in agreement; some is imperative, some merely 'take it or leave it'; some is painful, some joyous; some is a matter of life or death, some just in-flight entertainment; some is frankly mysterious; and some is completely fantastic or imaginary. Individual selfhood encompasses all this and more. As a concept, selfhood symbolises the distinctive cognitive and emotional complexities of real people – ourselves *to* ourselves, no less than others – so as to imbue those complexities with the minimal sense of consistency that we expect and require in everyday interaction.

Retrospection offers access to things that we have done or said, that others have done or said, and so on. Some of what is going on we observe as it happens. Other material is not retrospective: knowledge about how things are or how they might be. Other stuff is simply difficult to get at. And there are many other possibilities. More complicated than a structure of a few bits, this model is also more plausible. It allows for disagreement and dissensus. It allows for variability: some people may, for example, have a rich vein of material deriving from their parents, others may not. For some who do, the parental stuff may be very controlling, for others not. Etcetera.

A final problem with 'bits models' is their tendency to reduce process to structure. Mead, Freud and Berne might each argue that selfhood is dynamic, but when they draw maps of the self or people it with characters – even if only metaphorically – misplaced concreteness is added to the problems described above. This makes it even more difficult to place selfhood in interactional context. Although Mead, for example, consistently writes about selfhood as constructed within an intersubjective external world, his manner of talking about it makes that image difficult to hold. Despite Mead's protestations to the contrary, the human world for the Meadian self often appears to be internalised, condensed into a 'generalized other', part of the structure of the self rather than actually 'out there'.

EMBODIED SELVES

So then, what about the apparently elusive 'I'? If Ryle and Mead can't turn round in time to catch their 'I', it is because they *are* it. The self is a unifying point of view, and that point of view is always *here*. Thus, so am 'I': always here. When I reflect on myself I am not reflecting on someone – a 'me' – 'over there'. If I say, for example, 'That's just me, that is', I am either reflecting on myself *here*, which is also *now*, or I am reflecting on myself *then* (which could have been *here*, or in a range of *theres*). I am a complex character, capable of realising myself in different ways in different contexts, but I am me (and *vice versa*), and I am here, the centre of my own compass.

Where 'here' is requires further consideration, however. It is embodied, certainly. Selves without bodies don't make much sense in human terms. Ghosts or spirits, if we recognise them as human, once had bodies; even the disembodied world of cyberspace depends, in the not-so-final resort, on bodies in front of computer screens (Hakken 1999: 69–92). We reach out with our selves, and others reach out to us. The self participates in an environment of others; to recall Bateson, like mind selfhood does not stop at the skin. But it always *begins* – literally or figuratively – from the body. There is nowhere else to begin.

'Here' is not, however, limited to the spot which my body presently occupies. When, for example, a large number of people arrange to gather in a big room, it makes sense to ask, 'Is everybody here?' Thus there are various 'here's, depending on context. 'Here' from the point of view of an assembled group, and its individual members, is not the same as 'here' from the point of view of an individual performing solo. 'Here' can be a spot or a territory, as indeed can 'there' (a similar point to my earlier argument about the 'present': the here-and-now as a zone rather than an instant). As with all index words, point of view is crucial. Each individual is the embodied centre of a universe of self-and-others, the locus of perpetual internal–external comings and goings, transactional inputs and outputs, some of which are incorporated into the sense of selfhood and some of which are not.

Selfhood is constitutive of our sense of who and where we are, which also implies some sense of what we are doing. But the reciprocal entailment of mind and selfhood is more than logical. 'The mind' and 'the self' are different ways of referring to the same phenomenon, the embodied and developing point of view of the human individual, living with other human individuals (cf. Lakoff and Johnson 1999). While we distinguish cognition (mind) from emotion (selfhood), we also recognise their coexistence and relationships – it isn't easy to capture the simultaneity I am aiming for here – in the embodied point of view: it makes sense when we speak of our 'feelings' clouding our 'reason'. 'The mind' and 'the self' may not be the same thing, but they are ways of *talking* about the same thing.

Common knowledge and shared symbols – 'culture' – constitute mind and selfhood. Exploring this point illuminates the difference between the two: mind is more universalistic or collective than selfhood. Selves are interactional, but they are by definition individual. Mind is something else. It makes as much sense to talk of individual minds as of individual selves, but the ability to talk about 'mind', without the definite article, is telling. 'Mind' is not just 'cultural': in some senses it *is* 'culture'. We can be 'of one mind', but it makes no sense to say that 'we are of one self'.[5]

This all suggests that (the) mind and the self are not 'things' or 'objects', other than grammatically: they are processes. The mind and the self are perpetually in motion, even if it sometimes appears to be slow motion. They are perpetually in a state of 'becoming', even if what becomes is similar to what has been.

INDIVIDUALITY

To insist that minds and selves, whatever else they might be, are attributes of individuals is not to accept the 'primacy of the self' (Cohen 1994; Craib 1998; Vogler 2000). Selves and minds are *not* definitively private essences of individuals, ultimately causally prior to their behaviour. In what people do and say we witness minds and selves at work. Minds and selves are thus knowable. Not perfectly knowable, but nothing is. How we 'know' ourselves is basically the same as how we 'know' others, depending upon observation, retrospection and projection.

Selfhood does have its own particular status, however, in that it can be thought of as a *primary* (or basic) identification. This is not an allusion to the psychoanalytic concept of the infant's primary identification with an other. It draws, rather, upon the useful basic distinction between primary and secondary socialisation (Berger and Luckmann 1967: 149–57). Selfhood is arguably the earliest identification that humans develop, and the most robust (as well as the most vulnerable during its earliest formation). It can perhaps be understood as offering a template for all subsequent identities, a stem stock onto which they are grafted. During the initial emergence of self-recognition, the infant becomes aware of her presence as against others: her difference from and similarity to them. That she is one of them, but they are not her. The sense of self may be coloured with secure self-regard that reflects the regard of others. It may not. Her name enters into her identity. So do the names of other people and things, and her relationship to them. Subsequently, primary self-identification becomes elaborated in many ways: 'Mummy says I am a good girl', 'I hate Aunty Meg', 'I am bottom/top of the class', etc.

Selfhood is not the only identity which may be conceptualised as primary, in the sense of developing during primary socialisation and subsequently exhibiting great solidity. Gender is also best understood as a primary identity, organising the earliest experience and integrated into the individual sense of selfhood. Depending on local context, ethnicity may be, too (Jenkins 1997: 46–8). Mentioning gender and ethnicity in this context emphasises that primary identifications are neither fixed nor timeless. Identification is something that individuals do, it is a *process*. As decades of interactionist sociology has documented in detail, even the reproduction of the status quo requires perpetual work of one sort or another. What's more, primary identifications are only *resistant* to change, they're not set in concrete. Change is routine in the human world, occurring for all kinds of reasons, and selfhood, gender and ethnicity are in and of that world.

To characterise selfhood as a primary identity – perhaps even as *the* primary identity – doesn't imply that it is simply or only individual. Paying attention to others is at the heart of selfhood from the earliest moments. It is a species-specific trait:

> babies are born predisposed to learn about sounds and sights that are characteristic features of *people*. They are particularly attentive to shapes and patterns that are like faces and to sounds that fall in the frequency range of the female human voice. As babies they learn especially fast about stimuli that change in a way that is contingent upon their own behaviour.
>
> (Dunn 1988: 1)

The embodied point of view – mind and selfhood – emerges into, and within, an intersubjective human world of others and objects and the effects which the individual has upon them. Agency is central to selfhood and it is central to infancy.

Mind and selfhood, then, operate/exist within and *between* individuals. To focus on selfhood and self-identification, this is so in at least three senses.

First, individual human selfhood is initially realised *vis-à-vis* others: they are the necessary foils against which we come to know ourselves. The human developmental process is an interactive process and cannot be otherwise.

This process continues, second, throughout our lives, as our individual identities (and minds) adapt and change. Self-identification involves the ongoing to and fro of the internal–external dialectic. The individual presents herself to others in a particular way. That presentation is accepted (or not), becoming part of her identity in the eyes of others (or not). The responses of others to her presentation feed back to her. Reflexively, they become incorporated into her self-identity (or not). Which may modify the way she presents herself to others. And so on. As presented here, it appears simple, sequential and linear. It is in fact multiplex, simultaneous and often tortuous.

Third, the presentation and elaboration of self-identification draws upon a wide palette of accessories in the human world. These are often other people: family, sexual partners, children, friends, colleagues, etc. Who I have relationships with, and the nature of those relationships – who I identify with – contributes to who I am, and says something to others about me. What's more, other people can either validate who or what I claim to be, refute it, or attempt to float an alternative: power and authority are critical in determining whose definition counts. Nor are people the only resources that I can draw upon in self-identification: clothing, religious practice, house, residential location, music, car, occupation, pets. Things of all kinds can be put to use. The world, in this respect, seems to be our oyster.

The self is, therefore, altogether individual *and* intrinsically inter-actional. It arises and is maintained within the internal–external dialectic of identification. It draws upon the environment of people and things for its content. Even though it is the most individualised of identities – we might call it customised – selfhood is absolutely interactional. It depends for its ongoing security upon the validation of others, in its initial emergence and in the dialectic of continuing identification.

A unitary image of selfhood – rather than a model of the self as a collation of bits – doesn't imply a *simple* self. Quite the reverse: selfhood is complex and multifaceted, as is the lifelong process of self-identification, involving a range of others in a range of situations, and drawing upon a range of resources. Nor is a unitary self in complete charge of itself. In the first instance, the foundational experiences of early life are largely – although not completely – outside the infant's control. And they are extraordinarily consequential for later life. During that later life, during the ongoing dialectic of identification, the responses of others are, at best, only pre-dictable or manipulable to a degree. Nor is how we receive them and incorporate them into our self-identification likely to be within our full control. Everything that we know about individual psychology suggests that the early formation of selfhood – warm or cold, secure or insecure, rich in experience or poverty stricken, well fed or hungry – is enormously influential in equipping us with the resources required to respond to the categorisations of us offered or imposed by others.

Other constraints are grounded in embodiment. Selfhood is routinely entangled with identities that are *definitively* embodied, such as gender/sex, ethnicity/'race', or disability/impairment: the matter is infinitely more complicated than my attempt to deal with it via punctuation can communicate. Nor are the accessories of identification equally available to each individual. The world is not really *everyone*'s oyster. Various factors systematically influence access to the resources that are required to play this game: in any given context, some identities systematically enhance or diminish an individual's opportunities in this respect. The materiality of identification in this respect, and its stratified deprivation or affluence, cannot be underestimated.

In Chapter 3 I called my point of view 'pragmatic individualism'. As a sociological perspective this permits an engagement with the 'empirical selves' of real people acting in the world, who know what they are doing and who they are (although it doesn't follow that they know everything about what they are doing or who they are). As actual people they embody mind and selfhood as points of view located in space and time. As actual people they talk about themselves and others as 'persons'. But 'selves' and 'persons' don't fit together with any consistency. As I argued in the previous chapter, the two are not systematically distinguished in common sense: there is a loose equivalency, with the presumption that each or either word has a taken-for-granted and understood referent. Even where they are defined and differentiated – philosophically, for example – there is sufficient variety and lack of agreement, and so much conceptualisation by decree, that, when taken together with problems of translation between cultures and epochs, 'the risk of sheer incoherence is alarming' (Hollis 1985: 220).

So, as far as possible, I intend to avoid differentiating the *self* from the *person*. Instead I start from *unitary selfhood*, as the embodied point of view of the individual. It is the individual's reflexive sense of her own particular identity, constituted *vis-à-vis* others in terms of similarity and difference, without which she would not know who she was and hence would not be able to act. That particular identity, in this model, is always a to-ing and fro-ing of how she sees herself and how others see her. These represent opposite ends of a continuum, one her *self-image*, the other her *public image*. Each is constructed in terms of the other and in terms of her perceived similarity or difference to others. The difference is who is doing the perceiving, who is doing the constructing. This is the internal–external dialectic of individual identification.

And there are other issues about the choice of words. I have outlined two complementary understandings of the self: as the embodied point of view of each human individual in her or his context, and as a way of talking about the complex consistency – or the consistent complexity – of those human individuals. Each of these suggests that we should talk about *selfhood* rather than about *the self*. This usage minimises the pull towards reification implicit in '*the* self' and emphasises the processual character of selfhood. We are talking not about a 'thing', but about an aspect of the human condition.

The definite article must be retained in some circumstances, however. It makes sense, for example, to talk about the self or selves of a specific individual or individuals: *their* embodied point(s) of view. Nothing else will do if we are to remember that selfhood is an attribute of actual individuals, 'empirical selves' in Cooley's words. And indeed all identities must, at some point, refer to individuals if they are to have substance. Embodiment is not optional: just as all individual identities are inter-actional, so all identities attach or refer to individuals.

While some identities position individuals alongside other similarly identified individuals within collectivities, some identities differentiate individuals, *as* individuals, from each other. This distinction is crude and only analytical. Individuals differ from each other in their characteristic portfolios of collective identities, and the similarities of members of a collectivity typically presuppose their difference from the members of other collectivities. The interplay of similarity and difference is the logic of *all* identification, whether 'individual' or 'collective'. Allowing for these reservations, however, it remains useful to distinguish *individuality* from *collectivity*. The chapters immediately following focus upon identities which are, to differing degrees, and in different ways, individual.

6

ENTERING THE HUMAN WORLD

Any newborn human is the product of interactions that take place before birth. At least two people have to have had *something* to do with each other. There are family histories and a pre-existing context of emotion and relationships. There may be metaphysical and ethical debate about the status and identity of embryo and foetus. During pregnancy new identifications and relationships are constructed, tried out and worked into, particularly parenthood and particularly, perhaps, motherhood (Baker 1979; Smith 1991; 1994).

Nonetheless, birth, as the moment at which the embodied individual enters the human world, is a convenient point at which to begin here. Issues of identification attend every birth. Is the baby a boy or a girl? Who does he or she resemble? What is he or she to be called? There may be questions about paternity. There may be ritual initiation into the community concerned (baptism, circumcision, or a variety of other practices). Modern civil society requires the bureaucratic registration of name, place and time of birth, and antecedents, which may in turn establish the individual's claim to citizenship. In each of these cases, individual identification also locates the child within collectivities.

HUMAN-NESS

Some early questions of identification are, however, pointedly individual. The risks and uncertainties of pregnancy and birth, and the precariousness of life throughout most of human history, suggest that these must have been addressed by all people at all times. Perhaps the most pertinent is whether the baby is 'alright'. Depending on their severity and nature, perceived impairments can quickly raise doubts about the human person-hood of the child. Questions of individual human-ness are enormously consequential: although few, if any, mutual obligations are established on the grounds of fellow humanity, an attribution of 'non-human-ness' or 'sub-human-ness' has dramatic implications.

How human-ness is understood is locally and historically variable. Acceptable human-ness is attributed to individuals on the basis of explicit or implicit collectively defined criteria (Hirst and Woolley 1982). As a categorical problem, philosophers perceive it better than they can resolve it (Cockburn 1991). Modern medicine has rendered the issue more rather than less perplexing as fragile lives are increasingly maintained or prolonged. The question, 'Should the baby live?' is a big question, and no less so when it is implicit and unvoiced (Kuhse and Singer 1985; Lee and Morgan 1989; Singer 1994). On the other hand, modernity in the shape of National Socialist Germany's 'euthanasia' programme has also produced the most extensive and systematic attempt yet to kill those who fall short of acceptable human-ness (Burleigh 1994; Burleigh and Wippermann 1991: 136–67). Even then, however, when it might appear that the identification of the 'ab-human' was thoroughly routinised and collec-tivised, each decision required authoritative *individual* categorisation (in which it differed from the mass murder of the Jews and other peoples).

The question of whether a child should live does not always hinge on the individual attribution of flawed human-ness. It may be a response to environmental conditions: abandonment, infanticide or abortion in times of famine or other stress are well documented in the ethnographic and historical records (Williamson 1978). But even these practices are typically related to understandings of human-ness. Infanticide may be permitted at need if full human status – whether in terms of spirit, name or whatever – is understood as something children acquire, rather than possessing at birth.

There are also definitively collective identifications – 'race', for example – which may compromise human-ness in the eyes of others. At birth and in early infancy, however, the question of human-ness is posed individually. If selfhood is the primary identity of internal definition, human-ness is the primary identity of external definition. It is necessarily the work of others, with reference to perceived and interpreted bodily characteristics, to categorise individual neonates as acceptably human, or to decide the nature of their human-ness. More accurately, in the absence of evidence to the contrary, adequate individual human-ness is likely to be *assumed* at birth by significant adult others. Human-ness is largely taken for granted, and, once granted, human-ness is for most of us largely irrelevant thereafter. However, precisely because human-ness is axiomatic and vague it is at risk in the face of life's hardships. Subsequent factors such as perceived intellectual competence or acquired physical impairment may undermine it.

Human-ness and selfhood, as primary identities, are typically entailed in each other: there seems to be a close connection between perceptions of one and perceptions of the other. Anthropologist Robert F. Murphy, for example, in a moving account of his own progressive immobilisation by a spinal tumour describes profound disability as, in the eyes of others, 'a form of *liminality*' (a state of being betwixt and between), in which 'humanity is in doubt' (1990: 131):

> Alienation from others is thus a deprivation of social being, for it is within our bonds that the self is forged and maintained. This loss of self, however, is inherent in the social isolation of paralytics, who have furthermore become separated from their bodies by neural damage and from their former identities. Their plight is that they have become divided from others and riven within themselves.
>
> (Murphy: 227)

This relocation – not merely onto the margins of the human world but onto the margins of the human, a withdrawal of mutual recognition neither sought nor embraced by the individual concerned – is difficult to resist, even for adults equipped with resilient resources of selfhood. In this particular internal–external dialectic, others hold most of the cards. Human-ness is largely in the eye of the beholder. Murphy tells us of his vulnerability when other people neglected, or refused to continue to recognise, his full human-ness and individual selfhood. Others' definitions of the situation became so dominant as to carry the day. Thus as alienation from others feeds back upon self-perception and reflexivity, individuals become alienated from themselves and their sense of selfhood. Public image may become self-image. Our own sense of humanity, of who and what we are, is a hostage to the categorising judgements of others.

INFANTS, CHILDREN AND OTHERS

Birth inaugurates the process of individual initiation into the human world and the assumption of identities within it. While this process necessarily takes place from an embodied individual point of view, the human world is *always* a world of others, and during infancy the balance is in favour of the identificatory work done by those others. If Shotter's account (1974) can be accepted, an infant is not a being independent of its mother (or, presumably, other consistent carers). Shotter draws on Spitz to characterise the relationship between infant and carer as 'psychological symbiosis'. While this image acknowledges the infant's agency and predisposition to learn, it recognises the indispensible role of the other(s) in the infant's development of mind, selfhood and identity. For Shotter, 'making' a competent human infant is an intended project of the other(s).

This suggests that, to begin with, the symbiosis is neither symmetrical nor equal. Kaye, for example, reviewing the evidence in support of the notion of the 'mother–infant system', argues that, because the mother is in the first instance the locus of agency in the interaction, there is no system as such. Persons are not born, says Kaye, they are the creations of their parents:

> the temporal structure that eventually becomes a true social system will at first only have been created by the parent, making use of built in regularities in infant behavior rather than actual cooperation or communication. Another way of stating this is that evolution has produced infants who can fool their parents into treating them as more intelligent than they really are . . . it is precisely because parents play out this fiction that it eventually comes to be true: that the infant does become a person and an intelligent partner in intersubjective communication.
>
> (Kaye 1982: 53)

Kaye's interpretation relies on a strict notion of agency: because the infant is at first doing what seems to come naturally, her behaviour doesn't count. Two comments about this are necessary. First, it may be a naive observation, and obvious, but agency is integral to human nature – an evolutionary endowment – and much of it, whether in adulthood or childhood, is neither deliberate nor reflexive. Second, the evidence Kaye was surveying – evidence that has since grown (e.g. Mehler 1994) – can be interpreted otherwise:

> The mind of the infant is neither simple nor incoherent. They do not develop intentional integrity by the linking up of sensory–motor reflexes through conditioning, as the behaviourists said they did. They seem, rather, to be seeking to refine their reactions to particular events and formulate specialised skills within a coherent general ability to perceive and understand both physical objects and persons. They are born with

> several complementary forms of knowing, and they use these to develop
> experience of the particular world they are in, assisted by communicating.
>
> (Trevarthen 1987: 363)

The difference between these versions of early human development isn't total. They agree that human infants are utterly dependent, that they have the necessary instincts or reflexes – such as suckling – to ensure survival, that they are not blank slates, and that the contribution of others to their very early development is determinate. Much recent developmental psychology seems to see no paradox in a vision of active infants-in-their-own-right who require the work of others to realise their potential (see Lindesmith *et al.* 1999: 217–82). That vision is, in fact, pretty much the image of human nature that informs the account of identification offered here.

So, what is the place of identification in the processes by which the infant is 'routinely completed as a cognitive and social being' (Harré 1981: 98)? First, the infant recognises self and significant others (in the beginning, perhaps, significant *other*). Turn-taking is arguably the most basic – or even, recalling Mead's 'conversation of gestures', the *only* basic – interaction process (Goffman 1983: 7). To call it the atom of the human world may be no exaggeration. It provides the framework for attachment and mutuality of recognition. It is also the context within which language is acquired: recognising names, being able to ascribe them correctly, acquiring appropriate discursive forms. The capacity to make others respond bestows upon them significance, creating signifier and signified. Objects as well as persons fall into the identification process: their materiality and their uses, the practical possibilities that they afford (Gibson 1979; Winnicott 1965). Learning who she is, and her place in the world of others and objects, is an integral part of the infant's acquisition of language, and *vice versa*.

Identification is a two-way process between infant and caretaker, but in its early stages the exchange is dominated by incoming signals. Some of the earliest contributions to identification may, what's more, come from interactions that don't involve the infant, taking place away from her. Gendering, for example, often begins, unknown to the infant, from day one (or even before, now that the foetus can be sexed). In Britain, for example, naming aside, accessories such as clothing, toys and nursery colour scheme may be brought in to play, creating a gendered world that the infant encounters and takes for granted, and that structures the responses to her of others.

Gender is only the most obvious aspect of infant identity that is partly constructed during interactions between others. Being 'a grandchild' is another example, perhaps less momentous. Grandparents may open savings accounts for their grandchildren, attempt to influence this or that aspect of their upbringing, or revisit inheritance plans. They may vie with each other for position in the politics of the family. And in the process 'grandchildhood' is constructed as much during interactions between others – largely in the circle of parents and grandparents – as between grandparents and infant grandchildren (and in that process, of course, 'parenthood' and 'grandparenthood' also come into being).

Infants *very* rapidly become babies, however, and just as rapidly children. Incrementally, they enter into relationships with others that are increasingly autonomous of other relationships. They identify themselves as they identify others, and as they are themselves reciprocally identified. Dunn (1988) argues that self-efficacy develops in the child early in life, hand in glove with a concern about and with others. From at least as early as eighteen months, children exhibit an understanding of the world of self and others as a moral world in which actions have consequences; from about three years old they begin to show signs of interest in and understanding of minds, of their own mental states and those of others (see also Cicchetti and Beeghly 1990; Kagan and Lamb 1987).

There is a distinctively human pattern in this process, although specialists may dispute its detailed chronology, and local variation modifies it. Poole's overview of far-flung ethnographic and other evidence (1994: 847–52) suggests the following general sequence for the routine 'emergence of identity in childhood'.

- An individualised attachment to mothers and caretakers becomes apparent by seven to nine months.
- From twelve months onwards naming and categorisation emerges and is directed to an understanding of the human world.
- By the age of two basic conversational capacity is established.
- Thereafter the child's capacity to represent and act out everyday individual others and their practices in the abstract – 'in pretend' – grows in complexity.
- By early childhood (two to four years), the child's narratives and understandings of self and others indicate, 'the appearance of a more elaborated map of persons in an experientially expanding sense of community', entailing 'Self-identification of and with other persons through observation, differentiation, imitation and affiliation' (Poole 1994: 850).
- During the same period, gender becomes an important dimension of selfhood.

- By middle childhood, from five or six years, the child begins to assume a degree of interactional and moral responsibility for her actions, begins to understand the statuses she occupies, with their related roles, begins to acquire a public 'face' to control how she is perceived by others, and (ideally!) begins to do as she would be done by.
- As the child moves through middle childhood, towards adolescence, the peer group, often segregated by gender, begins to replace the family as the primary context within which identification occurs and develops.

It is necessary to question the late timing in this scheme of the child's attachment to mother or other carers, and the universality of phases such as 'early childhood', 'middle childhood' and 'adolescence'. However, viewed as a broad-brush impression rather than a technical drawing, Poole's account offers a useful ideal-typical model of some very general processes that draws comparatively upon a wider range of sources than most.[1]

The 'new' sociology and anthropology of childhood that coalesced during the 1990s (e.g. Corsaro 1997; James 1993; James *et al*. 1998; Jenks 1996) also has much to teach us about identification processes during childhood. Species-specific developmental patterns such as those summarised by Poole notwithstanding, the founding propositions of this revisionist approach are:

- that children and childhood are experienced and understood differently in different places and times, and
- that children should be understood, and approached by researchers, as active contributors to and makers of the human worlds of which they are members.

This is a matter of 'personifying children' (James 1993: 31), of treating them as conscious human persons possessing agency. Children are actors in their own right, not merely appendages of the adults in their lives, and there is no universal, objective category of 'childhood':

> Although clearly childhood can be seen as a permanent feature of any social structure, the particular social and cultural parameters which define and regulate . . . 'childhood' . . . are all temporally – that is generationally – situated. Any account of the unfolding of childhood in children's lives must therefore acknowledge the effects of such historical structuring.
>
> (James *et al*. 1998: 64)

although children may share in a common biology and follow a broadly similar developmental path, their social experiences and their relative competences as social actors must always be seen as contextualized, rather than determined, by the process of physiological and psychological change . . . Global paradigms, it is suggested, may over-standardize models of childhood as a particular segment of the life course by according priority to age and thus induce a determined and determining conformity which might underplay the impact of local social and environmental contexts on the everyday lives and experiences of children.

(Christensen and James 2000: 176)

'Childhood' is thus a matter of time, both historically and in the everyday lives of children: it is a matter of collective definition (by others) and individual becoming (on the part of children).

The implications of this approach for our understanding of identification are obvious. Accepting that there is an early imbalance in favour of 'external' moments in the internal–external dialectic of identification, and that young humans rarely have the cognitive, experiential or other resources available to older humans, there is no reason to imagine the post-infancy world of childhood as strikingly different to, or isolated from, the human world(s) experienced by adults. They are in large part the same world(s). Children actively construct their own identities – and, indeed, the identities of others – and identification *works* for children much as it does for adults. The everyday processes involved, rooted in the internal–external dialectic, are no different.

The new sociology and anthropology of childhood, in insisting that childhood is socially constructed, relative and relational, also reminds us that childhood is not a 'stand-alone' identification or state of being. Much as similarity and difference cannot make sense independently of each other, childhood and adulthood depend on each other for their meaning. Nor can either be understood outside of a more complex set of identifications and identificatory processes that make local collective sense out of, and order, the organically embodied changes of individual human ageing: the life course is among the most powerful institutionalised domains of identification (Hockey and James 2003) and among the most consequential in the lives of individuals.

GENDERED IDENTIFICATION

One of the developmental processes on which Poole focuses is the assumption of 'social personhood' (1994: 851). He defines personhood in contrast to selfhood, and much as discussed in Chapter 3: a public moral career with connotations of responsible agency and jural entitlements (ibid.: 842), which he sees as developing in middle childhood. Unfortunately, his version of the self–person distinction confuses institutional identification (jural entitlements) with individual cognitive and emotional development (responsible agency), and conflates an analytical category of 'the person' with local categorisations of agency and status. One reading of his account, for example, might suggest an equivalence between adulthood – as locally defined – and personhood, while another might question whether, within many local understandings of gender differentiation, women can be considered persons at all.

Poole's scheme is, however, a useful peg on which to hang the exploration of a number of general themes. For example, if, as already suggested, selfhood and human-ness are *the* primary identities *par excellence*, then gender is something similar. Gender differentiations, rooted in biological differences (Jenkins 2002: 119–29), are ubiquitous in the human world. Their specifics and content are locally variable, but that there *is* differentiation is not. Human infants are defined in terms of gender from their earliest appearance, the environment of infancy is structured in terms of gender, and children come early to an embodied identification of themselves as gendered (Damon and Hart 1988: 30–1).

It may be objected here that gender is a collective rather than an individual identity. It isn't that simple, however. While the biology of human sex differentiation has considerable generality, and some collective characteristics (generic male domination, for example), and gender, as the local coding of sex differences, is enormously significant in everyday life, no *general* principle of attachment, obligation or even mutual recognition is collectively established between actors on the basis of sex *or* gender. In any local context there may be, but it isn't universal (very far from it, indeed).

To introduce a distinction of which more will be made in subsequent chapters, gender is a *categorical* collective identification before it is a principle of *group* formation. In this it differs from kinship or ethnicity, which are in the first place – and by definition – principles of group identification. Furthermore, the gender of every individual must be established at birth, it isn't predictable from the local coordinates of birth, unlike kinship or ethnicity. One is not born into a gender in the same way, for example, that one is born into a family, a lineage, a community or an ethnie.

At which point it's necessary to qualify the argument further: despite the individuality of gender, all human communities and all local views of the world are massively organised in gender terms. This is a collective matter. Gender is one of the most consistent identificatory themes in human history, and one of the most pervasive classificatory principles – arguably the most pervasive – with massive consequences for the life-chances and experiences of whole categories of people.

Gender is thus simultaneously individual and collective in equal degree, and in this it may be distinctive. Although all human identities, individual or collective, are definitively interactional, where the individual emphasises difference, the collective is weighted towards similarity. Gender identities are fairly evenly balanced in this respect. Gender is a binary classificatory scheme, and the demographic distribution of the root male–female differentiation is approximately equal. Thus each main gender is the classificatory intersection of one basic relation of difference and one basic relation of similarity.

The internal–external dialectic of identification is also relevant. Gender as a category, no matter what else it may be, is always massively externally defined. This is so with respect to initial individual identification, and subsequent practices of identification. In the institutional constitution of the human world and its rewards and penalties, an individual's gender becomes interactionally real in large part because of their membership of a collective category. On the other hand, gender – rooted as it is in sex differences – is at the centre of the embodied point of view of selfhood and the internal moment of the dialectic of individual identification. Collectively, the sharing of similar life-experiences, which may be powerfully embodied, also allows gender to be a principle of group formation: this is the internal moment of collective identification. The twentieth-century women's movement can, for example, be understood as an attempt to transform individual identification based on categorical differentiation into collective group identification asserting shared similarity.

How do selfhood, human-ness and gender relate to each other? A sense of gender is typically powerfully incorporated into the embodied individual point of view of selfhood. Collective gender differentiation, on the other hand, may relate to local conceptions of human-ness, via gendered notions about 'human nature' or embodied models of the 'natural' or the 'normal'. For example, behaviour that is locally gender-inappropriate may be identified by others as 'un-natural', and the individual may perceive herself to be 'un-natural' too, or must struggle not to do so.

PRIMARY IDENTIFICATIONS

The model of an internal–external dialectic of identification fits with both Poole's account of child development and the recent renovation and expansion of the sociology and anthropology of childhood. During early-life experience, however, the external moment of that dialectic is necessarily the more significant. Very young humans are dependent: there is much that they must discover about the world and their place in it. All other things being equal, they are hard-wired to be voracious learners, and they must learn who's who and what's what. But if they do not learn this from others, they will never know. Children soon begin to exercise autonomy in this respect as in so many others, but it comes after, and only on the back of, a somewhat different early experience.

This suggests that identities that are established during infancy and childhood may be less flexible than identities which are acquired subsequently. There are a number of reasons for making this suggestion. On the face of things, identification is neither remorselessly permanent nor frivolously malleable. The most adamantine identity has some leeway in it, if only as a sense of possibility. Identities are flexible because the dialectic of identification is, in principle, never wholly closed. Given the uncertainty and unpredictability of life this is useful, even vital. Arising within and out of bilateral processes of mutual recognition which are often rooted in specific situations, identities are generally contingent, 'for the time being', and somewhat tolerant of inconsistency or contradiction.

But the more unilateral the internal–external traffic, the less negotiable the resultant identity is likely to be, the smaller the room for manoeuvre. Identifications entered into in early life are experienced as more authoritative than those acquired subsequently: at most, infants and very small children can only muster weak responses of internal (self-)definition to modify or reject them. Assumed during the most foundational learning period, they become part of the individual's axiomatic cognitive furniture: 'the way things are'. *Pace* Mead, this is all the more so given that children are learning to talk during this period, and language, and talk in particular, is central to identification (Antaki and Widdicombe 1998; Gumperz 1982). Very young humans lack the competence to counter successfully their identification by others. They have limited capacities to question or resist, even if they are disposed to. And they may not be: during and before the process of language acquisition the powerful human learning predisposition leaves the individual open to forceful and consequential definition by others. Further, inasmuch as gendered identity (for example) is incorporated into individual selfhood, a powerful set of mutual reinforcements, with change posing a threat to the security of selfhood, are likely to be set in place.

The security of selfhood has, of course, sources other than authoritative inculcation during early childhood. As Giddens has argued (1984: 50ff.; 1990: 92–100), individual ontological security – the common sense that all that is solid, including oneself, does *not* melt into air – relies upon routine and habit. This is arguably more so for children than for adults. Certainly infants and children are well known to resent the disruption of their routines: insisting upon routine may be among their earliest interventions in the human world. Further, the world of early childhood is often largely, if not totally, sheltered within an immediate domestic group. Routine is easily established, carers well known, and the world relatively simple. Under such circumstances, primary identities are acquired in ordered settings which the child experiences, and to some extent creates, as homogeneous and consistent. Minimal disruption may encourage the experience of primary identification as universal, globally independent of context and situation, providing the individual with a subsequent taken-for-granted 'thread of life', to borrow a phrase from Wollheim (1984).

This is, of course, an ideal-typical – even idealised – representation of early childhood.[2] None of it is inevitable: insecurity and inconsistency are to be expected. Not all parents and carers are or can be committed to their infants to the same degree. Interaction with baby, the all-important turn-taking, is perhaps as often neglected as not. The emotional climate of family life and kin networks is variable. Child-rearing practices vary enormously. For parents and carers, the demands of the adult world routinely conflict with the demands of childrearing. More dramatically, children are rarely insulated from the tempests of the outside world: when life is turned upside down, they are turned upside down too.

Secure consistency and relative calm in the formative years may, therefore, be as much the exception as the rule. But this doesn't mean that the human world is peopled by individuals with fragmentary or insecure senses of selfhood and identity. Rather, I am suggesting that although most people, most of the time, experience life from the embodied point of view of relatively unitary and consistent selfhood, they are no strangers to uncertainty and insecurity either. Usually we know who and where we are, but not always. And if on occasions our security is threatened (or worse), it need not mean our internal moment of identification is fragile or wavering. The human world can be unpredictable, challenging and unsupportive, and our bodies are vulnerable.

Even so, the primary identifications of selfhood and gender are much more robust than most other identities. Human-ness – a taken-for-granted assumption, ascribed by default – is different, but it can still be described as primary in that ascriptions of *compromised* human-ness are unforgivingly robust. What's more, although human-ness and gender may be distinct from selfhood, they are are acquired so early, are so consequential and are so definitively embodied, that they should be regarded as reciprocally entailed in selfhood.

Can any other identifications be called primary? One obvious candidate is kinship. The kin group is one obvious source of enduring individual primary identification. No matter when or where, one of the most important elements in individual identification, by self and others, is kinship (Harris 1990; Keesing 1975). Kin-group membership epitomises the collectivity of identity, locating individuals within a field that is independent of and beyond individually embodied points of view. Naming, the identification of individuals in terms of collective antecedents and contemporary affiliations, is central to kinship and is given substance by the rights and duties of kin-group membership. Kinship identity establishes relations of similarity with fellow kin in terms of descent; it differentiates the individual from non-kin and, in classificatory terms, other members of the descent group. Kinship may also establish equivalence – similarity – with non-kin: principles of exogamy and alliance relationships between groups identify potential marriage partners, ritual or exchange partners, political allies, and so on.

Looking at the internal–external dialectic, her individual name is among the earliest things a child learns. For most of us our name, for better or worse, is as it has ever been: there and part of us, we can't remember a time pre-name. Try imagining yourself by another name . . . it's not impossible (and people do change their names, or become called other names) but it isn't easy. From learning her own name follows a child's ability to name her parents, other significant kin, where she lives, etc. Thus kin-group membership – name and place – is likely to be significantly entailed in selfhood. The emotional charge on kin-relations is also significant. That kinship may be represented in terms of embodied family resemblance further encourages the incorporation of descent into self-identification. On the other hand, however, resemblance is in the eye of the beholder. And, certainly in childhood, our name isn't usually an identity which we bestow on ourselves. More generally, we should remember the old adage: unlike friends, one can't choose one's family.

Nor is kinship universally salient: in some local settings kinship is all, in others it has limited significance. It may be less significant within the immediate kin group (where it may be taken for granted) than in relationships outside it. Kin identification doesn't travel well, either. For example, outside the family itself my family membership only matters in the face-to-face local context from which it draws its relevance. Elsewhere, my family name ceases to be a multi-stranded identification *with* others, becoming instead a uni-dimensional means of differentiating me *from* others.

The other possibly primary identification is ethnicity. There is some debate about whether ethnicity is *primordial*, essential and unchanging, or *situational*, as manipulable as circumstances require or allow (Jenkins 1997: 44–8). The notion of primary identification opens up some middle ground for this debate. As a collective identity that may have a massive presence in the experience of individuals, ethnicity – including, for the moment, 'race' – is often an important and early dimension of self-identification. Individuals often learn frameworks for classifying themselves and others by ethnicity and 'race' during childhood, certainly by about ten years old.[3] The ideologies of collective descent that frequently underpin ethnicity imagine it as distinctively embodied. And embodiment, even if stereo-typical, is always individual and part of the point of view of selfhood. Although 'race' is likely to be more visible than ethnic differentiation based on behavioural cues, either may be established relatively early, albeit probably not as early as gender. Ethnicity may involve emotion and affect (Epstein 1978; Memmi 1990), suggesting that it can become significantly entailed in selfhood. Ethnicity, when it matters to people, *really* matters. The circumstances under which it matters are relevant, however. Ethnicity depends on similarity and difference rubbing up against each other collectively: 'us' and 'them'. Ethnic identification weaves together the fate of the individual with collective fate in a distinctive fashion, and it can be enormously consequential.

On the other hand, the research of Barth (1969) and others suggests that ethnicity can be *very* negotiable. Individuals may, under appropriate circumstances, change their ethnicity, and sometimes they do. Even the embodied categorisations of 'race' have their flexibilities: 'passing' is not unheard of and, more important, the definitions and significances of 'race' are historically and locally variable. Nor does ethnicity as an organising principle of interaction and relationships, or a presence in early experience, have the same salience everywhere. All of which suggests that ethnicity is *not* primordial. It *may* however – depending on the situation – be a primary identification (which need not deny it some situational flexibility).

Thus whether kinship or ethnicity are primary identifications is always a local question. Unlike human-ness, selfhood and gender, they are not *universal* primary identities. Kinship or ethnicity may be salient early in the individual experience of identification, they may be enormously con-sequential, they may be entailed in selfhood. That both involve embodied criteria of identification – family resemblance, physical stereotypes, 'race'

– is likely to reinforce this. But neither kinship nor ethnicity are necessarily primary individual identifications. Depending on local circumstance and individual history they may be more negotiable and flexible than humanness or gender.

THE 'OUTSIDE' WORLD

A gradual shift in the dynamics of the childhood dialectic of identification, towards increasingly bilateral relationships of mutuality and reciprocation, occurs sooner rather than later. Selfhood becomes more secure and consistent. Children become increasingly knowledgeable and competent actors. These changes are systematically entangled, and on each count the child develops greater resources with which to assert her internal moment of identification. She has a burgeoning, more confident and fuller sense of who she is. Infants soon become children, children eventually become adults.

There is more to it, however, than individual development or progress through local age-based identity categories. Although this will vary from place to place, she isn't very old before she starts to move in ever-widening networks. Increasingly she has to relate to other children, with whom interaction is more equitable and more of a contest. Families may have their politics, but the peer group is definitively political. Relationships with others become more negotiable and more negotiated (James 1993). And much less predictable. Other children need to know who she is. She needs to know who they are and what to expect of them. Who's who and what's what. Skills of self-presentation are acquired, and she learns to identify others on the basis of a range of cues. Reputation, public image in the eyes of peers, becomes important. If indeed it ever was, the regard of others is no longer unconditional. Hierarchy must be negotiated and status begins to matter. Friendship begins to be an affective domain of its own, distinct from kinship. Projective play – 'let's pretend' – provides opportunities for role-playing and the rehearsal of identities. And increasingly children cultivate the capacity to mobilise 'face' and 'front'. A sense of private selfhood begins to be important.

Before long the peer group competes with the domestic group for the child's attention. She also has more adults to deal with, and proportionately fewer of them are familiar. Increasingly she is a member of formal institutional settings. Negotiating a path through and round these ever more complex environments, she is increasingly required to be self-resourcing and resourceful and is expected to function autonomously to some extent. This entails the gradual assumption of more and more responsibility for her actions. One thing for which she may increasingly have to accept responsibility is her impact, acting in the part of the other, on the identification(s) of those with whom she interacts.

Most strikingly, every child has to learn to live with her public image. This may differ from her self-image, is not always within her control, and may vary from context to context. The internal–external dialectic of identification, the problematic relationship between how we see ourselves and how others see us, is now a central concern and theme of her life. Whether wholly consciously or not, identifications are increasingly entered into as projects, or resisted when they are imposed and unwelcome.

The face-to-face world of children very quickly comes to resemble the adult world in its strategies, its games, its stratification and its rules. It is, indeed, a model for the world of adulthood. This is the everyday world that Erving Goffman called the 'interaction order'. Goffman's work is one of the places where the next pieces of the jigsaw of identity will be found.

7

SELF-IMAGE AND PUBLIC IMAGE

Erving Goffman's work is approachable and subtle, combining sociology, social anthropology and social psychology in a manner that challenges petty disciplinarity. He is also among the most mundanely useful of writers. How many other social scientists can illuminate the full spectrum of our face-to-face encounters, from an evening in relaxed good company to the most formal of life-cycle rituals? He has no rivals in the sociological interpretation of everyday life. Even so, there are four established criticisms of his work:

- that, if not merely descriptive, it isn't a systematic body of theory;
- that it doesn't integrate the everyday world within 'social structure';
- that his analyses are too specific to the modern (American) human world to be generalisable; and
- that his actors are hollow shells, that he offers no account of the formation of selfhood and only a cynical account of motivation.

Responses to the first three are not vital here. For those who are interested, Collins (1988) and Giddens (1984: 68–73) offer discussions of the issues which are sympathetic to Goffman's project. The fourth criticism is, however, relevant.

SELFHOOD, MOTIVATION AND EVERYDAY LIFE

Hollis is representive of this strand of critique, arguing that, 'Goffman owes us a theory of self as subject . . . to sustain an active base for its social transactions . . . Notoriously the debt goes unpaid' (1977: 88). He goes on to say, somewhat contradictorily perhaps, that Goffman's actors are pure individualists, bent only on the public pursuit of purely private ends and interests (ibid.: 102–3). MacIntyre is one of Goffman's harshest critics in this respect:

> Goffman . . . has liquidated the self into its role-playing, arguing that the self is no more than 'a peg' on which the clothes of the role are hung . . . For Goffman, for whom the social world is all, the self is therefore nothing at all, it occupies no social space.
>
> (MacIntyre 1985: 32)

This, too, seems contradictory: if MacIntyre is correct, if Goffman's self is merely its role-playing, then that self, such as it is, can *only* be 'social'.

What does Goffman himself say? There are two interdependent themes running through his work, the better-known of which concerns *the routines and rituals of everyday interaction*. It can be summarised under four headings. First, there is the *embodiment* and *spatiality* of interaction. The individual has, and is, a physical presence in the world. The embodied actor is always, for Goffman, spatially situated: *vis-à-vis* others, and regionally, in terms of the local staging of interaction. The two main interaction regions are front-stage and back-stage, public and private (Goffman 1969: 109–40). The body, particularly the upper body and most particularly the face, is the interactional presence of selfhood. Goffman's unit of analysis is the embodied individual, and the embodied self has its territories, preserves of space which can be respected or violated (1971: 51–87). So while Goffman's self is embodied, its boundaries extend into interactional space.

Second, he uses two metaphors to understand everyday routines or rituals: interaction as a *performance or drama* (1969) – hence front-stage and back-stage – or as a *game* (1961; 1970). In each, interaction is cooperative, organised, ordered, rule-governed. However, it occurs in a world of nego- tiation and transaction which interactional routines enable and create: a universe in which implicit and explicit rules are resources rather than determinants of behaviour.

The variability and multiplexity of life and experience are summed up, third, in Goffman's concept of *framing* (1975). From the individual point of view, and in the institutional constitution of the human world, specific settings are 'frames' – each with characteristic meanings and rules – within which interaction is organised. Individuals experience life as a series of different sets or stages, organised formally or informally. While each individual may have different understandings of these settings, and of what's happening within them, the shared frame creates enough consistency and mutuality for interaction to proceed. Frames are bounded in space and time and in this sense substantial. Frame analysis is thus a compromise between the relativism of social constructionism, in which the 'definition of the situation' is all (but all there is), and a common-sensical epistemology which recognises that there is a 'real' world out there.

All of these merge, fourth, in Goffman's notion of *the interaction order* (1983): the face-to-face domain of dealings between embodied individuals. Remote dealings, over the phone or by letter, are not excluded, but the emphasis is on the physicality of co-presence. It is an orderly domain of activity, in which the individual and the collective become realised in each other. Although, in Goffman's own words, this is the terrain of 'micro-analysis', the notion of the interaction order may be regarded as his contribution to bridging the 'individual–collective' gap. The interaction order and 'social structure' are implicated in each other in a relationship of 'loose coupling' (1983: 11): each is entailed in the other, but neither determines the other.

One major problem with this framework is its vision of the human world as rule-governed, scripted or ritualised. Goffman himself glossed these possibilities as 'enabling conventions' (1983: 5), which is helpful, but the image of explicit and directed organisation lingers. A further problem is the implication that individual means–ends rational calculation is the wellspring of behaviour. Of course, much interaction is observant of rules or conventions, and means–end rationality is often important. But, *contra* rules or calculation, much of what people do is necessarily either habitual or improvisational. There is no scriptwriter – although there are repertoires – and rules can never be sufficiently flexible or comprehensive to deal adequately with the variability and unpredictability of life.

The importance of habit and habitualisation in human life is well known (e.g. Berger and Luckmann 1967: 70–85). In fact, habit provides the space within which rational decision-making operates: if we had to make a decision about everything, we'd never be able to make a decision about anything. Goffman's emphasis upon ritual, routines and frames indicates his awareness of this. Apropos *rules*, however, Goffman overstates the case. Bourdieu is on the right lines (1977; 1990), in theorising practical dispositions as embodied habit – habitus – and emphasising the improvisatory, non-rule governed nature of much of what we do. In many situations neither habit nor rules nor calculation offer a way ahead; so, necessarily, we improvise. Improvisation can, however, be reflexive, resembling rational calculation, or spontaneously unreflexive, in which case it looks more like habit. Improvisation may also pay attention to rules and conventions in the ad hocery of the moment. Habit, rule-observance, calculation and improvisation, as ways of doing things, are, at best, only analytically distinct. Things are a lot less tidy in every interaction.

IMPRESSION MANAGEMENT

The other important theme in Goffman's work is *identity*. Individuals negotiate their identities within the interaction order. Mobilising interactional competences within situational ('framed') routines, individuals present an image of themselves – of self – for acceptance by others. In my terms, this is the internal moment of the dialectic of identification with respect to public image. The external moment is the reception by others of that presentation: they can accept it or not. Individual identification emerges within the ongoing relationship between self-image and public image.

Goffman's work suggests that, interactionally speaking, the internal–external dialect of individual identification involves a number of elements. There are the arts of impression management: the interactional competences which 'send' particular identities to others and attempt to influence their reception. These include dramatic style and ability, idealisation (by which Goffman means individual identification with collectively defined roles), expressive control, misrepresentation and mystification. Many of these derive from early socialisation, and are routinised in embodied non-verbal communication in addition to language.

Interactional regions are resources for revealing and concealing particular identities. Back-stage one can, to some extent, be free of the anxieties of presentation, it is the domain of self-image rather than public image. Hence the idea that I can 'be myself' in private. I can rehearse the presentation of an identity in a backstage area before trying to carry it off in public. As a teenager, for example, I learned to play guitar in my bedroom, but I also practised something more awkward, 'being a guitarist'. Front-stage, work is required by performer and audience, to collude in the mutualities of identification. Under some circumstances audience tact is required if the performance is to 'come off' and the public image established in the setting in question.

Burns (1992: 270ff.) discerns two understandings of self-presentation in Goffman. In *The Presentation of Self in Everyday Life* (1969) selfhood lies in expressive performance: hence the metaphor of all the human world as a stage, and the criticisms of Hollis and MacIntyre. In *Frame Analysis* (1975), however, selfhood – as the thread of consistency from frame to frame – has become the source of the performance, sufficiently autonomous of context to be able, at need, to achieve distance from it. These visions of selfhood are complementary, not contradictory. Nor, arguably, is the second absent from *The Presentation of Self*: it is implicit in the discussion of discrepant roles (1969: 123–46), and clear in Goffman's distinction between the performed self-as-character, 'some kind of image, usually creditable, which the individual on stage and in character effectively induces others to hold in regard to him' (ibid.: 223), and the performer, 'a harried fabricator of impressions involved in the all-too-human task of staging a performance' (ibid.: 222). The individual as character is a public construct; the individual as performer is partly a psycho-biological creature and partly a product of the 'contingencies of staging performances' (ibid.: 224).

Apropos character in another sense, Hollis and MacIntyre are simply wrong: Goffman's individual is a moral creature, inhabiting a moral universe. Giddens correctly stresses (1984: 70) the emphasis in Goffman on interpersonal trust: on tact, collusion, interactional damage-limitation and repair. Goffman's actors want to appear creditable to others; they want (or need) to make a good impression. Thus most people most of the time extend to others the minimal interactional support which they require themselves if their own identity performances are to succeed (or, at least, not fail). Do as you would be done by seems to be the basic axiom. Thus the dialectic – a word which Goffman himself uses (1969: 220) – of identification has a moral dimension, rooted in reciprocity.

> when an individual projects a definition of the situation and thereby makes an implicit or explicit claim to be a person of a particular kind, he automatically exerts a moral demand upon the others, obliging them to value and treat him in the manner that persons of his kind have a right to expect. He also implicitly forgoes all claims to be things he does not appear to be and hence forgoes the treatment that would be appropriate for such individuals.
>
> (Goffman 1969: 11–12)

If this were all Goffman had to say, his would be a mildly utopian model of a world in which actors do their best to get on with each other in a relatively equitable fashion. Fortunately, he also knows that things do not always go smoothly.

LABELLING

In particular, Goffman recognises that identity can be 'spoiled'; that identification, particularly within institutions, can be heavily biased in favour of its external moment; and that identification is often a matter of imposition and resistance, claim and counterclaim, rather than a consensual process of mutuality and negotiation. Leaving institutional identification until later chapters, what does he mean by 'spoiled identity'?

The key text, *Stigma* (1968a) is arguably the least satisfactory of Goffman's books. Under the rubric of spoiled or stigmatised identity he includes a range of things – from having a colostomy, to being a criminal, to being a member of an ethnic minority – which don't have much in common, even at second or third glance. The book is concerned with how individuals manage discrepancies between their 'virtual social identity' – their appearance to others in interaction (often on the basis of superficial cues) – and the 'actual social identity' which closer inspection would reveal them to possess. Individuals with a discreditable actual identity want to be 'virtually normal': stigma is the gap between the virtual and the actual, and the shame which attaches – or which would attach – to its discovery by others. Stigmatisation is, moreover, a continuum of degree. We are all disreputable in some respects, and the information management skills required to control who knows about them, and to what degree, are routine items in our interactional repertoires.

In *Stigma*, Goffman also distinguishes between 'social identity' and 'personal identity'. Personal identity combines relatively consistent embodied uniqueness and a specifically individual set of facts, organised as a history or a biography. This is *not* reflexive selfhood: 'Social and personal identity are part, first of all, of other person's concerns and definitions regarding the individual whose identity is in question' (1968a: 129). These distinctions – social and personal, virtual and actual – are less rather than more helpful. Apropos the social and the personal, *all* human identities are, as I have already argued in Chapter 1, 'social' identities. What's more, Goffman's notion of personal identity relies heavily on the self–person distinction which I have been avoiding. Finally, the virtual–actual distinction is problematic in that the use of 'actual' implies that one is more 'real' than the other.

However, *Stigma* offers much that is useful. It emphasises the demands that others make of us on the basis of our public image. As a consequence, trajectories that are anything but those we would choose can be thrust upon us. Others don't just perceive our identity, they actively constitute it. And they do so not only in terms of naming or categorising, but in terms of how they respond to or treat us. In the dialectic of individual identification the external moment can be enormously consequential.

In *Stigma*, Goffman drew upon the labelling perspective in the sociology of deviance.[1] Intellectually, this is an offspring of Mead, on the one hand,

and Chicago sociologists such as W. I. Thomas and Everett Hughes, on the other. Beginning with the early work of Tannenbaum (1938), the labelling perspective was shaped into a coherent model by Becker (1963), Lemert (1972), Matza (1969) and others. Against the conventional view that social control was a reaction to deviance, the labelling school argued that social control necessarily produced deviance. This labelling theorem comes in three versions:

- rule-breaking is routine and endemic and only becomes deviance when it is authoritatively labelled as such;
- actors become deviants because they are so labelled; and
- rates of deviance are the product of the activities of social control agencies.

The classificatory logic of these arguments is unimpeachable. Compare, for example, Becker's view, that 'social groups create deviance by making the rules whose infraction constitutes deviance' (1963: 9), with Douglas's proposition, that 'Dirt is the by-product of the systematic ordering and classification of matter' (1966: 48). Disorder is the product of ordering; definition generates anomaly; and similarity begets difference.

The labelling perspective has its vigorous critics (Gove 1980; Taylor *et al.* 1973: 139–71). *Inter alia*, they argue that it isn't a systematic theory; that it is so relativist that nothing is *really* deviant; that it neglects power and structure; that it is an over-simple model of process; and that it sees actors as uni-dimensional at best and utterly determined at worst. Much of this resonates with the standard critique of Goffman, and as with Goffman, the labelling model has its staunch defenders (Plummer 1979).

BEING AND BECOMING

Although much of it isn't relevant here, some aspects of the labelling perspective are significant for a wider understanding of identification. Lemert, for example, distinguishes between *primary* and *secondary* deviance (1972: 62–92). Primary deviance is the basic act of deviance, with its origins in any number of physiological, psychological or interactional factors. Generally it is not dramatised as deviant, being normalised away or negotiated around. Excuses are made, mitigating circumstances discovered, the act redefined as not 'really' deviant, or whatever. We all do deviant things sometimes (or could otherwise be considered deviant) but hardly any of us *is* 'a deviant'. This is an individual identification that definitively requires the identificatory work of others. Depending on circumstance and the nature of the deviance, primary deviance may be recognised and defined as deviance, and the individual labelled deviant. Deviance is very much in the eye of the beholder. Secondary deviance is the internalised identity of 'deviant' produced by the act of labelling, and the subsequent deviance that identity generates.

The labelling perspective emphasises secondary deviance, the process whereby people are identified as deviant and come to identify themselves as deviant. In terms of my model, the external moment of identification is turned round on, and incorporated into, the internal. The individual's subsequent behaviour and biography become organised – by herself and by others – with reference to an identification which is now internal as well as external. Becker (1963: 25–39) refers to this as the *deviant career*, during which the initial external identification of 'deviant' becomes an internal identification. This internalisation occurs in the context of authoritative social control processes in which identification as deviant generates real consequences; in which the identity of deviant is sufficiently powerful to nudge or propel a rule-breaker towards 'becoming a deviant'. It is a question of whose definition of the situation, *and of the individual*, counts. The affinities with Goffman, and with my argument that identity must be understood processually, are clear: we should always be concerned with processes of identification, trajectories of *being* and *becoming*.

The labelling model is, of course, neither sufficient in itself to understand identification nor without shortcomings. In particular, it needs to recognise more clearly the capacity of individuals to resist external identification. More attention to the decision-making of individuals who are identified as deviant is also required. Insufficient attention is paid to *why* primary deviance occurs, not least in terms of motivation. Furthermore, much deviance is definitely not the secondary deviance of labelled individuals: unlabelled 'primary' deviants often know that they are being deviant, and precisely how deviant they are being. White-collar crime is illustrative of this. With respect to 'lifestyle' deviance – and the jazz musicians about whom Becker wrote are actually a good example – individuals may actively seek out an identification in part because it *is* deviant. Classifications of deviance are public knowledge, they are altogether collective, and they can be drawn on and manipulated in different ways with respect to identity.[2] An individual does not have to be labelled a deviant to know that some of the things she does count as deviance.

Allowing for these undoubted failings, the labelling perspective underscores the processual character of identity, and allows us to contextualise the internal–external dialectic of individual identification within the everyday realities of the interaction and institutional orders:

- it insists on the role of external identification in individual identification;
- it offers a way of thinking about *how* external definition becomes internal definition;
- it extends the dialectical model beyond primary socialisation;
- it offers a further view of the way in which collective identifications – of deviance in this case – can become incorporated into self-conscious individual identification;
- it emphasises the capacity of particular agents, occupying particular *positions* – the police, social workers, psychologists, judges and juries, and so on – authoritatively to identify others in consequential ways, moving us beyond the interaction order, into the institutional order.

The usefulness of the labelling perspective isn't limited to the analysis of deviance, either. Education is just one area in which labelling models have proven insightful (Cicourel and Kitsuse 1963; Mehan *et al.* 1986; Mercer 1973). The perspective is particularly suited to examining formalised practices of identification, but labelling operates with as much force in informal interpersonal settings.

In fact, the labelling perspective provides the basis for a *general* model of the external moment of individual identification. There is no reason to suppose that positive, valorised identities aren't internalised in similar ways to negative, stigmatising identities: they too are labels and they too have their consequences. Perhaps the best-known piece of research to make this point is Rosenthal and Jacobsen's experiment (1968) in which the academic performance of individual children was found to correlate with the expectations of their progress that the researchers had foisted upon teachers via a spurious testing procedure. Those pupils who were identified as about to experience a learning 'spurt' subsequently achieved more academically than their peers, presumably as a consequence of the extra attention, stimulation and encouragement offered – whether consciously or unconsciously – by their teachers.

NOMINAL AND VIRTUAL IDENTIFICATION

The 'expectancy' version of the labelling model exemplified by Rosenthal and Jacobsen's research brings me to the distinction between the 'nominal' and the 'virtual'. The *nominal*, in this context, is the label with which the individual is identified. The labelling perspective insists that a label alone is not sufficient for an identity to 'take': just because I call you a deviant, or a gifted child, doesn't mean that you will think of yourself as a deviant or clever, or that other people will. Nor is it enough for *you* to think of yourself as a deviant or clever. What is required is a cumulative labelling *process* over time, in which the label has consequences for the individual. This will be even more effective if that process is endowed with institutional legitimacy and authority. That the consequences lie in the responses of others to the labelled individual as well as in her responses to the identification, means that labelling individuals with the same identification doesn't mean that they will be similarly affected by it. In each of their lives, for myriad reasons, the consequences of being so identified – generated in the internal–external dialectic between the behaviour of others and their own actions – may differ widely. Being labelled is neither uni-directional or determinate.

It is in the consequences of identification that the *virtual* can be discerned. Putting aside Goffman's unfortunate distinction between the virtual and the actual, and the use of virtuality to refer to cyberspace, the 'virtual' in its *Oxford English Dictionary* definition is something that exists for practical purposes rather than in name or by definition. Thus virtual identification is what a nominal identification means experientially and practically over time, to its bearer. Distinguishing the nominal and the virtual is important for several reasons:

- Identification is never just a matter of name or label: the meaning of an identity lies also in *the difference that it makes* in individual lives.
- A label and its consequences may not always be in agreement. Only if they are is there likely to be substantial internalisation.
- The consequences or meaning of any specific nominal identification can vary from context to context and over time. The nominal may be associated with *a plurality of virtualities*.
- Individual identities and differences are to some considerable extent constructed out of collective identities. We need, therefore, a means of distinguishing the unique particularities of the individual from the generalities of the collective. Distinguishing the virtual from the nominal allows us to do that: *some part of the virtual is always individually idiosyncratic*.

Two examples may illustrate these points. There is, first, the situation where the virtual and the nominal are in disagreement. Nominally, people with learning difficulties over the age of eighteen in the United Kingdom are regarded by those who make policy about and for them, and provide them with services, as adults. However, the wider legal framework defining the adult status of people with learning difficulties is less clear: the matter is, at best, ambiguous (Jenkins 1990). On the other hand, the routine everyday responses to people with learning difficulties of many significant others – family, friends, care workers, or the anonymous public – serves to compromise their adulthood (even though due lip service may be paid to the notion). Subject to an almost constant supervision that is generally inappropriate to their competences (Davies and Jenkins 1995), they are *nominally* adult but *virtually* something else, the precise status of which is unclear. Although people with learning difficulties may be called adults, they are consistently treated otherwise. As a result it is therefore difficult for them to become adults, in their own eyes or in the eyes of others.

Apropos the individual and the collective, second, being a gay male is an important identity which, in any individual case, becomes publicly nominal once it is 'out' and visible. But although there are relatively consistent collective templates or stereotypes of male homosexuality, what it means virtually depends on individual circumstances. It is one thing to be a gay television producer, another to be a gay doctor, and quite another to be a gay clergyman. Being gay in London, with a flourishing and supportive gay scene, is likely to be quite different from being gay in, say, a rural village in Norfolk. The same nominal identity produces very different virtual identifications and very different experiences. Nor is it only context and the responses of others which constitute the virtualities of identification: individuals construct the consequences of their own identification as and how they can, in engagement with a human world bursting with others. There are many ways to be gay, in Norfolk as in London.

Neither the nominal nor the virtual is the more 'real': both are real in the lives of individuals, both have their own substance. Nor are they separate in everyday life. The nominal and the virtual are aspects of the same *process*. In fact, we should speak not about nominal and virtual identities, but about nominal and virtual identification. On the one hand there is the labelling or naming of individuals, by themselves and by others. On the other, the individual's actions and the responses of others are consequential experience. All identification combines the nominal and the virtual. It is in the interaction between them that identity careers, drawing together the individual and the collective, emerge as meaningful elements in biography.

8

GROUPS AND CATEGORIES

Individual identification emphasises uniquely embodied differentiation. During primary and subsequent socialisation, in everyday interaction and in institutionalised practices of labelling, individuals are identified, by themselves and by others, in terms which distinguish them from other individuals. Individual identification is, however, necessarily about similarity too. Selfhood, for example, is a way of talking about the similarity or consistency over time of particular embodied humans. And public individuality in the interaction order is in part an expression of each person's idiosyncratic combination of collective identifications.

Collective identification evokes powerful imagery of people who are in some respect(s) apparently similar to each other. People must have something significant in common – no matter how vague, apparently unimportant or apparently illusory – before we can talk about their membership of a collectivity. However, this similarity cannot be recognised without simultaneously evoking differentiation. Logically, *in*clusion entails *ex*clusion, if only by default. To define the criteria for membership of any set of objects is, at the same time, also to create a boundary, everything beyond which does not belong.

It is no different in the human world: one of the things that *we* have in common is our difference from *others*. In the face of their difference our similarity often comes into focus. Defining 'us' involves defining a range of 'thems' also. When we say something about others we are often saying something about ourselves. In the human world, similarity and difference are always functions of a point of view: our similarity is their difference and *vice versa*. Similarity and difference reflect each other across a shared boundary. At the boundary, we discover what we are in what we are not.

Put even as superficially as this, it is possible to see an internal–external dialectic of identification at work collectively, to begin to understand how the same basic processual model of the construction of identity may be applicable to individuals and to collectivities. This is not to say individuals and collectivities are the *same*. They very clearly are not (Jenkins 2002: 81–4). It is, rather, to suggest that there may be much to be learned from addressing the similarities as well as the differences between individuals and collectivities.

UNDERSTANDING COLLECTIVITY

Collectivity and collective identifications are vital building blocks in the conceptual frameworks of sociology and social anthropology (social psychology, as we shall see later in this chapter, is somewhat different). Without some way of talking about them, we can't think sociologically about anything. Even the intimacies of selfhood incorporate identifications such as gender, ethnicity and kinship which, whatever else they are, are also definitively collective. However, although the 'individual' is an easy enough notion to grasp – in the sense that the human world is people by real bodies that are also persons – a 'collectivity' is more abstract and elusive. So what might 'collectivity' mean?

Similarity among and between a plurality of persons – according to whatever criteria – is the clearest image of the collective that I have offered so far. In sociology and social anthropology it is generally taken for granted that a collectivity is a plurality of individuals who either see themselves as similar, or who have in common similar behaviour and circumstances. The two facets of collectivity are often conceptualised together: collective self-identification derives from similar behaviour and circumstances, or *vice versa*. This understanding of collectivities dominated sociology during the late nineteenth and early twentieth centuries and still informs much contemporary social theory. It underpins most, if not all, attempts to apply models of causality to the human world, allowing regularities in behaviour to be translated into the principles which are believed to produce that behaviour.

It also exposes a major fault line within social theory: between an approach which prioritises people's own understandings of their interpersonal relationships, and another which looks for and classifies behavioural patterns from a perspective which is outside the context in question. Somewhat crudely, this is the difference between the *verstehen* of Weber and Simmel, and the positivism of Durkheim, between 'the cultural' and 'the social' (Nadel 1951: 75–87), and between 'subjectivism' and 'objectivism' (Bourdieu 1977; 1990).

This might suggest that there are two different types of collectivity, and hence two different modes of collective identification. In the first, the members of a collectivity can identify themselves as such: they know who (and what) they are. In the second, members may be ignorant of their membership or even of the collectivity's existence. The first exists inasmuch as it is recognised by its members; the second is constituted in its recognition by observers. Nadel is, however, correct to emphasise (1951: 80) that these are not two different kinds of collectivity. They are, rather, *different ways of looking at* interaction, at 'individuals in co-activity'. He is equally right to insist that neither is more 'real' or concrete than the other: both are abstractions from data about 'co-activity'.

These different kinds of abstraction provide the basis for the fundamental conceptual distinction between *groups* and *categories*:

> *category*. A class whose nature and composition is decided by the person who defines the category; for example, persons earning wages in a certain range may be counted as a category for income tax purposes. A category is therefore to be contrasted with a group, defined by the nature of the relations between the members.
>
> (Mann 1983: 34)[1]

This is a methodological distinction – expressed in social psychology, for example, in the contrast between sociological categories and psychological reference groups (Turner and Bourhis 1996: 28) – which constitutes the human world as a manageable object for empirical inquiry and theoretical analysis. Whether a collectivity is seen as a group or a category is a consequence of how it is defined. However, since in each case the definition is that of the observer, the difference is less clear than it appears. By this token a group is simply defined sociologically according to a more specific criterion – mutual recognition on the part of its members – than a category, which may, in principle at least, be defined arbitrarily, according to any criteria.

At this point Bourdieu's strictures against substituting 'the reality of the model' for 'the model of reality' (1977: 29) are worth considering. He warns – as indeed does Nadel – against the reification of interaction, against the linked fallacies of misplaced concreteness and misplaced precision. We should beware, for example, of investing collectivities with the kind of substance or agency with which embodiment allows us to endow individuals. It is not that collectivities lack substance or the capacity to do things – if that were so they would be of little sociological interest – but they differ in these respects from individuals. Similarly, the boundedness of a collectivity is different in kind from the bodily integrity of an individual. Where a collectivity begins and ends is not mappable using the sociometric equivalent of a dressmaker's tape. Nadel and Bourdieu are also reminding us that our necessarily systematised and draughted view of the human world is, after all, just that, a *view*. A necessarily abstract and simplified view which we should not mistake for reality. And, what is more, a view that is always *from* a point of view.

However, nor are groups and categories *just* sociological abstractions. Social scientists have no monopoly over processes of definition and abstraction, of identification. Sociologists engage in the identification of collectivities, but so does everyone else, in a range of everyday discourses and practices of identification. The sociological definition of 'group', above, recognises this. Group identity is the product of *collective internal definition*. In our relationships with significant others we draw upon identifications of similarity and difference, and, in the process, generate group identities. At the same time, our self-conscious group memberships signify others and create relationships with them. Thus categorisation is also a general interactional process, this time of *collective external definition*. I have, for example, already suggested that the identification of others – *their* definition according to criteria of *our* adoption (which they may neither accept nor recognise) – is often part of the process of identifying ourselves. More generally, categorisation is a routine and necessary contribution to how we make sense of, and impute predictability to, a complex human world of which our knowledge is always partial. The ability to identify unfamiliar individuals with reference to known categories allows us at least the illusion that we know what to expect of them.

Thus, although in the strictest of senses groups and categories exist in the eye of the sociological beholder, the conceptual distinction between them mirrors routine interactional processes, external and internal moments of collective identification: *group identification* on the one hand, *categorisation* on the other. This means that groups and categories are something more than products of the sociological imagination. But what?

THE POWERS OF CATEGORISATION

It is an article of sociological faith for all but the most obdurate positivists that if people think that something is real, it is, if nothing else, real in terms of the action that it produces and in its consequences. Therefore it is 'socially' and intersubjectively real. Deriving from W. I. Thomas at Chicago in the early decades of the last century, this injunction recommends that sociologists not bother themselves too much with ontology and get on instead with the pragmatic business of trying to understand the inter-subjective realities in terms of which people act. How people define the situation(s) in which they find themselves is thus among the most important of sociological data.

From this point of view, a group is intersubjectively 'real'. Group members, in recognising themselves as such, effectively constitute that to which they believe they belong. In the first instance processes of internal collective definition bring a group into existence, in being identified by its members and in the relationships between them. However, a group that was recognised *only* by its members – a secret group – would have a very limited presence in the human world. What's more its discovery (and categorisation) by others would be perpetually immanent. Furthermore, even if secrecy were maintained, such a group would necessarily be shaped to some extent by the categorising gaze of others: one of its identifying features in the eyes of its members would be precisely its freedom from external recognition. Thus categorisation by others is part of the reality of any and every group.

A category, however, is less straightforward, since its members need not be aware of their collective identification. Here we must focus on consequences. Can the extreme case – a category which is unrecognised by those who are identified by others as belonging to it, and which has no impact upon their lives – be said to have any reality? Such cases are not common; a category is not generally a secret to its members. But there is no reason why it could not be. Among the obvious possible examples are the classificatory schema of the social sciences.[2] These are often distant from the people to whom they refer, and their uses apparently arcane and remote.

It seems unlikely, for example, that anthropological debates concerning the Nilotic peoples of the southern Sudan – about whether 'the Nuer' are a definite collectivity in their own right, whether 'the Nuer' and 'the Dinka' are separate collectivities, whether one is the other, or which one is which (Burton 1981; Hutchinson 1995; Newcomer 1972; Southall 1976) – have been audible to Dinka or Nuer themselves or have had any consequences for their lives. A similar point could be made about sociological debates concerning the categorisation of populations in terms of social class (e.g. Erikson and Goldthorpe 1993; Goldthorpe and Hope 1974; Marshall *et al*. 1988; Stewart *et al*. 1980; Wright 1985; 1989). It doesn't seem likely that technicians, for example, spend much time pondering whether they are members of the 'service class', the 'non-manual working class' or some other analytical category.

However, these examples oblige us to ask whether categorisation can ever be disinterested. In the first place, neither example is wholly divorced from the people who are the objects of the classificatory exercise: 'Nuer' and 'Dinka' are locally recognised identities in Sudan, are part of the present political landscape (embroiled in the conflict between the Khartoum regime and the south), and earlier had resonance for colonial government (who also tried to 'pacify' them). Similarly, people in industrialised societies routinely identify themselves according to class, and those identifications have implications for everything from voting to courtship, housing and schooling choices – or their absence – and policing patterns. The precise ways in which these categories are defined and refined may not be part of the local common knowledge of the people to whom they are applied, but the categories themselves are locally grounded. They are not secrets to their members.

The role of categorisation in the production of disciplinary power is also worth considering. Foucault (1970; 1980), Hacking (1990), and Rose (1989) argue that the categorising procedures of the social sciences are part of the bureaucratic practices of government of the modern state, and thus not wholly disinterested. Scientific notions of 'objectivity' and 'truth' derive their epistemological power in part from their grounding in procedures of categorisation. In turn, assumptions of objectivity and truth underpin the bureaucratic rationality that is the framework of the modern state. The categorisation of individuals and populations that is the stock in trade of the social sciences is one way in which humans are constituted as objects of government and subjects of the state, via censuses and the like. The reference to taxation in the definition of 'category' quoted earlier was apposite. More pointedly, 'objective' knowledge about the human world provides one basis – whether that is its rationale or not – for the policing of families and the private sphere which characterises the modern state (Donzelot 1980; Meyer 1983).

So, even the most apparently aloof categorisation is only apparently so. Whether directly, via the commissioning, direction and use of social science research by the state or other agencies, or indirectly, via the contribution of theory and research to the fecundity and potency of the categorical point of view of government (Foucault's 'governmentality'), categorising people is always *potentially* an intervention in their lives, and often more.[3] Although they may not be aware of their categorisation, that they have been categorised is always at least immanently consequential for a category's members.

It's more common that people know that they have been lumped together in the eyes of others, but aren't aware, or fully aware, of the content and implications of that categorisation. A category may be recognised by its membership without its implications for their lives being clear or obvious to them. We have probably all had the experience of realising that we are being categorised in a particular fashion – in a new workplace, perhaps, or on moving into a new neighbourhood – without knowing what this means in terms of the responses or expectations of others. Imbalances of this kind may be thoroughly institutionalised. Policies such as 'normalisation' and 'empowerment' may encourage individuals with learning difficulties, for example, despite their awareness of the general categories 'retarded', 'stupid', or whatever, to deny that these apply to *them* (Davies and Jenkins 1996). The consequences may be unintended, but the extent to which those categorisations shape their lives and exacerbate the routine cruelties of the world are concealed. Both nominal and virtual are obscured.

This highlights another characteristic of categorisation. Group membership is a relationship between members: even if they do not know each other personally, they can recognise each other as members. Membership of a category is not a relationship between members: it doesn't even necessitate a relationship between categoriser and categorised. Any interpersonal relationships between members of a category only involve them as individuals. Once relationships between members of a category involve mutual recognition of their categorisation, the first steps towards group identification have been taken.

Categorisers are the other side of the coin. Categorisation may be more significant for categoriser(s) than for categorised. Our categories don't have to be consequentially 'real' to the people to whom they refer, in order to have consequences for us. Although categorising others is one aspect of identifying ourselves, this need not involve explicit notions of difference *vis-à-vis* ourselves and those others. Nor need we have any expectations of them. The examples of the Nuer–Dinka, or social class, can help again to make the point. The most important themes of these categorisations are not 'Nuer–Dinka are different from us anthropologists', or 'the working class are different from us sociologists' (although these sub-themes may be present). As aspects of their disciplinary world views, categorisations such as these do other kinds of identificatory work for anthropologists and sociologists: recently, for example, Brubaker and Cooper (2000) used the Nuer case to establish their own distinction with respect to other social theorists of identity. Disagreements over categories produce boundaries internally, between different 'sides' of the argument: in the case of class, for example, competing classificatory schema are associated with intra-disciplinary groupings and sociological feuds of some longevity and bitterness.

Another example may further illustrate what I mean. Style is an arbiter of youth identities in western industrialised societies. One of the ways in which styles are delineated is through the categorisation of music and musicians. In my youth, for example, questions such as whether white musicians could play the blues, or whether Tamla-Motown counted as soul, had an urgency which seems disproportionate only in retrospect: the answers were a significant part of style and 'who's who and what's what'. Thus the categorisation of others is a resource upon which to draw in the construction of our own identities.

That categorisation has consequences, even if only trivial or immanent, returns the discussion to the distinction between the *nominal* and the *virtual*. Collective identification also has nominal and virtual dimensions. The nominal is how the group or category is defined in discourse, the virtual how its members behave or are treated. As with individual identification these are conceptually distinct. In practice they are chronically implicated in each other, but there is no necessary agreement between them.

SIMULTANEITY AND PROCESS

I argued in Chapter 3 that although the dialectic of internal–external definition might imply sequence – one, then the other – simultaneity is what I am trying to communicate. Collective internal definition is group identification; collective external definition is categorisation. Each is an interrelated moment in the collective dialectic of identification, suggesting that neither comes first and neither exists without the other. But is this actually the case?

Group identification probably cannot exist in a vacuum. Short of imagining an utterly isolated – and implausible – band, small enough to lack significant internal sub-groupings, then it seems sensible to suggest that groups necessarily exist in relation to other groups: to categorise and to be categorised in turn. Group identification therefore proceeds hand in glove with categorisation. Although it makes figurative sense to talk about groups being constituted 'in the first instance' by internal definition – after all, without their members relating to each other, and defining themselves as members, there would be nothing to belong to – this should not be misconstrued literally and chronologically, to mean *first* group identification, *then* categorisation.

There may, however, be situations in which group identification is generated by prior categorisation. But although categorisation necessarily conjures up a possible group identity, it doesn't inevitably create an actual one. Marx understood this when he talked about the difference between a 'class in itself' and a 'class for itself'.[4] He argued that the working class is constituted *in itself* by virtue of the similar situation of workers, their common alienation from the means of production within capitalism. By virtue of their shared situation, workers have similar interests (i.e. things that are in their interest). Marx argued that these interests cannot be realised until workers unite into a class *for itself*, and realise for themselves what their interests are. This, for Marx, signifies the emergence of the working class as a collective historical agent. The process of group identification encourages and is encouraged by class struggle. Subsequent refinements of this model, particularly by Lenin in *What is to be Done?*, emphasised that class struggle would not 'just happen' as a consequence of the conflict of interests between classes; it has to be inspired or produced. Hence Lenin's notion of the 'vanguard party', and hence the need for politics.

Whether or not we agree with this, it illustrates my argument. Given appropriate circumstances, groups may come to identify themselves as such because of their initial categorisation by others. The point is that there was no class 'in itself' until its common interests were perceived and *identified*. The categorical constitution of the working class as a class in itself with a situation and interests in common – by socialists and other activists, on the one hand, and, as a 'dangerous class', by capitalists and the state, on the other – was a necessary although not a sufficient condition for the birth of the class for itself and, hence, for working-class politics (if not necessarily revolution). Before the working class could act *as* a class, working people had to recognise that it *was* – or they were – a class. In this recognition the working class was constituted as a politically effective group.

Distinguishing the necessary from the sufficient suggests that for a category to be defined it must be definable. There has to be something that its members share. In principle this can be completely arbitrary. One could, for example, decide that all married persons with ingrowing toenails were a category. But would this ever amount to more than an abstract, logical category? To become a category, it would at the very least have to be recognised by appreciable numbers of others. In order for that to happen the combination of being married and suffering with ingrowing toenails would have to possess some significance to those others. They would have to have an *interest* in the matter, there would have to be a *point* to it. In the case of the working class, capitalist wage-labour produced the common interest and the point, without which there would have been nothing 'in itself' to recognise. Although categorisation may in principle be arbitrary, it is actually unlikely ever to be so.

People collectively identify themselves and others, and they conduct their everyday lives in terms of those identities, which therefore have practical consequences. They are intersubjectively real. This is as true for categories as for groups. Or, to come closer to the spirit of this discussion, it is as true for categorisation as for group identification, since neither groups nor categories are anything other than emphases within ongoing processes of identification.

Two further points flow from adopting this position. First, collective identities must always be understood as generated simultaneously by group identification *and* categorisation. How we understand any particular collective identity is an empirical matter, for discovery. In one case group identification may be the dominant theme, in another categorisation, but, as argued above, both will always be present as moments in the dialectic of collective identification, even if only as potentialities. Second, identificatory processes are pre-eminently practices, done by actually existing individuals. There is thus nothing idealist about this argument. Collectivities and collective identities do not just exist 'in the mind' or 'on paper'.

The distinction between groups and categories is an analogue of the general *processes* of group identification and categorisation. Collective identities are no less processual than individual identities, and group identification and categorisation have practical consequences. Rather than reify groups and categories – as 'things' – we should think instead about identities as constituted in the dialectic of collective identification, in the interplay of group identification and categorisation. In any particular case it is empirically a question of the balance between these processes. Group identification always implies categorisation. The reverse is not always the case. Categorisation, however, at least creates group identification as an immanent possibility.

THE INDIVIDUAL AND THE COLLECTIVE REVISITED

Groups and categories are fundamental to the social psychology of identity inspired by the work of Henri Tajfel (1970; 1978; 1981a; 1982; Tajfel and Turner 1979). Sometimes these are distinguished from each other in the way that I have done here: groups are defined by and meaningful to their members, while categories are externally defined without any necessary recognition by their members (e.g. Turner and Bourhis 1996: 27–30). More consistently in this approach, however, the distinction between groups and categories is weak and only implicit: a group is an actually existing concrete point of reference for its members, while a category is a collectively defined classification of identity, part of local common knowledge.

Looking for an alternative to the individualism that he saw as prevalent in social psychology and inspired by his earlier research on social perception, Tajfel was concerned to understand prejudice and conflict as something other than inevitable 'facts of life' and to reconcile cohesion and differentiation within one model of human group relationships. The resultant 'social identity theory', and its immediate development 'self-categorisation theory' (Turner 1985; Turner *et al.* 1987), can be summarised thus:[5]

- 'Personal identity', which differentiates the unique self from all other selves, is different from 'social identity', which is the internalisation of, often stereotypical, collective identifications. Social identity is sometimes the more salient influence on individual behaviour.
- Group membership is meaningful to individuals, conferring social identity and permitting self-evaluation. It is a shared representation of who one is and the appropriate behaviour attached to who one is.
- Group membership in itself, *regardless of its context or meaning*, is sufficient to encourage members to, for example, discriminate against outgroup members. Group members also exaggerate the similarities within the ingroup, and the differences between the ingroup and outgroup.
- Society is structured categorically, and organised by inequalities of power and resources. It is in the translation of social categories into meaningful reference groups that 'social structure' influences or produces individual behaviour. Social identity theory focuses on how categories become groups, with the emphasis on intergroup processes.
- Social categorisation generates social identity, which produces social comparisons, which produce positive (or negative) self-evaluation. Universal species-specific processes mediate between social categories and individual behaviour: cognitive simplification, comparison and evaluation, and the search for positive self-esteem. These processes bring groups into being.
- The cognitive simplification that is required to manage the information overload produced by a complex world generates stereotypes of collectivities and their members.
- Comparison and evaluation between groups is generically bound up with the establishment and maintenance of ingroup distinctiveness, in an interplay of internal similarity and external difference.
- Groups distinguish themselves from, and discriminate against, other groups in order to promote their own positive social evaluation and collective self-esteem.
- Individuals and groups with unsatisfactory social identity seek to restore or acquire positive identification via mobility, assimilation, creativity or competition.
- Moving from intergroup to intragroup matters, self-categorisation theory focuses on the universal psychological processes that produce

group cohesion. Accentuating the in–out distinction, self-categorisation as a group member – the internalisation of stereotypes – generates a sense of similarity with other group members, and attractiveness or esteem.

• Individuals, in using stereotypical categories to define themselves thus, bring into being human collective life.

• Individuals will self-categorise themselves differently according to the contexts in which they find themselves, and the contingencies with which they are faced.

This is merely a thumbnail sketch of a complex and growing body of research and literature that has become an established social psychological paradigm in its own right (see Capozza and Brown 2000; Robinson 1996; Worchel *et al.* 1998). Nor does it do justice to the twists and turns along the way. Tajfel, for example, in his last word on stereotyping (1981b) goes beyond cognitive simplification as an explanation, adding the defence or preservation of values, the creation or maintenance of group ideologies, and positive ingroup differentiation (see Chapter 11 for a further discussion).

As might be expected, three decades of development has generated considerable debate about 'social identity theory', within the approach itself and with external critics. One of the most pertinent issues concerns the empirical underpinnings of Tajfel's – and Turner's – foundational propositions. These data derived from explicit, controlled laboratory experiments, most characteristically the 'minimal group' approach. This method involves, typically small, artificial coalitions of subjects, doing tasks in the outcome of which they have no material or other interest. Among the most significant findings here is that, placed in otherwise meaningless groups by an experimenter, research subjects tend to discriminate against members of the experimental outgroup, even though they stand to gain or lose nothing by doing so (Tajfel 1970; Tajfel *et al.* 1971).

Questions have been asked by supporters and critics about whether 'social identity theory' can be generalised beyond its experimental context (e.g. Maass *et al.* 2000; Skevington and Baker 1989). To stick with the example above, it may, for example, be at least partly *because* a minimal group is a simplified, no lose–no gain situation that experimental subjects discriminate against the outgroup in this way. Within the checks and balances of the everyday human world, in which actions have real consequences, choices are likely to be more complex (or may not be available at all). More specifically, there are questions about whether the evidence supports generalisations about themes such as intergroup evaluation and bias (Crisp and Hewstone 1999; Hewstone *et al*. 2002), intergroup negative discrimination (Migdal *et al*. 1998), the cognitive simplification effects of stereotyping (Oakes 1996: 98–100), and the maximisation of self-esteem (Rubin and Hewstone 1998; Wetherell 1996: 277–80).

It is, obviously, important to be clear and cautious about what we can learn from laboratory experiments (which is not the same thing as rejecting them). To a sociologist or social anthropologist, reservations about the minimal group approach seem to be uncontroversial: ambitious generalisations about large-scale collective processes deriving from the investigation of micro-micro-level situations – whether experimental or not – require considerable modesty in their formulation, even when they are not completely unsafe. This issue has, however, been hard fought and has yet to be accepted by most social psychologists, working as they do in a field in which the experiment is still the gold-standard research design.

From my point of view, there are other criticisms of psychology's 'social identity theory', not least its problematic basic differentiation between personal and social identity (as discussed in previous chapters). The equally fundamental problem of how to differentiate in this approach between its own concepts of social categorisation in general and social identification in particular shouldn't be underestimated either (McGarty 1999: 190–6). What's more, despite Tajfel's original ambitions, 'social identity theory' remains an individualist perspective, perhaps because of the centrality of experimental methods: groups are, at best, present as simplified and reified features of the human landscape, actual interaction is largely ignored and identification appears to take place solely 'inside people's heads'. With respect to interaction, the particular lack of attention to the emergence of identification during talk and other discourse is noteworthy (Antaki and Widdecombe 1998; Billig 1996: 346–51), as is the frequent dependence on assumptions about weakly conceptualised motivational factors such as 'esteem', 'attraction' and 'liking'.[6]

These criticisms aside, some recent research within this paradigm resonates loudly with the arguments advanced in this book. Deschamps and Devos (1998) have, for example, explored the relationship between similarity and difference and 'personal' and 'social' identity, while Deaux (2000) has looked at the range of motivations for social identification and the varying intensity of group identification. Abrams's account (1996) of how, depending on situational factors and goal-orientations, self-identification and self-attention may vary in their salience and interact to produce self-regulation of varying intensity, suggests fruitful lines of inquiry into the hows and whys of identification's variability.

Specific research findings aside, important general themes running through this approach support the model of identification that I am exploring and advocating here:

- In the general spirit of earlier theorists such as Mead, 'social identity theory' offers a vision of identification as rooted in basic and generic human processes, part of our species-specific nature.
- The minimal group experiments suggest that group identification is one of those generic processes, and is *in itself* a powerful influence on human behaviour.
- These experiments further suggest that categorisation, in my definition – i.e. external identification, the process of placing people, in this case arbitrarily, into collectivities – is also an important generic process, which can contribute to group identification.
- The approach understands collective identification as not just an internal group matter, but as coming into being in the context of *inter*group relations: thus groups identify themselves against, and in their relationships with, other groups.
- 'Social identity theory' also recognises that collective identifications are real for individuals – that they mean something in real experience – and seeks to understand how that reality *works*.
- 'Self-categorisation theory' acknowledges the situational variability of identification.
- There is a general appreciation of the necessary interplay within identification of similarity and difference.
- Although not well thought through, the significance for identification of the distinction between groups and categories is acknowledged.
- Finally, the emphasis – certainly in Tajfel's own writings – on power and inequality, while it may be underdeveloped, is an important reminder of the realities of the human world.

With benefit of considerable hindsight, one of the striking things about this school of thought is its apparent isolation from scholarship outside social psychology that, some time before Tajfel's seminal statements, outlined a vision of how identification works which, in some of its fundamentals at least, resembles 'social identity theory'. As I shall discuss in the next chapter, during the 1960s Fredrik Barth, standing on the shoulders of earlier anthropologists and sociologists (not least Goffman), began to put together some *very* similar propositions. The resultant shift in the understanding of ethnicity and other collective identifications – the establishment of what I have called 'the basic anthropological model'

(Jenkins 1997) – seems to have been unremarked by Tajfel and his associates, despite its conceptual harmony with much of what they were saying.

I doubt that this was mainly due to 'academic trade barriers' on the part of social psychologists eager to establish a distinctive niche for themselves within their discipline (Condor 1996: 309–10). Probably more to the point are personal factors, the nature of the discipline in question, and the power of normal science. Reading his own words and what his ex-students say about him – even when, like Billig (1996), they now seem to be at odds with much of his intellectual legacy – Tajfel's influence as a teacher and the force and direction of his intellectual leadership shine through. He seems to have been *trying* to establish a distinctive school of thought. The context for that project was an academic disciplinary field, psychology, in which natural science, rooted in the laboratory, held sway (even today, 'humanist' approaches remain a peripheral minority interest, often located outside mainstream psychology departments). Tajfel himself was committed to the natural science model: it isn't obvious that anthropology, for example, or the work of Goffman, would have interested him. Finally, once established, the social identity and social categorisation theorists pursued their work within a taken-for-granted normal science paradigm. Most of them don't seem to have seen any need to look elsewhere for ideas: the work they had in hand was enough.

Nor, to be fair, should this mini intellectual history single out for comment the social psychologists. After all, what goes on within groups, and how their members identify themselves, is also a function of what goes on *between* groups. And there is no evidence that the anthropologists showed any interest in, or were aware of, what Tajfel and his followers were doing (almost certainly for reasons similar to those that I have just sketched in). With little communication between the two camps, their relationship, if it can be called that, seems to have been characterised by distance and mutual ignorance rather than stoutly defended boundaries. 'Trade barriers' weren't necessary. That was a shame: each might have benefited from talking to the intellectual Other. That they didn't, however, is no more than might have been expected: they simply got on with doing their own stuff. It's a tribute to the force of disciplinary identifications and boundaries that, by and large, it's what they're still doing today.

9

BEYOND BOUNDARIES

Identification is the production and reproduction during interaction of the intermingling, and inseparable, themes of human similarity and difference. Collective identification emphasises similarity – although it is only a matter of emphasis – and this will be the focus of the next chapter. The collective identification of *differences*, as process and with respect to its consequences, is the distinctive intellectual territory of Norwegian anthropologist Fredrik Barth, and the focus of the present chapter.

Barth hasn't had the recognition he deserves. Compared to stars such as Bourdieu or Geertz, his work remains little known outside anthropology. This may be a consequence of being based in Oslo, rather than in Princeton or Paris, it may be a consequence of intellectual fad and fashion. Whatever the reasons, however, Barth's body of work is one of the richest and most imaginative in anthropology (and social science more widely). A theorist of greater significance than his lack of wider reputation might suggest, the consistent project of his life's work has been:

> to explore the extent to which patterns of social form can be explained if we assume that they are the cumulative result of a number of separate choices and decisions made by people acting *vis-à-vis* one another . . . patterns are generated through processes of interaction and in their form reflect the constraints and incentives under which people act.
>
> (Barth 1966: 2)

Barth wants to understand how collective forms exist, and what collectivity *is*, given that the human world is, before it is anything else, a world of individuals. That he understands collectivities as generated in and out of interaction between individuals doesn't mean that 'society' is simply the sum of individuals and their relationships:

> Indeed, 'society' cannot defensibly be represented by *any* schema which depicts it as a whole made up of parts . . . The complexities of social organization can neither be bounded in delimited wholes nor ordered in the unitary part-whole hierarchies which the schematism of our terminology invites us to construct.
>
> (Barth 1992: 19)

In this 1992 paper he cautions against identifying any 'particular area of the world' in which we are interested as a 'society' (to which I'd want to add that we shouldn't talk about a 'culture' either). The world is not as neat and tidy as that. It is a further consistent theme in his work that, in addition to the relatively stable patterns and forms of the human world, we should recognise, in the open-endedness of everyday life, the routine imminence of change and transformation. Each, in a sense, gives rise to the other.

ETHNIC GROUPS

In 1969 Barth edited *Ethnic Groups and Boundaries*, a symposium on ethnic identification that was subtitled 'the social organisation of culture difference'. This indicated that ethnicity and 'cultural' difference are connected, and suggested that the 'social' and the 'cultural' are not separate domains. Although this framework addressed ethnic identification, it is also applicable to other collective identification.

Although Barth's model of ethnic identity broke new ground for social anthropology, it wasn't an immaculate conception (Jenkins 1997: 9–13). Its important elements all had their antecedents. Individual behaviour and decision-making – organisation rather than structure – had long been themes in the work of anthropologists such as Malinowski, Firth and Nadel. Barth's key insight that ethnic identities are flexible – if not totally fluid – over time can be found, albeit less systematically expressed, in Leach's earlier study of Burma (1954), and the situational variability of ethnic identity had already been explored by, for example, Moerman (1965). Barth's theorising also owes much to Goffman and, through him, to Chicago sociologists such as Everett Hughes.[1]

However, Barth superseded existing conceptualisations in depth and detail, theorising ethnic identification within a wider set of arguments about interaction and collective forms. This line of thought began with his study of politics in Swat, north-western Pakistan (1959), which focused on how political groupings develop and change as the result of interpersonal strategising and transactions. His understanding that collective forms are not fixed, but are brought into being by, or emerge out of, interaction, was taken further in *Models of Social Organisation* (1966). That work's insight that the foundation of collective pattern was laid in the processes of individual lives was the primary theme in Barth's thinking. It continued in his exploration of ethnic identification.

Barth's 'Introduction' to *Ethnic Groups and Boundaries* (1969) begins by observing that the persistence of differences between ethnic groups, indeed the groups themselves, had been taken for granted. The existence of ethnic groups (or 'tribes') was just 'the way things were' and anthropology had not problematised how such groups maintained their distinctiveness or reproduced themselves. Although Barth made the pragmatic assumption that it was sensible to continue to talk about groups, he was moving away from a structural-functionalism that over-solidified them, as Durkheimian 'social facts'. 'Societies' are not to be seen as *things*. That people in interaction produce groups is his basic theorem, and anthropologists need to look at how the membership of ethnic groups is recruited, rather than simply assuming an obvious process of birth-and-death reproduction.

He went on to insist that groups 'exist' even though whatever separates them is osmotic rather than watertight: 'boundaries persist despite a flow of personnel across them' (ibid.: 9). Barth declared his interest in, 'social processes of exclusion and incorporation whereby discrete social categories are maintained *despite* changing participation and membership in the course of individual life histories' (ibid.: 10). Bearing in mind that his use of the word 'category' is not tightly defined like mine – something else he shares with the social psychologists discussed in Chapter 8 – Barth is arguing that ethnic collectivities are independent of the individuals whose membership constitutes them. Members come and go, if only (but not only) as a consequence of human mortality. An ethnic group can also survive the fact that individuals in the course of their lives may change their ethnic identities. In Haaland's analysis, for example (1969), individual members of sedentary Fur communities in the western Sudan may adopt a nomadic lifestyle, eventually becoming members of Baggara communities. But a difference between Fur and Baggara, as collective identifications, remains clear even though it may be blurred in individual biographies.

Barth's model of how ethnic identification works is built out of three basic elements:

- Ethnic identities are *folk classifications*: ascriptions and self-ascriptions, held and understood by the participants in any given situation. They thus contribute to the organisation of interaction. In W. I. Thomas's sense they are 'socially real'; in terms of the 'social identity theory' discussed in Chapter 8, they are 'psychologically real'.

- Barth is interested in the *processes* that generate collective forms, rather than in their abstract structure. He is primarily concerned with what people do; his is a materialist (and pragmatist) concern with the behaviour of embodied individuals.

- As a consequence, rather then looking at the 'content' of ethnicity – cataloguing the history or 'cultural' characteristics of ethnic groups – the focus of investigation shifts outwards to processes of ethnic *boundary maintenance* and *group recruitment*. This involves looking at inter-ethnic (i.e. intergroup) relations. By these tokens, shared common sense, common knowledge and behaviour are better understood as products of processes of boundary maintenance, rather than as defining characteristics of group organisation.

The model can be summarised by saying that the interactional construction of (external) difference generates (internal) similarity, rather than *vice versa*. It follows that:

> we can assume no simple one-to-one relationship between ethnic units and cultural similarities and differences. The features that are taken into account are not the sum of 'objective' differences, but only those which the actors themselves regard as significant . . . some cultural features are used by the actors as signals and emblems of differences, others are ignored, and in some relationships radical differences are played down and denied.
>
> (Barth 1969: 14)

This characteristic of ethnic identities allows individuals *in principle* to move in and out of them. It also means that ethnic identities are not immutable. They are capable of change over time, a process in which the nominal and virtual aspects of identification may come into play. To be German in 1995, for example, involves emphasising or de-emphasising different things than being German would have done before reunification; and both would be very different to nominally equivalent identifications in 1938, or 1916, or 1871. There is also likely to be considerable variability between contexts. What it means to be English – what is required to maintain the identification, and the kinds of responses from others which it generates – is one thing when an English person interacts with, say, a Nigerian person in England; it is likely to be another thing altogether in Nigeria.

Thus difference is organised, in the first instance, by individuals in interaction. But not all interactions are equally significant in this respect. The continuity of ethnic collectivities – a better expression for the moment than groups or categories – is particularly dependent upon boundary maintenance. This is managed during interaction *across* the boundary, with Others (for whom we are, in turn, their Other). Referring at this point to Goffman's 'presentation of self', Barth (1969: 16) argues that all inter-ethnic relations require recognised rules to organise them. Although 'rules' may be too strong a word, implying a degree of conscious formulation that is implausible, these interactional conventions or habits do not just delineate difference. They define the limits of the interaction, and permit either side to participate with only the barest agreement about acceptable behaviour in common.

Barth doesn't, however, neglect relationships within the boundary, between co-members. He emphasises the importance to ethnic identity of shared value orientations, the 'standards of morality and excellence' with which behaviour is evaluated. His emphasis upon being recognised, as well as recognising oneself, is congruent with Mead and the symbolic interactionist tradition, as well as Goffman. Internal and external meet, inasmuch as claiming an ethnic identity, 'implies being a certain kind of person, having that basic identity, it also implies a claim to be judged, and to judge oneself, by those standards that are relevant to that identity' (Barth 1969: 14). In belonging to a collectivity, an individual accepts the right of co-members to judge, and seeks to be to be accepted and judged by Others only in particular ways.

For Barth, ethnic identities are processual or practical: 'for acting . . . rather than contemplation' (1969: 29). All identification is, what's more, part of a larger universe of experience, which is, in turn, part of 'the material world of causes and effects' (Barth 1981: 3). Collectivities exist within the realities of ecological constraint and possibility, which frame their relations with Others and relations among their members. Intergroup competition for resources within specific ecologies is important in the generation of boundaries. Further, in the embodied face-to-face world of everyday life – and making a distinction which is homologous to that between the nominal and the virtual – he argues (1969: 28) that although ethnic ascription does not require access to assets (conceived in the widest possible way), the satisfactory performance of an ethnic identity does. It is not enough to claim an ethnic identity, one must be able satisfactorily to perform it, to actualise it. That may require resources.

What counts as a successful performance, however, varies from situation to situation, place to place, and time to time. Nor is success guaranteed. Nominal 'ethnic labels' and the virtualities of experience feed back on each other: 'under varying circumstances, certain constellations of categorization and value orientation have a self-fulfilling character . . . others will tend to be falsified by experience, while others are incapable of consummation in interaction' (Barth 1969: 30). Drawing once again upon Goffman,[2] Barth means by 'self-fulfilling' that participants will typically do their best, using 'selective perception, tact, and sanctions', to maintain identifications conventionally appropriate to the situation. If for no other reason, they do this because it is generally easier than coming up with alternative identifications or definitions of the situation. Thus although change and flux in ethnicity are possible – and common – the persistence and stability of the everyday common sense of ethnic identification is likely to be routine. This is a tribute to the 'organizing and canalizing effects of ethnic distinctions' (ibid.: 24). Identity revision only takes place when it is either manifestly incorrect ('untrue in any objective sense') or proves to be consistently unrewarding. What counts as unrewarding is, of course, moot in terms of the pragmatics of the situation. What counts as 'objective' is more problematic: I will return to this below.

It is implicit that identity change occurs only when interaction must be maintained, when disengagement isn't a practical option. It is also implicit, given Barth's insistence that interaction across the boundary is the *sine qua non* of ethnic identity, that its persistence or revision is a dialectical process of collective identification, with internal and external moments. Ethnicity is always a two-way street, involving 'them' as well as 'us'. The fact that not all identificatory performances 'work' draws our attention to the role of significant others in validating identity: internal identification and external identification are mutually entangled. Although in Barth's own work, and its appropriation within anthropology, the emphasis has fallen upon group identification ('us') rather than categorisation ('them'), this emphasis is not inevitable (Jenkins 1994; 1997).

TRANSACTIONS, POLITICS AND POWER

Although he seems never to have aspired to leadership of a school of thought, such as psychology's 'social identity theory' discussed in Chapter 8, Barth's understanding of ethnic identification as *transactional* and *situationally flexible* is now almost conventional anthropological wisdom (e.g. Eriksen 1993). It has, indeed, become the 'basic anthropological model' (Jenkins 1997). However, the same themes in Barth's *general* social theory were fiercely attacked during the 1970s (Asad 1972; Evens 1977; Kapferer 1976; Paine 1974), and these criticisms can be applied to his arguments about ethnicity. In particular, he was taken to task for individualism, means–ends voluntarism and neglecting power.

Barth has responded at length to these criticisms (1981: 76–104), so I shall be brief here. That he emphasised individuals, and their decision-making in the pursuit of their interests, was at that time unusual – although not novel – within anthropology. That it is more routine today reflects a gradual recognition of the need to acknowledge agency, practice and subjectivity. But Barth focuses on more than individuals anyway. His critics have largely overlooked his central interest in the processual generation of collective forms (such as identities) as the unintended consequence of interaction. He has described this aspect of his work as the most significant (1981: 76), and it is the theoretical path he has continued to tread (e.g. 1987; 1992). If a body of work of great substantive range and theoretical variety can be characterised in one keyword, 'generative' would undoubtedly do.

Since 1969 Barth has addressed issues which further mitigate the charge of individualism. Discussing pluralism in complex societies (1984; 1989), he talks about 'universes of discourse' or 'streams of tradition'. These are less clear-cut than 'cultures'; individuals participate in them differentially, typically in several at the same time, and with varying intensity or depth. Writing about Bali, Barth describes it thus: 'People participate in multiple, more or less discrepant, universes of discourse; they construct different partial and simultaneous worlds in which they move; their cultural construction of reality springs not from one source and is not of one piece' (Barth 1989: 130). While the imagery suggests movement and activity, these universes or streams are to a considerable extent historically stable.

In part these ideas are a response to the persistence with which anthropologists and sociologists – despite his arguments of 1969 – continue to reify ethnic groups as possessing coherence and definite boundaries: 'We must abandon the physicalist comforts of seeking to anchor plural cultural components universally in some construct of population segments' (Barth 1984: 80). Ethnic identification is, let us remember, processual, generated during and an expression of interactional give and take. For Barth, this implies that 'dichotomized cultural differences . . . are vastly overstated in ethnic discourse'; 'the more pernicious myths of deep cultural cleavages . . . sustain a social organization of difference' but are not 'descriptions of the actual distribution of cultural stuff' (1994: 30).

Criticism of Barth's neglect of power is, of course, related to the accusation of individualism. And it has some force. Much of the relevance of Barth's argument with respect to power is at best implicit in his work. That doesn't, however, mean it is absent. A consistent theme running through Barth's work since the 1950s has been the fundamentally *political* nature of interaction. Competition and manoeuvre are ubiquitous, as are constraints of ecology and resources. Emphasising choice and decision-making does not mean that they only take place in a situation of equality between persons. Quite the reverse (and the echo of Marx is surely no accident):

> choice is not synonymous with freedom, and men and women rarely make choices under circumstances chosen by themselves. What is more, the unfortunate circumstance of a gross disadvantage of power does not mean that strategy is unavailing – indeed it may be all the more essential to the actor and all the more pervasive in shaping his behaviour.
>
> (Barth 1981: 89)

In emphasising the importance of assets for successful performance, and exploring the circumstances under which ethnic identifications are *not* validated, Barth is implicitly indicating the importance of power, in this case the power to define the situation successfully. Stressing that the dialectics of group identification and categorisation (to use my terms) are rooted in interpersonal transactions does not mean that each is equally important in specific situations. One is likely to dominate; *which* is a question likely to be decided by power differentials.

Barth's argument is, however, vulnerable to other criticisms. In suggesting that shared common knowledge, common sense and patterns of behaviour (similarity) come into being as a result of processes of identification (differentiation) at the boundary, rather than *vice versa*, he misses the dialectical simultaneity of identification. Neither similarity nor difference 'come first'. Subsequently, and somewhat contradictorily, however, in highlighting the role of values in orienting decision-making, he takes for granted a substantial degree of shared common sense and knowledge. This is part of his emphasis upon 'feedback', most evident in his 1966 *Models of Social Organisation*: upon how values change as a result of interactional experience. As Barth himself admits, he may have 'overestimated the potential power and adequacy' of the concept of 'value' (1981: 91). If nothing else, an emphasis upon values falls foul of the difficulty of attempting to know what is going on in other minds (Geertz 1983: 55–70; Holy and Stuchlik 1983). Nor, as discussed in Chapter 7 with respect to Goffman, are notions of choice and decision-making unproblematic. Exactly the same cautions apply in Barth's case.

Perhaps the most significant problem with Barth's work, however, attaches to the notion of 'boundary'. As we have seen, Barth himself has always recognised the danger, in subdividing the human world into distinct 'segments', of reifying collectivity. It's clear that he understands identity boundaries as somewhat indefinite, as ongoing emergent products of interaction, particularly between people holding different identities. It is in these ongoing transactions that what is or is not relevant as markers of the identities in question – and what 'being A' or 'being B' *means* in terms of consequences – comes into being. However, with its topological or territorial overtones, 'boundary' is a metaphor the use of which demands vigilance; witness the ease with which one talks about *the* boundary. It may be precisely Barth's emphasis on boundaries that has allowed many other anthropologists to draw on his work while persisting in the reifying view of the ethnic group as corporate and perduring which he intended to demolish (Brubaker and Cooper 2000: 21–5; Cohen 1978: 386–7; Jenkins 1997).

Recently, Barth has looked further at this issue (2000). Acknowledging that talking about boundaries may help us to think about collectivity, he insists that we must bear in mind two cautions:

- that to make a distinction between things is not necessarily to establish a definite boundary between them, and
- that 'boundary' is *our* analytical notion, which doesn't necessarily travel well: it isn't clear that all local traditions of human thought and being understand collectivity in a definitely bounded fashion.

For Barth, whether collective boundaries 'exist' – in the sense of being locally meaningful – is always a matter of discovery, a matter of respect for the observable realities of any local human world (for all that they may be Other-wise and difficult to comprehend or translate). The presence or importance of boundaries shouldn't be assumed.

Even where it can be said to exist, it's far from clear 'where' or 'what' the boundary of any particular identity 'is'. This is not surprising, since 'it' is not, really, any*where* or any*thing*. Boundaries are to be found in interaction between people who identify themselves collectively in different ways, which can in principle occur anywhere or in any context. Identification is not a simple matter of the 'cultural stuff' which is associated with any specific identity, and which may appear to constitute the solid criteria of membership. Identity is about boundary *processes* (Wallman 1986) rather than boundaries: it is a matter of identification. As interactional episodes, processes of identification are temporary checkpoints rather than concrete walls (and even the latter are permanent only in their makers' conceit: witness Maginot and Berlin). Boundary processes may be routinised or institutionalised in particular settings and occasions – something which I will discuss subsequently with respect to the institutionalisation of identity – but that is a different matter.

Finally, Barth's notion that revision of an identity occurs if it is 'objectively' incorrect requires more attention. As a moderate caution it is very sensible: the capacity of humans to define the reality of the human world in the face of 'the material world of causes and effects' is finite. But there is more to it than Barth's mention of the environment. Harking back to discussions in earlier chapters, the embodiment of identification is a case in point, for example. Gender is the obvious case. As the lives of transsexuals and transvestites attest, it is to some extent manipulable, but the definitive embodiment of female and male means that the scope for and ease of revision and change are limited. The same is true for other identifications that are defined in embodied terms, such as 'race' or age.

Embodiment aside, there is a more general point that is not to be denied. Albeit that it is 'socially constructed', the human world has its observable realities and these demand our respect if we are to understand that world (Jenkins 2002). A group of people without Norwegian passports, with no discoverable historical connections to Norway and speaking no Norwegian, cannot, for example, simply arrive at the Norwegian border and have any expectation of mounting a plausible claim to Norwegian identity or nationality. Even categorisation – the thoroughly external moment of identification – can never, as I argued in Chapter 8, be *wholly* arbitrary. There needs to be something to work with.

Thus actors' definitions of the situation cannot be unilaterally paramount. To begin with, not everything is thinkable in any given context; not everything that is thinkable is situationally practical; and not everything that occurs in practice is thinkable (or, at least, thought). And the matter of *whose* definition of the situation counts is always significant, returning us to the importance of power, authority and resources. In recognising this, Barth – like Goffman – is espousing a middle-of-the-road materialist realism that resonates with the core themes of pragmatism.

This is but one sense in which Barth stands in a line of thought which, via Goffman and the Chicago sociologists of the 1940s, reaches back to Mead and beyond. However, whereas Mead begins with the whole (the collective human world) and goes to the part (the individual), Barth works from individuals to the collective. Each makes his biggest error in conceptualising the matter in terms of a vector of one to the other. And in each case, the error is largely one of expression: they actually both imply models of the relationship between the collective and the individual as a perpetual and more or less simultaneous dialectic or feedback.

BEYOND ETHNICITY

Barth's is among the most developed, and the most convincingly empirically supported,[3] explorations of the interaction between internal and external collective identification, between group identification and categorisation, and between the individual and the collective. In this respect there are two themes, intimately related to each other, that stand out in his work:

- He is concerned to understand how difference is organised during, and arises out of, interaction. Rather than taking identity differences and boundaries for granted and then looking at how they affect interaction, Barth's approach is the reverse. He wants to know – and he *really* wants to know, rather than paying the idea lip service – how identification, difference and boundaries are socially constructed.
- In exploring what he has called (1994) the 'median' level of human collective life – analogous perhaps to the 'interaction order' (or Merton's 'middle range') – he offers a bridge between individuals, their practices and identifications, and collective forms and identifications.

Accepting these rather general propositions, it's now time to justify in more detail my earlier remark that Barth's arguments apply to identifications other than ethnicity.

Oblique confirmation of this proposition comes from a paper by Yehudi Cohen that appeared at the same time as Barth's ethnicity symposium (1969). In a discussion which appears to owe nothing to reading Barth, drawing heavily instead on the literature about networks, Cohen develops a model of 'boundary systems' that is remarkably similar to Barth's – intra- and intergroup relationships are seen as mutually dependent across a boundary – and applies it to collective identifications such as kinship and town membership. To anticipate the discussion in the next chapter, further indirect support for the argument can be drawn from the studies inspired by Anthony Cohen's model of communal belonging – rooted as it is in Barth's ideas – which deal with identities other than the ethnic.

In *Ethnic Groups and Boundaries*, however, Barth himself said little about this issue. In a tantalising aside, he suggested, for example, that, like 'sex and rank':

> ethnic identity implies a series of constraints on the kinds of roles an individual is allowed to play, and the partners he may choose for different transactions . . . ethnic identity is superordinate to most other statuses, and defines the permissible constellation of statuses, or social personalities, which an individual with that identity may assume.
>
> (Barth 1969: 17)

But that was all. Fifteen years later, however, in a study of everyday life in Sohar, Oman (1983; 1984), Barth painted a picture of the organisation of difference using a wider palette, albeit with a fine brush:

> the diversity of identities that entails membership in distinctive culture-carrying groups in Sohar was not one that I had expected. I arrived in the field with the expectation that ethnicity would provide the primary ordering identities . . . The dismantling of this picture . . . [was] my response to empirical findings in Sohar.
>
> (Barth 1983: 81fn.)

To understand the pluralism of the town of Sohar, it proved necessary to develop a model of diversity (Barth 1983: 81–93; 1984) which could encompass the following 'universes of discourse' or 'streams of tradition':

- *ethnicity* (Arab, Baluchi, Persian, Zidgali, Indian Banyan), each with its own language, with Arabic as the *lingua franca*;
- *gender*, including institutionalised transsexualism (Wikan 1977), in Barth's view the deepest and most ubiquitous distinction of all;
- *history* and *descent* (10 per cent of the population are the stigmatised descendants of former slaves);
- *religion* (Sunni Islam, Shiah Islam, Ibhazi Islam, Hindu);
- *occupation* and *class*; and
- *settlement* and *lifestyle* (the distinction between townspeople and recently settled Bedouin).

To this list, although Barth might not conceptualise them as aspects of pluralism, one could append further universes of discourse such as kinship or age.

The domains of identity that Barth explored in Sohar are bounded, but only very weakly: there is coming and going across them, and little in the way of mutual reinforcement between them. The overlaps are complex. There is a varied range of processes of group identification and categorisation. Some people, some collectivities, are in a stronger position to construct their identities and resist the imposition of identification by others; some are in a weaker position.

Soharis in their daily lives, and in the pursuit of their varied interests, spin the different strands into distinctive threads of biography and individual identity. In their transactions and interactions they weave a carpet of complex plurality. In doing so, the mundane preoccupations of their daily lives emerge out of and are channelled by the histories to which they further contribute, and the local is brought to bear upon and is framed by wider networks and 'external' events and processes. The town is a 'kaleidoscope of persons' (Barth 1983: 165).

This summary of the ethnographic riches of Barth's study, and that of his collaborator, Wikan, makes a *prima facie* case for arguing that his model applies to a universe of identification wider than ethnicity. It also supports Barth's latter-day observation, perhaps a little tongue-in-cheek, that the original ethnicity symposium,

> contains, perhaps, one of the first anthropological applications of a more postmodern view of culture. Though we lacked the opaque terminology of present day postmodernism, we certainly argued for what would now be recognised as a constructionist view. Likewise in our view of history: we broke loose from the idea of history as simply the objective source and cause of ethnicity, and saw it as a synchronic rhetoric – a struggle to appropriate the past, as one might say today.
>
> (Barth 1994: 12–13)

His recent discussion of boundaries, in which he mentions ethnic groups, corporate groups, households and formal institutions, is further evidence that he sees his approach as widely applicable (Barth 2000).

So Barth offers us a *general* model of collective identification, within which all the domains of identification (my term) or universes of discourse (his) encompassed by the Sohar study are understandable. The same general model was quite clearly present, even if implicit, in 1969 in *Ethnic Groups and Boundaries*:

- Identification is *processual*, part of the ongoing organisation of interaction and everyday life. It is not to be understood as part of a superstructure of 'culture'.
- The analytical emphasis falls on the social construction of identities in interaction at and across the *boundaries* that they share with other identities, and upon processes of recruitment.
- Collective identification and its boundaries are, thus, generated in

transaction and interaction and are, at least potentially, *flexible*, *situational* and *negotiable*. Barth begins with embodied individuals in interaction and works up to collective forms.

- Identification is a matter of *ascription*: *by* individuals of themselves, and *of* individuals by others. Collectively, the same holds good: group members identify themselves and are categorised by members of other groups.

- Finally, it is an important implication of Barth's emphasis upon transaction that collective identification is inherently *political*.

This is a model of the collective dialectic of identification, of the entanglement and interplay of group identification and categorisation, and of how that occurs in interaction between individuals. It has the widest possible application. However, in emphasising the social organisation of difference, Barth arguably underplays the question of similarity. It is to this that I now turn.

10

SYMBOLISING BELONGING

Although the previous chapter focused on the role of *difference* in collective identification, it still makes sense to say that the emphasis in collective identification falls upon *similarity*. Group identification, by definition, presupposes that members will see themselves as minimally similar. Categorisation is predicated upon the proposition that those who are categorised have a criterion of identification in common. Collectivity means having something in common, whether 'real' or imagined, trivial or important, strong or weak. Without some commonality there can be no collectivity.

These issues have a long history in social theory, particularly the theme that the less stuff people have in common with each other, the more problematic collective cohesion becomes. Marx's writings on alienation, and his subsequent discussions of class conflict and mobilisation, are about this. When Ferdinand Tönnies, writing in 1887, posited a historical shift from *gemeinschaft* ('community') to *gesellschaft* ('association') he, too, was concerned with what people had in common and how it was changing. Durkheim's distinction in *The Division of Labour in Society*, first published in 1893, between the mechanical solidarity of traditional rural life, in which similarity bound people together – an image reminiscent of Marx's description, in *The Eighteenth Brumaire of Louis Bonaparte*, of the French peasantry as 'potatoes in a sack' – and the differentiated complementarity, or organic solidarity, of the newly industrialised world, evokes the same theme. So does his notion of the *conscience collective*.

Ever since Durkheim, the classic territory within which these themes have been explored has been 'the community'. Thinking about community probably has its deepest roots in the romantic intellectual tradition in European social thought, in response to the uncertainties and conflicts of rapid modernisation and industrialisation. 'Community' called up an imagined past in which horizons were local, the meaning of life was relatively consensual, cooperation prevailed, and everyone knew everyone else and 'knew their place'. However, in a post-1945 world characterised by affluence, mobility and consumerism on the one hand, and conflict, the shadow of genocide and a gradual retreat from socialism on the other, 'community', and the approach to empirical research known as the 'community study', became increasingly contentious (Bell and Newby 1971; Stein 1960). Agreed definitions of the basic notion became ever more elusive and, facing competition from theoretical newcomers such as 'culture', 'community' slowly withdrew to the margins of the syllabus (where it would eventually be joined by 'class'). Postmodernism's celebration of diversity, flux and decentred polyvalence looked like the final nail in the concept's coffin.

However, 'community' does not belong to intellectuals. It is a powerful everyday notion in terms of which people organise their lives and understand the places and settlements in which they live and the quality of their relationships. It expresses a fundamental set of human needs (Doyal and Gough 1991; Ignatieff 1984). Along with the idioms of kinship, friendship, ethnicity and faith, 'community' is one way of talking about the everyday reality that the human world is, collectively, more than the sum of its individual parts (Jenkins 2002: 63–84). As such 'community', and its analogues in languages other than English, is among the most important sources of collective identification. Whatever we do with it, it isn't to be ignored.

It probably isn't too surprising, therefore, that the idea of 'community' has experienced a recent revival within the social sciences (Crow and Allen 1994; Delanty 2003). Whether in Bauman's cautious rediscovery of the post-postmodern virtues of collectivity (2001), in communitarianism and the critical responses to it (Etzioni 1993; Sennett 1998), in the notion of 'social capital' (Putnam 2000), in lively anthropological debates (Amit 2002; Amit and Rapport 2002), in discussions of 'communities of practice' (Wenger 1998), and in empirical studies of aspects of 'community' (e.g. Bellah et al. 1991; 1996; Blokland 2003; Keller 2003), the idea shows signs of returning to a centre-stage position that would have seemed unlikely twenty years ago.

SYMBOLISING COMMUNITY

Despite this recent renaissance, in order to understand better community and collectivity I am going to turn to a framework that is, in fact, just about twenty years old itself. Not only is it a previous generation of intellectual software, but, to make matters worse, it has recently been repudiated by its author, Anthony Cohen. Drawing on his argument (1994) that selfhood, identification and consciousness are rooted in an irreducible and interior essence of stable, private, self-consciousness Cohen has now taken to task his own work, *The Symbolic Construction of Community* (1985), criticising it and himself for: 'the attribution to identity of the characteristics of relativity and an ephemeral nature; and concomitantly, the denial to identity (communal or individual) of constancy' (Cohen 2002: 166).

It isn't the notion of community itself that bothers Cohen. Rather, he is resisting the notion that communal boundaries are by definition negotiable and shifting, merely a matter of who stands where, and deploring the neglect of relatively autonomous communal self-identification that he sees as resulting from the emphasis on transactions at the boundary. Both these elements of his original argument derive, interestingly enough, from Barth.[1] Collective identification, he seems to be saying, has to be something more solid, something more authentic.

I make no apologies, however, for insisting that Cohen's original model of the 'symbolic construction' of communal and other collective identities remains useful (Cohen 1982; 1985; 1986). More than useful, in fact: it's indispensible, exploring how people construct a sense of themselves and their fellows as 'belonging' *in* a particular locality or setting of relationships and interaction, and *with* – if not *to* – each other. This is what Cohen meant by 'community' in the 1980s and it seems to be pretty much what he still means (2002: 168–9). Although, the argument was developed during his work in peripheral communities within large-scale polities, his framework offers a set of general, and generalisable, propositions about communal life:

- community membership depends upon the symbolic construction and signification of a mask of similarity which all can wear, an umbrella of solidarity under which all can shelter;
- the similarity of communal membership is thus imagined;
- inasmuch as it is a potent symbolic presence in people's lives, and community is not, however, imaginary.

Like most social theory, Cohen's was a creative synthesis. Drawing on the Durkheimian tradition of British social anthropology – emphasising the role of symbolism in creating solidarity – Cohen's understanding of the significance of communal boundaries, as has already been pointed out, owed much to Barth. With respect to the politics of symbolism, he acknowledged the influence of the Manchester School of social anthropologists, particularly Max Gluckman (1956), Victor Turner (1967) and Abner Cohen (1974), while his emphasis upon meaning derived from Geertz (1973; 1983) and, ultimately, Weber.

Cohen's starting point was that 'community' encompasses notions of similarity and difference, 'us' and 'them' again. This focuses attention on the boundary, which is where the sense of belonging becomes most apparent:

> The sense of difference . . . lies at the heart of people's awareness of their culture and, indeed, makes it appropriate for ethnographers to designate as 'cultures' such arenas of distinctiveness. . . . people become aware of their culture when they stand at its boundaries.
>
> (Cohen 1982: 2, 3)

Recognition of a 'sense of us' and community stems from the awareness that things are done differently *there*, and the sense of threat that poses for how things are done *here*. The debt to Barth is obvious: in particular note that collective forms – such as 'cultures' – are produced by the local sense of difference at the boundary.

However, 'community' in this model is not material or practical in the way that identity is generated interactionally for Barth. But neither is it 'structural'. It is definitively 'cultural', and as such – anticipating Cohen's later arguments about selfhood and identity – mental or cognitive:

> culture – the community as experienced by its members – does not consist in social structure or in 'the doing' of social behaviour. It inheres, rather, in 'the thinking' about it. It is in this sense that we can speak of the community as a symbolic, rather than a structural, construct.
>
> (Cohen 1985: 98)

Emphasising the symbolic construction of 'community', Cohen advanced three arguments:

- *Symbols generate a sense of shared belonging.* A sports team, for example, can excite the allegiance of, thus uniting, all or most of a community's members, coming, in time, to symbolise the community to its members and to outsiders. Shared rituals – whether weddings and funerals, or rituals of community such as the annual fête or the works outing – can also act *for* the community as symbols *of* community.

- '*Community*'[2] *is itself a symbolic construct upon which people draw, rhetorically and strategically.* Claims to act in the best interests of the 'community' or to represent the 'community' are powerful. We're all supposed to be in favour of 'community': it's a feel-good word carrying a powerful symbolic load, hence its political uses, as in 'community care', for example (Bulmer 1987). 'Community' is ideological: it not only says how things are, it says how they *should* be. It's also 'essentially enshrined in the concept of boundary' (Cohen 1985: 14): it symbolises *exclusion* as well as *inclusion*. Hence its rhetorical potency in ethnically divided situations such as Northern Ireland.

- *Community membership means sharing with other community members a similar 'sense of things', participation in a common symbolic domain.* This does not entail either a local consensus of values or conformity in behaviour: 'community', for example, means different things to different community members. So do symbols of community. The rugby club in a south Wales valley, for example, will be experienced and understood differently by an ex-player, by a teacher who has only recently come to live locally and by the wife of an unemployed man who spends too much money in the club bar. But each of them may see themselves as supporters of the team, particularly if it's doing well in the Cup, and to each the club may represent 'the community'. What matters is not that people see or understand things the same, or that they see and understand things differently from other communities, but that their shared symbols allow them to *believe* that they do.

Whether we are talking about 'symbols *of* community' or 'community *as* a symbol', the power of the notions and images thus mobilised depends on the capacity of symbols to encompass and condense a range of, not necessarily harmonious or congruent, meanings. By definition, symbols are abstract to a degree, imprecise to a degree, always multifaceted and frequently implicit or taken-for-granted in their definition. As a consequence, people can to some degree bestow their own meanings on symbols; they can say and do the 'same' things without saying or doing the same things at all. This returns us to the distinction between the nominal and the virtual. The nominal – the name or description of an identification – is always symbolic. In addition to language, it may be further symbolised in heraldry, dress, ritual or other material and practical forms. Which is precisely why the nominal can be associated with a wide range of virtualities without change or abandonment.

So the sense of homogeneity or uniformity that is apparent within local communities is just that: *apparent* and every inch a collective – and symbolic – construct:

> the members of a community may all assent to the collective wisdom that they are different from other communities in a variety of stereotypical respects. But this is not to say that they see each other, or themselves, manifesting these differences similarly.
>
> (Cohen 1986: 11)

Using an expression which recalled Barth (1981: 12, 79–81), Cohen argued that the ties or bindings of 'community' *aggregate* rather than *integrate*: 'what is actually held in common is not very substantial, being *form* rather than content. Content differs widely among members' (Cohen 1985: 20).

Differences of opinion and more – of world view, cosmology and other fundamentals – among and between members of the same community are normal, even inevitable. They are masked by a semblance of agreement and convergence generated by shared communal symbols, and participation in a common symbolic discourse of community membership which constructs and emphasises the boundary between members and non-members. Thus members can present a consistent face to the outside world. One might also say – although Cohen didn't put it like this – that the symbolic construction of community allows people who have to get on with each other to do so without having to explore their differences in damaging detail.

Here Cohen, once again anticipating his later arguments about self-identification, introduced a distinction between the public and the private:

> The boundary thus symbolises the community to its members in two quite different ways: it is the sense they have of its perception by people on the other side – the public face, or 'typical' mode; and it is their own sense of the community as refracted through all the complexities of their lives and experience – the private face, and 'idiosyncratic' mode. It is in the latter mode that we find people thinking about and symbolising their community.
>
> (Cohen 1986: 13)

This is almost a communal 'I' and 'me'. The symbolisation of community is, once again, to be found in 'thinking' rather than in 'doing'.

Cohen rounded his argument out with the suggestion that symbolic boundaries – of hearts and minds – become more important as boundaries of place and locality become less important, with political centralisation, lifestyle standardisation and national integration. The more pressure there is on communities to change as part of this process, the more vigorously boundaries will be symbolised. Difference will be constructed and emphasised and *we*-ness asserted in opposition to *them*. A symbolically contrived sense of local similarity may be the only available defence. In some cases the hardening of an apparently 'traditional' identity may actually serve as a smokescreen, behind which substantial change can take place with less conflict and dislocation.

Various criticisms can be made of Anthony Cohen's original framework. For example, his contrast between 'thinking' and 'doing' is problematic (Jenkins 1981), as is his distinction between 'social structure' and 'culture'. In particular, the epistemological difficulties of his emphasis upon what people *think* cannot be underestimated. Discussing the private 'thinking of community' (Cohen 1986: 9) he anticipated his recent insistence on the essential privacy of meaning and individual identification (1994), discussed in Chapter 4. As suggested there, any analysis developed on these terms is opaque, relying on assertion rather than evidence.

Fortunately, in his original work on *collective* identity, Cohen's emphasis upon individual private thoughts was almost irrelevant. Advancing his argument by means of apt ethnographic case study and illustration, he presented, over and over again, accounts of people *doing* things: saying this or that, participating in rituals, mounting political protests, fishing together, or whatever. It's in and out of what people *do* that a shared sense of things and a shared symbolic universe emerge. And it's in talking together about 'community' – which is, after all, a public *doing* – that its symbolic value is produced and reproduced.

There are other problems, too. Focusing on the anthropologised margins, Cohen overemphasised the homogenising, flattening effect on communities of their integration into nation-states and wider polities. Even more important, he exaggerated the uniformity, and the monolithic tendencies, of large-scale political units. Doing what many anthropologists do – treating 'beyond the community' as the modern equivalent of 'here be dragons' on a medieval map – he didn't attend to the complexity, divisions and tensions of state and nation and their constituent institutions. Which is ironic. Almost every thread in his analysis of the 'symbolic construction of community' could have been woven into a model of the 'symbolic construction of the nation' (and indeed, in many respects, it already had: see, for example, Anderson 1983). The 'community' of locality and settlement is no less imagined than the 'community' of the *nation*, and no less symbolically constructed.

A related difficulty is that he didn't explore situations in which collective communal solidarity is *not* symbolically reasserted in the face of external pressure. He replaced structural-functionalism's image of consensus with a model of *imagined* consensus or homogeneity that is no less unlikely to fit all situations. How, one wonders, would Cohen accommodate the fractured towns and villages of Sicily and Calabria,[3] or inner city neighbourhoods in the United States,[4] within his framework? The ethnographic evidence suggests that while the conventional understanding of 'community' doesn't fit the bill, situations such as these can't be explained away as anomic disorder either. Cohen's model *can*, however, be expanded to include them, at least in principle. There is ample evidence of collective identification – within families, networks, churches, gangs or informal associations, for example – that could quite easily be grist to his analytical mill. But the mask of *community* has slipped: that *particular* umbrella is in tatters. That Cohen neglected to take on the local fragmentation of communal identification – its symbolic *de*construction, if you like – was an opportunity missed to widen the scope of his theoretical framework.

Allowing for these criticisms, however, his original framework brings much to the sociology of identification. In the first place, he recognised that his analysis wasn't confined to localities of physical co-residence (1985: 97–118). Although the emphasis on community as a mental construct created problems, it permitted the application of his model to a wide variety of collectivities: communities of interest, geographically extensive ethnic communities, occupational communities, religious communities, transnational communities, cyber-communities, and so on (see, for example, Howell 2002). These are all collectivities to which one can 'belong'. Cohen's arguments are relevant beyond the village or the neighbourhood. In his edited volume about 'Identity and Diversity in British Cultures' (Cohen 1986), for example, households, kinship, adolescence and a farm are among the communities of identification discussed by the contributors.

Second, his original framework complements Barth's, offering a more developed model of the relationship between boundaries of identification and their 'contents' – the common sense, common knowledge and patterns of behaviour shared by the people inside the boundary – while still emphasising the possibility of flexibility and variability. Bearing in mind his emphasis upon cognition and concomitant de-emphasis of inter-action, Cohen's original understanding of boundaries was more 'definite' than Barth's (thus already implying, perhaps, his subsequent self-critique). But in taking seriously the 'cultural stuff' within the boundary, and emphasising symbolisation rather than values, Cohen offered an advance on

Barth (which further suggests that his critique of his own neglect of collective self-identification is probably a little harsh).

Collective identities are not 'internally' homogeneous or consensual. They can and do change; they can and do vary from context to context; they can and do vary from person to person; and yet they can and do *persist*. Cohen's self-critique overlooks the fact that it is precisely the 'constancy' of collective identification that his original framework helps us to understand. Without emphasising the symbolic dimensions of identification – in addition to the transactional and interactional – the enduring more-than-the-sum-of-parts of collectivity cannot, in fact, be fully understood.

SIMILARITY AND DIFFERENCE REVISITED

Symbolisations of community are umbrellas under which diversity can flourish, masks behind which a considerable degree of heterogeneity is possible. In my terms, the mask or umbrella is a *nominal* identification. This is always symbolised: in language, but also potentially in other forms, whether visual, musical or whatever. The practice and experience of community membership, *vis-à-vis* other members and outsiders, is the *virtual* dimension of communal identification. It may, in large degree, be individually idiosyncratic. Both nominal and virtual have internal and external moments of identification; both are a dialectic of group identification and categorisation. Each feeds back upon the other (to return to Barth). The distinction between the nominal and the virtual allows an emphasis upon process and the practices of embodied individuals to be integrated into Cohen's original scheme.

Cohen was saying, most convincingly, that the similarity emphasised by collective identities is a construction, an ongoing historical contrivance, reminiscent perhaps of Bourdieu's 'cultural arbitrary'. It stems from the minimal sharing of a symbolic repertoire. But, of course, and I think Cohen would not disagree, in that the individuals concerned believe in it – in the sense of organising their lives with reference to it – it is not only 'socially real', it is consequential. And sometimes very powerfully consequential. A flag may only be a symbol of national unity, but there are too many historical examples of individuals perishing in its defence to take it anything but seriously. There is no such thing as *just* a symbol. Nor can a community ever be imaginary (even though it can never be anything other than imagined).

And Cohen was saying more: if communal identification is a collective contrivance, it is contrived within a comparative framework of similarity *and* difference. It evokes our difference from them as well as our similarity to each other. But that's not all. Throughout Cohen's argument, and in his choice of examples, he emphasised that the 'belonging' of 'community' is symbolically constructed by people in response to, even as a defence against, their categorisation by outsiders, whether they be the folk from the next village, tourists upon whose cash locals might depend, the representatives of an oil company, environmental protesters or the officers and impersonal agencies of the state. Against these foils difference is asserted and similarity symbolically constructed; it is in their face that communal identification is necessary. It is here in Cohen's original framework that we see the internal–external dialectic of collective identification at work.

To recall a point made elsewhere, words such as 'response' or 'defence' should not be misconstrued to imply necessary *sequence*. They do not mean that communal identification, the shared sense of belonging together, is absent until, one morning, along comes the outside world to conjure them up. There will always have been an 'outside world', even if only the next village. However, the outside world's salience, its power and size, and its perceived distance and difference from 'us', may all change. In the process, as part of an ongoing dialectic of collective identification, community may be more explicitly stressed and practices of communal symbolisation and differentiation increasingly called into play in the solidary affirmation of similarity and the defence of perceived collective interests. To reiterate another earlier point, collective identificatory strategies stressing symbolisations other than the strictly communal – family, friendship or whatever – may be alternatives to a communal response.

The similarities here with social psychology's 'self-categorisation theory' (Turner 1984; Turner *et al.* 1987) are sufficiently striking to deserve brief comment. That approach argues that in response to 'external' situational contingencies individuals select, from the available possibilities, and not necessarily self-consciously, collective identifications with which to identify themselves (and to identify themselves with). In the process, they contribute to the production and reproduction of the collectivities with which they are identifying, evoking and constructing intragroup similarities and intergroup differences. This theory, with something in common with both Barth and Cohen, could be described as another version of the internal– external dialectic of identification, albeit a very individualist one.

BOUNDARIES, RELATIONSHIPS AND EMBODIMENT

The internal–external dialectic allows us to think about boundaries of identification – A/not A – without reifying them. One metaphor for boundaries might be the dash between the internal and the external (a dash, after all, meaning nothing without whatever it connects). In another image, the boundary can be seen as the dialectical synthesis of internal thesis and external antithesis: the identity is in important senses the boundary. These ways of thinking about the matter converge, in that each involves at least two simultaneous points of view. The internal definition of A is external from the point of view of B, and *vice versa*. Similarly, A and B can be thesis, antithesis or synthesis, depending on one's starting point (of view). Boundaries are definitively relational, simultaneously connecting and separating one side and another.

This definitively relational nature of boundaries of identification is closely connected to the symbolisation of identity. In the first place, symbols only 'make sense' in relation to other symbols. Meaning is a product of system and relation; nothing means anything on its own. Similarity, for example, cannot be established without also delineating difference. The second place, however, is more interesting. This is, 'the line of argument of the French sociologists of *L'Année sociologique* . . . that the social relations of men provide the prototype for the logical relations between things' (Douglas 1973: 11). That line of argument stretches from Durkheim and Mauss, via Lévi-Strauss, to Michel Foucault, Mary Douglas herself and Pierre Bourdieu. In the present context, it points to a reciprocal mutuality of signification between symbolisation and identification. This means that identification is not just a sub-set of the general symbolic domain that we routinely, and carelessly, reify as 'culture'. As the symbolic constitution of relationships of similarity and difference between collectivities and embodied individuals, identification provides the basic template – via analogy, metaphor, homology, etc. – for the wider constitution of the world as meaningful. Identification thus emerges as fundamental to cognition, a view which resonates with the arguments of Marx and Mead, that interaction between humans is the *a priori* of consciousness, rather than *vice versa*.

If interactional relations provide the model for symbolic relations – i.e. for *meaning* – then it is important to remember that those are relations between individuals, and that those individuals are embodied. This is recognised by, among others, Douglas (1973), Bourdieu (1977: 87–95; 1990: 66–79) and Lakoff and Johnson (1999). The collective point of view imagines a world with humanity at its centre; the individual point of view centres on the body. With respect to identity, this is perhaps most significant in that the (individual) human body provides a basic metaphor for symbolising and imagining collective identities. It's not only social scientists who 'see' the human world using organic analogies. In English, for example, we talk about 'the head of the family', 'the head of state', 'the heart of the community' or 'the backbone of the organisation'. We say that a particular group 'has guts'. Communities can be 'alive' or 'dead'. One could doubtless find many other examples. Even collective identification, it seems, draws symbolically on embodiment as a model or evocation of its consistency and integrity.

The symbolisation of identification offers a further perspective on the processes during which the embodied individual and the abstract collective converge. Individual and collective identifications are inherently symbolised, particularly in the symbolic interaction of language (remember the discussion of Mead in Chapter 4). Language allows individuals to participate in the collective domain; according to Mead, it permits reflexive selfhood, in the capacity to take on the role of the Other. In summarising what might otherwise be vast amounts of information about people, condensing it into manageable forms, the symbolisation of identification also allows us, sociologically and in everyday life, to think about and to model – in other words to imagine – collectivities and the relations between them. Symbolisation permits the necessary abstraction of individuals and collectivities, and of the relationships between them, which is the constitutional basis of the notion of 'society'.

Among the most important aspects of the symbolisation of identity in this respect is that it allows individual diversity and collective similarity to coexist within the human world. There is no need to wonder about why people who 'are' the same don't all 'do' the same. For practical purposes and in certain contexts, we simply imagine them as more or less the same. And that imagining is 'socially real'. The symbolisation of identification works, what is more, in a similar fashion whether individually or collectively. One way of talking about selfhood, for example, is as a symbolisation of the complexities of individuals, a means of glossing them with enough consistency to allow others to decide how to act towards them. The identification of individuals with respect to their membership of collectivities contributes in the same way to the expectations that others have of them. The point is not that this consistency is 'objectively real', but that it provides a plausible basis for a minimum of predictability during interaction and in the course of relationships between people.

The unity of selfhood is in one sense an umbrella or mask, under or behind which the diversity and contradictions of the individually embodied point of view over time and across situations can coexist, back-stage, without having to be perpetually in the front-stage public limelight (to the likely confusion of self and others). The parallel with the 'symbolic construction of community' is clear: selfhood is no less imagined than any other identity. Identification, whether individual or collective, is always symbolically constructed.

THE INESCAPABLE ABSTRACTION OF EVERYDAY LIFE

Looking at symbolisation draws our attention to the necessary abstraction of identification. Sociologically speaking, images of identity – selfhood, community or whatever – look very like what Max Weber called *ideal types* (1949: 90–106). An ideal type is an abstract model of any particular collective pattern or form, with two basic characteristics:

- An ideal type is a synthesis of/from a myriad of 'more or less present and occasionally absent' collective phenomena. Not everything that is a specified feature of an ideal type is necessarily present in any actual case.
- Phenomena are included as elements of an ideal type on the basis of the 'accentuating' point or points of view – in the sociological case, theoretical positions and interests – from which it is constructed.[5]

Among the examples of social scientific ideal types that Weber offered are the 'city-economy', 'capitalistic culture', 'feudalism', 'the state' and 'Christianity'. The construction of ideal types by social scientists is a heuristic procedure that permits comparison and hypothesis formulation in the face of the extreme diversity and density of everyday life.

Weber recognised that many ideal types are not only *analytical* models, but are also meaningful *folk* models (which harks back to the discussion of groups and categories in Chapter 8). Sociologists are not the only people who need to compare things, or frame working hypotheses. Nor do they have any monopoly on the complexity of collective life. Alfred Schutz (1967: 176–250) expanded upon Weber's conception of the ideal type to make this point more thoroughly. Schutz argued that all of our knowledge of the world – whether common-sensical or sociological – is in the form of ideal typifications. Given the inherently symbolic nature of language this is perhaps no more than we might expect.

Schutz distinguishes our direct face-to-face knowledge of our *fellows* in the everyday human world, from our indirect experience of *contemporaries*, who we have never met and may never meet.[6] Our ideal typical models of our contemporaries are likely to be more abstract than the typifications – based in direct experience – which we draw upon to understand and render more predictable people who we 'know'. There is a continuum, from more concrete to more abstract, which Schutz expresses from an ego's point of view, as a move from *We* to *Thou* to *They*. From the direct vividness of my face-to-face interaction with known others, the human world becomes ever more 'remote and anonymous' as I look out into the world of my contemporaries. Eventually the boundary of that world is reached in artefacts which 'bear witness' to their meaning for some unknown Others, but don't identify those Others to me. Beyond that boundary my contemporaries are inaccessible. What Schutz is saying here is relevant to our understanding of similarity and difference:

> All our knowledge of our fellow men is in the last analysis based on personal experience. Ideal-typical knowledge of our contemporaries, on the other hand, is not concerned with the other person in his given concrete immediacy but in what he is, in the characteristics he has in common with others.
>
> (Schutz 1967: 193)

This resembles closely my proposition that individual identification emphasises difference, while collective identification emphasises similarity. The 'concrete immediacy' of our fellows differentiates one from another as complex individuals; our contemporaries have 'in common' their collective similarity as members of this or that particular category.

Schutz's distinction between fellows and contemporaries illuminates the nuances of the relationship between similarity and difference, as it is worked out differently with respect to individuals and collectivities. For example, despite Schutz's stress on what they have in common, it is clear that contemporaries are definitely individuals, even though they may be shadowy and anonymous. I know that the Mexican Navy, for example, is made up of real sailors; I don't recognise any of their faces, however. Even in the case of contemporaries with faces, in the absence of knowledge based in direct personal experience one relies on more superficial, less individualised knowledge about them, among which their participation in collective identifications, such as gender, ethnicity, residence, class or occupation, will be prominent. Allowing for that, however, that one of my fellows is, say, Mrs Oswald's daughter, baby Helena's mother and the owner of a red Mazda coupé, who dropped a bag full of groceries outside my door yesterday (which I helped her to pick up at the same time as having a chat about the new couple who have just bought the house two doors away), will probably be more relevant to me than her collective identifications as female, Afro-Caribbean, middle class and a lawyer.

But this example itself demands further elaboration. I cannot, for example, *forget* that Mrs Oswald's daughter is female. Otherwise she would be Mrs Oswald's son, and could not possibly be Helena's mother. And the relevance of gender depends upon point of view, whether 'I' am male or female, regardless of closeness of relationship and directness of knowledge (and not actually regardless: the nature of intimacy and its likelihood between individuals are both influenced by gender). Gender, the embodied intersection of one relationship of similarity and one of difference, is simultaneously and definitively a matter of individual fellowship and collective contemporaneity.

Nor is ethnicity – 'race' in this case – disregardable. 'My' ethnic point of view matters, depending on context. When I first encountered the woman who I now know to be Helena's mother, that she was Afro-Caribbean may have been the first and most significant thing that I noticed about her. And *is* Mrs Oswald Afro-Caribbean? And what might it tell me if she were not? Similarly the fact that her daughter owns the red Mazda tells me something about her class, which in itself may call up knowledge about her profession. And that she is a lawyer is a significant aspect of her individual identity as one of my fellows: you never know when you might need a bit of informal legal advice. Etcetera. No less important, there is also the place of collective identifications in *her* self-image, which none of the above even begins to touch on.

Our knowledge of our fellows – their individual identity in our eyes – can never, whether in the last analysis or not, be completely 'based on personal experience' as Schutz claims. I do not, for example, have to experience Mrs Oswald's daughter practising law to know, for all practical purposes and until otherwise proven wrong, not only that she is a lawyer, but also (approximately) what being a lawyer entails. That is a matter of the things she has in common with other members of the professional collectivity – lawyers – that she claims as her own. What we know about individuals as fellows in our everyday lives, and the plausible expectations we have of them, are as much a matter of their collective identifications as our direct experience of them.

Nor are our contemporaries only known to us in terms of their collective similarities to specified others. The President of the United States – as I write it is George W. Bush – is not one of my fellows. Even so, I would recognise him if I bumped into him in the High Street. In his case, however – unlike his predecessor, Bill Clinton – I could neither name nor recognise his wife. The media ensure that I know a great deal about Bill and Hilary – from their marriage, to their politics, to their business dealings – although I cannot personally vouch for the accuracy of my knowledge. More to the point, do I know any less about Clinton or Bush than I know about the neighbour with whom I pass the time of day every day, discussing only the garden and the weather, and is what I know any less accurate, less verifiable or less concrete?

One resolution of these questions might suggest that all our fellows are, in some aspects of their lives and in some circumstances, also our contemporaries. That this is so may, when it becomes apparent, be a potent source of distress in close relationships: 'To think I thought I knew her' is too common a theme to require elaboration. We simply can't have full direct experience of even our closest intimates. Each of our fellows is identified individually by us via their idiosyncratic combination of collective identifications and the synthetic, rolling account provided by our direct experience of them. And on the other hand we know about our contemporaries in vastly different degrees of detail and individuality.

The more people have to do with each other in everyday life, the more likely they will be to identify each other as *fellow* individuals, rather than primarily by reference to their collective identifications. Others, looking into the everyday human world from a distance or 'outside' will, however, be more likely to identify them first as members of a collectivity, as *contemporaries*. Whether someone is my fellow or my contemporary is always a function of my point of view. At the boundary, in encounters between 'insiders' and 'outsiders' – which is, once again, always relative, a matter of point of view – when insiders come to see themselves, in the internal–external dialectic of collective identification, as belonging, there is a constant interplay of similarity and difference. As symbolic constructions, each is imagined. In their consequences, however, neither is imaginary.

11

PREDICTABILITY

Collectivity may not require consensus, but a degree of *consistency* is important in the human world. The symbolisation of communal identity generates an imagined similarity, which, as Anthony Cohen argues, permits difference and heterogeneity to prosper. But if diversity were all, human life would be complex and unpredictable to the point of being unimaginable. Because communal identity, for example, is a cognitive and emotional reality to individuals – and it, therefore, influences their behaviour – it is 'socially real' in W. I. Thomas's sense. People may or may not think the same, but there must be *some* reciprocal and consistent similarity, even if not uniformity, in what co-members *do*. Identification is a practical matter – something that people do – and it involves similarity as well as difference.

Which brings me back to Barth, for whom consistent patterns of behaviour generate identity boundaries and collective forms more generally. Goffman alludes to this when he talks about 'routines' and 'presentation', and Schutz seems to imply it in his definition of a 'personal ideal type' – a model or typification of a particular kind of person and of what it is plausible to expect of them – as '*by definition* one who acts in such and such a way' (1967: 190, original emphasis). Should their behaviour not conform to the ideal type, then eventually the individual will be re-identified with reference to another ideal type.

CONFORMITY AND CONFORMISM

One way to look at *collective* consistency is in terms of conformity and conformism. Conventional social psychological wisdom (Aronson 1991:

12–55), which resonates with Mead and Goffman, suggests that two motivations inspire conforming behaviour: the desire to be correct, and the desire to remain in the good graces of others. The first has its greatest impact on back-stage private decision-making, the second on front-stage public behaviour. Each is rooted in primary socialisation and each is an emotional allotrope of the desire to *belong*. External factors that impinge upon conforming orientations vary according to local common sense and knowledge, situational contingencies and individual point of view. Non-conforming behaviour, deviance if you like, may come most easily to those whose group membership is secure in the mainstream. Insecure member-ship may thus encourage conforming behaviour, although one would expect to find a point of marginality beyond which this is no longer true. This puts a new spin upon Cohen's argument about the symbolic power of bound-aries to license or accommodate within them a degree of dissensus and heterogeneity.

Aronson recognises that conforming behaviour may have sources other than these conscious goal-orientations. *Compliance*, for example, is produced by compulsion. While it may only be weak *conformity*, which won't survive relaxation of the coercion, it is significant. *Identification* depends upon affective powers of attraction, in intimate dyadic relationships and in more collective or public contexts: here the result is conform*ism*. Identification, of course, is related to the desire to stay in the good graces of others. *Internalisation*, finally, results in this model from learning and rational-isation. Here, conformism results from doing whatever is thought – within local canons of rationality – to be the most sensible response to the demands of the situation; it is also routinely reflected in the thoughtlessness of habitual routines.

This social psychological scheme is not wholly straightforward, however. Attempting to distinguish 'internalisation' from the 'desire to be correct', for example, looks like hair-splitting: locally specific canons of 'correctness' are central to both, and in both there is a presumed motivation to be 'right' or, at least, to avoid being 'wrong'. Similarly, the perceived rational thing to do may be to stay in the good graces of others. Compulsion apart, therefore, the distinction between goal-oriented and non-goal-oriented conforming behaviour – or, which is a little different, between conformity and conformism – looks analytical, at best.

Max Weber's discussion of the nature of domination (1978: 53–4, 212–301) is pertinent here. From Weber's point of view, conformity and conformism are, in different ways, both product and expression of domi-nation. In his model the exercise of *power* – the capacity to dominate others through coercion of one kind or another – is the pursuit of compliance and conformity. The alternative to power, however, is more interesting and more routine: *authority* is legitimate domination, the conformism of those who accept its demand or expectation as justified (Smith 1960: 15–33). Identification and internalisation fall within Weber's categorisation of legitimate domination: the first as the basis of charismatic authority, the second of either legal or traditional authority. There are many modes of legitimate domination, and many sources of conformism. All of them are intimately bound up with ideology and the symbolisation of collective identification (cf. Bourdieu 1991; Bourdieu and Passeron 1977; Gledhill 1994). If for no other reason, this is because to identify oneself, or one's group, in a particular way, is to treat as axiomatic, and hence legitimate, the arbitrariness of one's way of life and relationships.

The social construction of conformity and conformism is also, partly, an attempt to render interaction predictable. This, it must be emphasised, does not imply 'objectively' accurate predictability: it is, rather, predictability for practical purposes and, even more important perhaps, the comforting *sense* of predictability. It is what affords individuals some expectations of the behaviour of others (and Others), on the basis of which they can proceed with their everyday lives without having to consider consciously everything in advance, and without excessive uncertainty. Conformity of a kind may also, however, emerge out of uncertainty. When one is unsure of local rules or customs, the behaviour of others may be the single most important source of information about the right thing(s) to do. Hence conformity. This is of major significance for childhood learning, but it remains important throughout adult life (think, for example, about driving in a foreign country), and offers another understanding of why behavioural conformity may be at a premium at the boundary.

Looking at these matters anthropologically, Mary Douglas (1966) argues that notions of ritual pollution and supernatural danger reinforce other pressures towards conformity. Both tend to be associated with the boundaries of identity: examples might be marriage rules forbidding certain alliances, or ghost stories associated with the territorial spaces between groups. Her particular emphasis is upon symbolic classifications and their boundaries: between different membership roles within groups, between appropriate and inappropriate behaviour, between dirt and cleanliness, etc. Without classificatory systems, everyday life is unthinkable. Every human group has such a system or systems, some competence or participation in which is a criterion of practical group membership. *Inter alia*, classification systems focus our attention on boundaries: of the group, of acceptable behaviour, of purity, of humanity, of whatever. Issues of classification are always issues of identification.

Ritual pollution and supernatural danger combine in the 'incest taboo'. Conventional anthropological wisdom suggests that a ban on incest, in one local form or another, is *the* universal regulation for humans – the ultimate boundary – and that incest is the ultimate transgression. From Frazer to Lévi-Strauss, and since, debates about incest have a long history within anthropology. Fortes brings out their relevance for this discussion.[1] He argues that the notion of incest, the identification of particularly close categories of kin between whom sex is prohibited, provides a basic 'us–them' template for the wider human world, creates a need to form relationships between us and them, and offers the basic model for the rules of everyday life in general. It is thus the foundation of the human world: 'without rules there can be neither society nor culture . . . it was the emergence of the capacity to make, enforce, and, by corollary, to break rules that made human society possible' (Fortes 1983: 6).

The argument is plausible (although one major qualification would be that organisation requires more than rules). Fortes posits an intimate relationship between identification and our capacity to live collectively integrated *human* lives. While one can overplay the notion that human experience is orderly, human relationships are certainly ordered. In this sense, the original sin of incest is to generate disorder, a confusion of identities. Incest places individuals in two incompatible places at the same time: how can one's mother also be one's sister, for example? Fortes further suggests that rules do not *create* identities. The message of incest prohibitions is that, if anything, it's rules that emerge from the classification and categorisation of individuals. By these lights, identification – knowing who's who, what's what, and what that involves – is an irreducible aspect of being human and living together.

MAKING SENSE

Stereotyping and attribution are important dimensions of classification and identification. A further social psychological conventional wisdom suggests that stereotyping, the labelling and classification of collectivities in a partial and incomplete fashion, simplifies otherwise excessive information flows in and about complex situations (Aronson 1991: 227–37; Tajfel 1981b). By this argument, stereotyping is but an extreme example of the general classificatory process of ideal typification. In its encouragement of everyday predictability – which, let me repeat, isn't 'objectively' accurate predictability – stereotyping underpins habituation and facilitates institutionalisation (Berger and Luckmann 1967: 74–5). I will return to this in Chapter 12. At this point, the important thing to grasp is the mundane nature of stereotyping. Although the word has in many quarters come to attract wholly negative connotations, stereotyping is a routine, everyday cognitive process upon which we all to some extent depend.

However, important as they are, stereotyping is about much more than the interactional and cognitive demands placed upon individuals by the demands of information management in a complex human world. Tajfel, for example (1981b), argues that stereotyping is also a collective process, involving the creation and maintenance of group values and ideologies, and the positive valorisation of the ingroup. In other words, collective boundary maintenance and symbolisation, *pace* Barth and Cohen, are also important (McDonald 1993). In a thoroughgoing revision of theorising about stereotypes, which is also an exhaustive historical account, Pickering (2001) emphasises their political role in the 'social exorcism of the Other', their extreme dramatisation of differentiation and boundaries.

All of which reminds us that stereotypes, almost before they are anything else, are powerful symbols: 'symbolic discourse . . . only retains from experience a minimum of fragments to establish a maximum of hypotheses, without caring to put them to the test' (Sperber 1975: 4). Stereotypes of the inhabitants of either side of an identity boundary demarcate its contours with a particular, albeit illusory, clarity. Stereotypes are at best partial and always – like all ideal typifications – constructed from a point of view. They are not, however, *necessarily* hostile: a stereotype can flatter (a similar point to that which was made in Chapter 7 about labelling). Apropos Schutz, and my general argument about collective identities, it is in the nature of stereotypes to emphasise a small number of putative similarities between the stereotyped rather than their infinite array of particularities and differences. Stereotypes are extremely condensed symbols of collective identification.

Attribution, the attempt to understand others, particularly the motivations of others, by inference from the limited information provided by their verbal and non-verbal behaviour, is also at work within stereotyping. Attribution is another attempt to understand the human world and render it more predictable: rather than cognitive overload and complexity, this is the other side of the coin, the fact that often humans don't have sufficient information to make sense of what's going on (Eiser 1990: 99–122). All people, all of the time, need to explain and anticipate the behaviour of others. To do so, we often need to go beyond the available information. Ambiguity and uncertainty in such situations lead, Aronson suggests, to the use of stereotypical attributions (1991: 229–37). It may, therefore, be no coincidence that, according to Douglas, anomaly and ambiguity are likely to attract a symbolic charge (1966: 41–53). Ambiguity or anomaly, uncertainty about which way to jump or what to do, are characteristic of boundaries and borders, hence the need to map them with imaginary precision or to dramatise them ritually (and it is, of course, precisely the ambiguity of boundaries that underlies Barth's understanding of them – and of identities – as fluid and permeable).

Before leaving this topic it is vital to remember, or insist, that stereotyping is but *one* aspect of cognition and identification. It's probably not even the most important. Returning to one of my central themes – the relationship between similarity and difference – humans attend to particularity and differentiation no less avidly than they do to stereotypical homogeneity (Billig 1985; 1987: 118–55). In order to live successfully in a complex human world we need to be equally concerned with each: that's the whole point of the model of identification presented in this book. If cognition were only a matter of simplification and stereotyping – regardless for the moment of *why* stereotyping happens – then we would have only the most rudimentary sense of who's who and what's what, and the human world would in all respects be a very different place indeed.

PRODUCING PREDICTABILITY

To recapitulate another core theme, although individual and collective identification are matters of symbolic classification and boundary maintenance, they are matters of classification *in interaction and practice*. Group membership, for example, demands, as a practical accomplishment, some behavioural conformity: some consistent similarity in what individual members do. Every member has to be able, to some extent, to 'bring it off'. As we have seen, however, this doesn't entail consensus. The symbolisation of group boundaries and identifications (the 'umbrella'), the distinction between private judgements and public behaviour, and the variety of types of domination, all suggest that normative consensus is not necessary for the existence of a shared identity.

Nor do marginality, deviance or non-conforming behaviour necessarily imply normative dissent. At the margins of the group, where the frameworks of predictability are less firm and intrusive, there is likely to be ambiguity about membership criteria and appropriate behaviour. Group boundaries may thus be generated by uncertainty, emerging as an ordering response to the relative unpredictability of encounters. Strong pressures encouraging conforming behaviour – with penalties attaching to deviance – may oppress most those whose membership or identity is insecure. Powerful signals about conformity and deviance, dramatising group membership and boundaries, are easily expressed as stereotypes of insiders and outsiders. This is the exorcism and dramatisation of the Other, to recall Pickering's argument (2001). For individuals on the collective margins, the price of admission may be some subordination of their own ambiguity, submission to the minor tyranny of the everyday predictability demanded by others. The less securely one belongs, or the more one wants or needs to, the higher that price is likely to be. And in this, once again, it is possible to see an internal–external dialectic of identification at work.

Symbolisation is central to more than individual and collective dialectics of identification, however. For Abner Cohen symbolisation underlies, 'the whole process of institutionalisation . . . Social relations are developed and maintained through symbolic forms and action' (1974: 5). Institutionalisation is one of the most consequential ways in which individuals participate in, or take on, collective identifications. It also contributes massively to the production and reproduction of environments of relatively predictable collective behaviour.

To follow the thread of the argument back as far as Mead, I have been considering predictability as an emergent and symbolically constructed property of everyday life. People identify themselves in particular ways at least in part in order that others may know what to expect of them. This involves a minimum of appropriate behaviour: a performance. In identifying *myself* within any setting where there is even a minimum of intersubjective understanding, I also render the behaviour of *others* easier to predict (or, at least, to imagine). In identifying myself, I can imagine their position or orientation *vis-à-vis* myself. In presenting myself, I may make an active contribution to their behaviour towards me. Similarly, identifying others in particular ways permits me to imagine that I know what to expect of them. I will, more often than not, orient my behaviour towards them in terms of their presentations of identity. And so on. Throughout, one can see the interactions of internal and external moments of identification, the emergence of individual and collective senses of who's who and what's what.

Nor, again, must predictability be 'objectively' well founded or accurate, or identification actually predictive of behaviour. It may be, but that isn't the point. Our ideal typifications of ourselves and others allow us to proceed in our everyday lives without fretting perpetually about what other people are going to do: we are afforded an intersubjective *sense* of the predictability of the human world. On the basis of who we think they are, who we imagine them to be, we accept them at behavioural face value until there is reason not to do so. Most people most of the time 'know' who they are, 'know' who others are and 'know' what to expect. This is fundamental to understanding identification.

To talk about institutions and institutionalisation, as I have begun to do in this chapter, necessitates going beyond the discussion so far. Institutions are organised, and organising, with respect to identification and behaviour. No less imagined than any other human phenomena, institutions are enormously consequential in everyday life. In the next chapter I discuss institutions and institutional identification, and explore further arguments about the importance of identity as a conceptual bridge linking the individual and collective within a unified understanding of the human world.

12

INSTITUTIONALISING IDENTIFICATION

Having understood that collectivities are more than the sum of their embodied parts, Durkheim, following Comte and Spencer, made an error in adopting an organic analogy in order to understand and communicate this: collectivity – 'society' – modelled as a corporeal entity, a 'living thing' with firm boundaries, complex functional internal relationships, and higher and lower systems. In this, he was adopting an essentially common-sensical symbolisation of collective identity. Margaret Thatcher, approaching the same issue, made what is arguably a worse mistake, however, in declaring that there is no such thing as 'society', other than 'you and me and our next-door-neighbour and everyone we know in our town' (Raban 1989: 29–30).

A worse mistake, but an easy one to make. Although their existential status is not straightforward, individuals are at least embodied and obvious. Collectivities, from the smallest network to the largest nation or global corporation, are altogether more nebulous; in their definitively collective aspects they may be difficult to 'see', whether in common sense or socio-logically. An army on the march or a stadium full of partisan sports fans have an embodied physicality that presents itself with material immediacy. But even their tangible presence – and many collectivities don't have that kind of presence – is a small part of what constitutes each as a collectivity. There must be something else if an aggregation of individuals is to be anything other than arithmetical (Jenkins 2002: 63–84). The fact of a lot of breathing human bodies occupying a territory is not enough to constitute a collectivity.

Collectivities and collective identifications are to be found, in the first instance, in the practices of the embodied individuals that generate or constitute them. Two different kinds of identificatory process have been outlined: group identification and categorisation, corresponding, respectively, to the internal and external moments of the process of collective identification. These processes take place most definitively at the boundaries of identity, which, at the risk of repeating myself once too often, doesn't mean a territorial boundary. Nor is it like the physical boundary of an organism. It is a cumulative social construction that occurs when people who are identified as, say, Laputans interact with others who are identified differently in any context or setting in which being Laputan matters. In the process the relevant criteria of membership of Laputa – Laputan identity – are rehearsed, presented and developed, as are the consequences of being Laputan. These are political processes: negotiation, transaction, mobilisation, imposition and resistance.

During these interactions, an image of similarity that is the defining characteristic of collective identities is symbolically constructed. But in the shade of that image a range of diversity and heterogeneity exists with respect to what people do: collective identity emphasises similarity, but not at the expense of difference. Similarity and difference being irretrievably entangled in each other, where the emphasis falls depend on the point of view. Difference is no less socially constructed than similarity: both are 'culturally arbitrary', to use Bourdieu's expression, but neither, to remember W. I. Thomas, is any less 'real'.

REALISING INSTITUTIONS

Individual and collective identifications coincide in complex ways. A useful starting point if we are to grasp these is the notion of *institutions*, understood in an open, minimalist definition:

- An institution is a pattern of behaviour in any particular setting that has become established over time as 'the way things are done'.
- An institution has intersubjective relevance and meaning in the situation concerned: people know about it and recognise it, if only in the normative specification of 'how things are done'.

Institutions are thus an integral part of the human world, with reference to which, and in terms of which, individuals make decisions and orient their behaviour.

The study of institutions is a staple of the sociological diet, and their constitution as appropriate objects for our attention is a matter of fundamental methodological importance. Institutions can be understood as ideal types, in both common-sensical and sociological discourse. Abstractions from the complex ebb and flow of interaction, they allow us to think about, to imagine, the patterns and regularities of everyday life. Once again, however, they are anything but imaginary: they are consequential and constraining. Institutions – much like identities, in fact – are as much emergent products of what people do, as they are constitutive of what people do. They don't 'exist' in any sense 'above the action'. Institutions are perhaps best understood as our collective ideal typifications of continuing processes of institutionalisation.

One of the most lucid accounts of those processes, rooted in the phenomenological ideas of Schutz (Schutz and Luckmann 1973), comes from Peter Berger and Thomas Luckmann in their classic, *The Social Construction of Reality* (1967: 70ff.). They identify *habit* – and whatever else we are, human beings are certainly creatures of habit – as the cognitive foundation of institutionalisation. The habitualisation or routinisation of behaviour brings with it two important practical advantages:

- Choices are narrowed to the point where many courses of action or ways of doing things do not have to be chosen (or, indeed, rejected) at all.
- Since we don't have to think and decide about every little aspect of our daily lives, space for 'deliberation and innovation' is opened up: there is no need for every situation to be perpetually encountered and defined anew.

More than simply rendering the human world predictable, habitualisation almost obviates the need for predictability in many situations: it creates a substantial, and secure, environment of 'the way things are', which may not be easy to reflect upon consciously, much less change (Bourdieu 1977; 1990).

Habitualisation may be a necessary condition for institutionalisation, but it isn't in itself enough. A degree of intersubjectivity – shared meaning – is required. When a number of people begin to share the same habitualised pattern of activity, to possess some sense that they are doing it, *and* to communicate to each other in the same terms about what they are doing, that is the beginnings of institutionalisation. If it persists for any length of time, a pattern of activity acquires a history. People encounter it as 'the way things are done'. It has become institutionalised as a taken-for-granted feature of the human world.

As part of this process, sanctions are likely to become associated with deviation from institutionalised routine: 'the ways things are done' may quickly become 'the way things should be done' (if, indeed, there is much difference in the first place). Institutions, perhaps before anything else, involve control. Lest this be misunderstood, however, Berger and Luckmann are clear that the very existence of the institution, as an axiomatic part of the human world — 'the way things are' — is the primary form of control. Doing things otherwise is simply difficult to imagine. Additional processes of control are necessary only if institutionalisation is less than complete or effective.

The human world that we encounter as axiomatic during early social-isation is a world of institutionalised practices. As the products of history, we encounter them as 'objective', as not to be questioned, and we seem to move in and out of their shadows. It is, of course, we who actually cast those shadows: 'Knowledge about society is thus a *realization* in the double sense of the word, in the sense of apprehending the objectivated social reality, and in the sense of ongoingly producing this reality' (Berger and Luckmann 1967: 84). This is how institutions 'hang together'. They are 'real' — W. I. Thomas again — because we *think* they are and *behave* as if they are. The logic which institutions appear to possess derives not (only) from their own organisation, but is imposed by the reflexive consciousness of actors. We 'know' that they are logical and integrated and therefore *de facto* they are. Language — discourse — is the pre-eminent source of this order, in the form of ritualised speech, rules and laws, written records, narratives, etc.

Institutions order everyday life, provide predictability, and permit actors to exercise lower levels of attention than might otherwise be demanded by the complexities of the human world. They provide templates for how things should be done. But they do require legitimation in order to be presented successfully to each new generation: 'The same story, so to speak, must be told to all the children' (Berger and Luckmann 1967: 79). The more intersubjective meanings are shared in any collectivity, the greater scope there is for the thoroughgoing and interpenetrating institu-tionalisation of everyday life. This we may call 'axiomatic legitimation' (Jenkins 1983: 7).

Where a range of constituencies each constructs the world from differing points of view — which is likely, no matter how 'simple' or 'complex' the setting in question — then the institutional order will be more fragmented or limited in scope. Legitimation is more problematic in the presence of alternatives. Berger and Luckmann (1967: 110–46), while drawing in the first instance on Weber, broaden the notion of legitimation to encompass more than the overtly political. They insist that the legitimation of the institutional order is a matter of *knowledge* rather than, or as well as, *values*. Legitimation emerges from the production and reproduction of 'symbolic universes': cosmologies, implicit and explicit specifications of the nature of the world and the place of people and their creations within it. In my terms, symbolic universes may be thought of as collective points of view or common knowledge:[1] 'bodies of theoretical tradition that integrate different provinces of meaning and encompass the institutional order in a symbolic totality . . . symbolic processes are processes of signification that refer to realities other than those of everyday experience' (Berger and Luckmann 1967: 113). One of the key words in here is 'processes'. At the heart of these processes is language, the primary constituent and framework of symbolic universes.

While wishing to avoid the reification which bedevils discussions of this kind, a symbolic universe is, if you like, the story which a collectivity tells about itself, the world and its place in the world. A symbolic universe – and Anthony Cohen later said something very similar – is, for Berger and Luckmann, the unifying umbrella under which the discrepant diversity of everyday life can come together. Nor is this only a collective matter:

> By the very nature of socialization, subjective identity is a precarious entity. It is dependent upon the individual's relations with significant others, who may change or disappear . . . symbolic universes . . . are sheltering canopies over the institutional order as well as over individual biography.
>
> (Berger and Luckmann 1967: 118, 120)

For Berger and Luckmann, then, symbolic universes are the sources of collective *and* individual consistency, continuity and constancy: 'psychology always presupposes cosmology' (1967: 196). Returning to the concerns of this discussion, one paraphrase of this might suggest that psychology is to cosmology, as individual is to collective identification.

Unfortunately, after all these kind words, it has to be said that Berger and Luckmann's conception of the 'symbolic universe' is perhaps a little grandiose. It is certainly much too integrative. A back-door functionalism, consensus in the final instance, lurks in the 'totality' of it all. As earlier chapters have argued, consensus – whether normative or cognitive – is neither necessary nor likely. We might, perhaps, do better to imagine the human world as a complex of greater and lesser symbolic universes – 'provinces of meaning' in the quotation above? – which interlock and conflict with each other in a variety of ways and with uncertain outcomes.

Modest examples of symbolic universes in this sense might be godparenthood, the medical profession, a neighbourhood community, a government bureaucracy or a voluntary organisation. Each of these rests on a minimal intersubjective definition of the situation, sufficient at least to actually conjure up the institution as a reality in the human world. Each also integrates within it a certain amount of institutional diversity in terms of detail and practice.

MATERIALISING INSTITUTIONS

The centrality to Berger and Luckmann's model of cognition – symbolisation and knowledge – is no less problematic. When it first appeared, *The Social Construction of Reality* was a welcome corrective to structural-functionalism's emphasis upon normative integration and values. However, as I have just suggested, the model of ultimate cognitive integration with which Berger and Luckmann replaced it shared many of the same problems. Even more serious – and there is a similar problem in Anthony Cohen's work – is their neglect of what Barth called 'the material world of causes and effects', and the contribution that it makes to the way that the human world 'hangs together'. This is most significant, in the present context, with respect to the location and sedimentation of institutions in embodied individuals, artefacts and territorial space.[2]

This of course varies, depending upon which institutions we are talking about. Marriage is an institution, for example. It exists, it hangs together and it persists, as a fairly abstract institution, because people believe in it as a symbolic universe within wider symbolic universes. But it also hangs together in a very material sense: in the sexual, domestic and economic practices of cohabitation, in common property, in the physical presence in the everyday world of married couples, in specific places which one has to attend and specific rituals – whether secular or religious – which one has to perform there in order to be married, in the ring and the ring finger, etc. Without the full symbolic consecration of marriage it is possible to be married after a fashion by *doing* it: cohabiting, behaving as a married couple, even wearing rings. And symbolic consecration alone may not be sufficient: without cohabitation, without *doing* 'being a married couple', is it a 'proper' marriage? Each scenario is recognised in British law and everyday discourse: one is a 'common-law marriage', the other constitutes grounds for divorce, or refusal of admission by an Immigration Officer. How often, for example, have we heard people say things such as, 'The marriage was *really* over years ago'? Nor do the everyday practices of marriage and its symbolic specification have to harmonise in order for the institution to make sense.

That, for many people, they appear not to harmonise or 'fit' at the moment doesn't mean that marriage, as an institution rooted in appropriate symbolic universes, is necessarily weakening.

A more straightforward example is a university. A university is an institution in two senses: as an example of 'the university' – a type of institution of higher learning – and as *this* particular university (of Poppleton, for example). Symbolically it is conjured up within and by a rich universe of statutes, traditions, ideals of scholarship, rituals of consecration, funding mechanisms, recruitment processes, and so on. This constitution has developed historically within the broader institutional field of education, although these days it also has something of the air of a business enterprise (does this undermine it as a university?). More mundanely, however, it also exists as a body of people and as a collection of buildings, a campus and playing fields. Getting off the train at Poppleton, for example, it is possible sensibly to ask for, and expect to receive, directions to 'the University'.

Thus one can see and encounter physically both marriage and a university. Metaphorically, where marriage is a shifting archipelago of particular and historically ephemeral marriages, a university is a substantial landmass (which is not to ignore its eventual historical impermanence). The point is not that Berger and Luckmann are wrong to emphasise the symbolisation of institutions. Quite the reverse: everything about the materiality of marriage and a university which I have described above is, in fact, definitively symbolised and cannot be otherwise. The point is, rather, that symbolisation is *always* embodied in very material practices, in their products and in three-dimensional space (which also involves time, since space doesn't make sense outside a temporal framework, and *vice versa*). In their desire to move beyond the materialist–idealist impasse this, perhaps, was something that Berger and Luckmann neglected. Collective life hangs together as much in the visibly embodied doing as in the thinking (and the two are, indeed, not easily disentangled). Berger and Luckmann's notion of 'society as objective reality', meaning symbolically objectified reality, does not take the embodiment of collectivity – in people and in things – seriously enough. Institutionalised collective forms may be imagined, but they are not imaginary: the practices of people, and their products, constitute them as tangible in space and time.

There are other criticisms of Berger and Luckmann. The cognitive and the normative, for example, are not as distinct as they sometimes seem to imply: the way things *are* done and the way things *should* be done often amount to much the same thing. The power of ideology resides precisely in its combination of the two. Nor is the distinction between habituation and institutionalisation always clear. There is a continuum from the individual to the collective in this respect: collective habit is a form of institutionalisation, and habit is often the individual expression of institutionalised patterns (hence Bourdieu's notion of the habitus).

Berger and Luckmann's underplaying of power and compulsion is more telling. Their emphasis upon legitimation is an important recognition of particular aspects of domination, and of the stratification which is an inherent characteristic of knowledge and symbolic universes. Nor do they wholly ignore power: 'He who has the bigger stick has the better chance of imposing his definitions of reality' (1967: 127), is only one example. But power could be more prominent in their model than it is. This is particularly important for our understanding of internal–external dialectics of identification. External identification does not have to be legitimated or accepted by those who are its subject and object – they don't necessarily even have to know about or recognise it – in order for it to be consequentially real for them.

INSTITUTIONS AND IDENTITIES

Such criticism notwithstanding, Berger and Luckmann's account of institutionalisation is plausible and straightforward, allowing us to think about flexible, fluid and loosely specified institutions, as well as those that are constituted more formally. It also helps us to understand the nature of collectivities and collective identification. While not every institution involves identification or membership – 'going for a walk' might be a mundane example, or 'having a bath' – all collective identities are, by definition, institutionalised: as 'ways of being' they are 'the way things are done'.[3] Thus ethnic identifications, for example, are institutionalised, as are locally specific gender norms and conventions, or the most loosely knit friendship group or temporary interest-based coalition.

To reverse the thrust of the argument, it's no less important that institutions, such as *events* (i.e. an annual village fête), *estates* (i.e. marriage) and *corporate groups* (i.e. universities), are sources and sites of identification. Even when they are not in themselves collective identities, they are productive – in Barth's terms, generative – of identifications. The village fête has an organising committee and a structure of tasks and offices that are occupied by individuals, whose incumbency differentiates them from each other and from those who merely attend the fête and may have wider resonance within the politics of the village. Being married differs from being single, being divorced or being widowed (all of which are, however, identifications that are necessarily rooted in the institution of marriage). Being a university lecturer is an identification constituted in and by the institution of the university, from which, at least in part, derive the frameworks of similarity and difference which situate it – and any *particular* university lecturer – with respect to, say, a university porter, on the one hand, or a lecturer in a college of further education, on the other.

As 'the way things are done', collectivities and collective identifications are institutionalised. And institutions are sources and sites of identification for individuals. But what, for example, is the relationship between institutional identities and the individuals who occupy them? Ralph Linton addressed this issue when he defined *status* and *role* (1936: 113–31). A status is an institutionalised identification viewed in the abstract, as 'a collection of rights and duties' (ibid.: 113). For example, 'husband' and Professor of Sports Marketing at the University of Poppleton are both statuses: the actual individuals who may be identified with the status are irrelevant. Every status has a practical element, in the role attached to and specified by it: this is what the occupant of the status does when acting in that status.

Linton's notion of role, with its implied theatrical analogy, anticipates some aspects of Goffman's dramaturgical model (see Chapter 7). Indeed, the status–role dyad – for they are inseparable concepts, each entailed in the other – was fundamental to the development of social theory. However, it is problematic in at least three key respects. First, as Merton pointed out (1957: 369), 'a particular status involves, not a single associated role, but an array of associated roles'. Merton preferred to refer to the 'role-set' attached to a status: 'that complement of role-relationships which persons have by virtue of occupying a particular social status'. Taking Merton's point further, any institutionalised identification – any 'status' – *can* be done in a variety of ways, depending upon the individual occupant(s), contextual constraints and possibilities, and the demands of significant others.

The second problem is that the practical concomitants of any institutionalised identification are unlikely to be as clear and unambiguous as both Linton and Merton appear to think. No doubt *some* of the practical requirements or expectations of any status are obvious and definite: fidelity is part of the role of 'husband' in western Christian societies, for example. But much will be situationally sensitive and, as recognised by Goffman and Bourdieu, improvisatory within the interactional ebb and flow of the human world. Another way of saying which is to remember that institutional identifications, like all human phenomena, are simultaneously in the individual, interaction and institutional orders. The role-expectations of a 'status' may be contradictory or incongruent: fidelity figures prominently in Christian marriage vows, but locally it may also be regarded as perfectly appropriate for a 'good' husband to discreetly take a mistress. But in that same local context, failure to take a mistress does not amount to failure as a husband.

The final problem with Linton's definition may in part account for the 'difficulties and weaknesses of general role theory' (Jackson 1972: 5). Put simply, if a 'status' is a collection of rights and duties, why do we need a further concept of 'role' in order to define its performative aspects, unless they are somehow different from the rights and duties concerned? Rights and duties are, after all, practical matters: rights are what you can expect of others, duties what they can expect of you. Since Linton, and many subsequent sociologists, have understood role as the operationalisation of the rights and duties of status, the former entailed in the latter, the concept of role looks redundant (Coulson 1972). What's more, 'status–role' looks suspiciously like a version of the problematic distinction between thinking and doing, and its associated allotropes of structure/action, and culture/society.

From the point of view of the beginning of the twenty-first century, 'status' and 'role' might, therefore, appear to be antediluvian; they are certainly no longer much used. But they don't deserve to be simply forgotten. For example, in suggesting that rights and duties are definitive of institutionalised identity, they shed further light on the internal–external dialectic of identification. Rights may be what I *expect* of others as an aspect of my institutional identity, but they have no effect – in fact they don't exist – if those others don't recognise them. I cannot simply *assert* this or that 'right': it has to be specified in a legitimate collective discourse about rights and the entailment of rights in particular identifications. This is, in fact, the point about institutionalisation. A similar point in reverse can be made about my duties: the call of duty may be *collectively* issued, but it has to be recognised – and that duty done – by me as an *individual*.

Thus status, as a collection of rights and duties, alerts us to the complexity of the dialectic of identification. Nor is it the only useful lesson to be drawn from Linton:

> A *status*, in the abstract, is a position in a particular pattern. It is thus quite correct to speak of each individual as having many statuses . . . However, unless the term is qualified in some way, *the status* of any individual means the sum total of all the statuses that he occupies.
>
> (Linton 1936: 113)

Although this is a little too simple, using the same word for both the *abstractly institutional* and the *concretely individual* encourages an appreciation of the interpenetration of the individual and the collective. Individual identification is revealed as, to a considerable extent, a customised collage of collective identifications.

The problems with 'status–role' seem to centre largely on the role side of the equation. The distinction between the *nominal* and the *virtual* may offer a more promising way forward, in that it allows us to think about the fact that abstractly collective institutionalised identifications (statuses) are occupied by embodied individuals, yet are also independent of them. The nominal in this case is the ideal typification of the institutionalised identity – its name or title, the notional rights and duties which attach to it, etc. – while the virtual is how that identification is worked out, given local vagaries of context and allowing for individual variation, by any particular incumbent. This permits comparison of the range of differentiation in everyday life between *individual* incumbents of the same institutionalised identity, such as 'husband' or lecturer at the University of Poppleton. At the same time we can compare *local* differences in typification and practice with respect to institutionalised identities: we might look, for example, at lecturers at the universities of Poppleton and Old Sarum to see what these identities have in common and how they differ. Rather than persisting with the concepts of *status* and *role*, we might therefore talk about *institutionalised identities in their nominal and virtual aspects*. This has the further advantage of reducing the scope for confusion between the Weberian notion of 'status' – that dimension of stratification which relates to 'social honour' or 'social standing', judged according to a range of ascribed or achieved criteria (Turner 1988) – and 'status' as abstract institutionalised identification.

ORGANISATIONS AND IDENTITIES

So far I have been talking about institutions in very general terms. But what about different kinds of institutions? Clearly there is, for example, a difference between 'marriage' and an event such as the village fête. Both are institutionalised, and both are sources of identifications, but I don't have to be a sociologist to appreciate that they are not really the 'same kind of thing'. A first move towards clarity is to distinguish *institutions* from *organisations*.

Institutions have already been defined. Organisations require a slightly more complex definition, as particular kinds of institutions in which:

- there are always members;
- members combine in the pursuit of explicit objectives, which serve to identify the organisation;

- there are criteria for identifying, and processes for recruiting, members;
- there is a division of labour in the specification of the specialised tasks and functions performed by individual members; and
- there is a recognised pattern of decision-making and task allocation.

By this definition, the category of organisations stretches to include many real life possibilities: from a rhythm'n'blues band, to a New Guinean men's house, to an Ashanti matrilineage, to a bowling club, to the CIA, to Microsoft, to the United Nations. Thus, marriage is not an organisation – although any particular marriage may be – while the village fête organising committee is.

The sociological study of organisations is well established. Building on Weber's initial observations about bureaucracy, there is a huge literature, on formal organisations in particular,[4] that doesn't need to be reviewed here. But looking at organisations does help us understand the interplay between individual and collective identifications. Organisations are composed of members, actual individuals. My organisational memberships are an aspect of my individual identity, although each is not equally relevant. Being a member of the University of Sheffield has greater salience than being a member of the National Trust. Once again, however, this depends on point of view and context: to its staff my membership of the Trust is likely to be my *only* significant identification.

Organisations are also networks of specialised nominal identifications: positions, offices and functions organised as 'jobs'. This is where the organisation as a division of labour comes into its own. Although occupied at any point of time by individuals, these positions are identified with or part of the organisation: at least in principle, their existence is independent of their occupancy by specific individuals. Organisations create, in fact, the possibility of specific, concrete identities that are not, at any particular point in time, embodied (whether individually or collectively). That a post or an office is vacant does not necessarily mean that it ceases to exist.

The organisation of identification is an important part of what social scientists talk about, often with a glibness that does them little credit, as 'social structure'. If 'social structure' is to be found anywhere other than in the aggregate abstraction of statistics, if it is to have anything approaching an intersubjective reality in the human world, it is in institutions and organisations, and the pattern of relationships between organisations and their members. In the organisation of identification, the interaction order and the institutional order are routinely and mutually implicated in each other.

I suggested in Chapter 1 that a theoretical appreciation of identification is vital if we are to steer the debate about structure and agency – the collective and the individual – out of its present doldrums. In any local setting in the human world, organised processes of identification are central to the allocation of rewards and penalties, resources and costs, honour and shame. Organisations and identifications are at the heart of the production and reproduction of hierarchy and stratification. Furthermore, since the degree to which identity is organised is likely to be a function of complexity – scale and institutional heterogeneity – there is also something more to be said in this respect about modernity and identity. These issues are explored further in the closing chapters.

13

ORGANISING IDENTIFICATION

In English, the word 'organisation' can refer to the *act* of organis*ing*, to the state of *being* organis*ed* or to an organis*ed* system. Each meaning emphasises activity: process and practices. Organisations are bounded networks of people – distinguished as members from non-members – following coordinated procedures: *doing* things *together* in interrelated and institutionalised ways. These procedures are specified explicitly or tacitly, formal or informally, in bodies of organisational common knowledge: organisationally specific symbolic universes, which may be subject to revision or confirmation and are transmitted to members through processes of organisational socialisation. Organisations are also networks of identifications – individually and collectively – which influence strongly who does what within those procedures, and how. These identifications – positions, offices, functions, jobs – are specified informally and formally by and in organisational common knowledge, as are the procedures for allocating or recruiting individuals to them.

Understood in this way, everything from families to nation-states (and beyond) can be described as organisations. That might suggest that the term is too vague and general to have analytical value. I don't think so, however. First, as discussed in Chapter 12, not all institutions are organisations. Second, not all collectivities are organisations. Categories, for example – collectivities that cannot speak, do not in fact know their own name – are not organisations. Nor are spontaneous collectivities (crowds, audiences, mobs, refugees in flight, and so on). Nor are loosely knit networks of individuals pursuing the same or congruent goals but lacking organised divisions of labour or authority structures (Boissevain 1968; Mayer 1966; Wellman 1999). The word 'organisation' covers most collectivities, but not all.

In terms of identities, organisations are constituted simultaneously in a distinction between members and non-members, on the one hand, and in an internal network of differentiation among members, on the other. An organisation without internal differentiation doesn't make much sense: organisation is the harnessing and orchestration, under a symbolic umbrella, of difference. Thus between the members of any organisation there is a relationship of similarity and a range of relationships of difference.

If organisations were only concerned with their own internal affairs they would be of limited sociological interest. However, organisational members rarely live their lives all day and every day wholly within the organisation: the 'total institution' (Goffman 1968b) is the exception rather than the rule. Nor are most people members of only one organisation. Furthermore, an organisation's *raison d'être* is the coordination of the activities of a plurality of individuals – not all of whom will necessarily be members – in collective pursuit of some specified purpose. This defining purpose is the organisational charter; it is what calls it into existence, another, and hugely important, part of the common knowledge of the organisationally specific symbolic universe. An organisation's purposes are rarely, however, purely or even mainly internal: they are typically oriented towards and located in the wider, external human world. Organisations are open to and part of their environments. So much so that their boundaries may be permeable and osmotic; it isn't always easy to see where they are drawn.

Another defining feature of organisations requires emphasis: without relations of authority (or, indeed, power), the successful coordination of activities would be impossible. Some subordination to others is the reciprocal precondition of individual autonomy, in the same way that similarity is the precondition of difference and rules create deviance. Organisations – small or large – are institutionalised networks of hierarchical relationships, of sub- and superordination, of power and authority. Organisational collectivity is, in fact, the source of the legitimacy without which authority carries no weight.

For the purposes of this discussion, I will concentrate on two aspects of organisations:[1]

- the ways in which individuals become identified as organisational members (and as particular organisational members), and

- the ways in which organisations influence the identification of non-members.

Surveying the historical, local and institutional variety of either, let alone both, would be a task more appropriate to an encyclopedia. Instead, in order to illustrate the range of possibilities, I shall discuss a limited selection of procedural types or cases with respect to each, as examples of general organisational processes. I will also discuss the consequential nature of organisational identification with respect to the lives of individuals and the production and reproduction of patterns of differentiation: hierarchy, stratification, inclusion and exclusion, etc. In this chapter I focus on organisations and their members; in the next, on their impact on non-members.

RECRUITMENT

Without personnel renewal and replacement, the lifespan of any organisation could be no longer than that of its most long-lived individual member. Since a characteristic of organisations is that they can persist despite routine attrition of personnel, procedures for recruiting replacement members are vital. There are two basic trajectories of organisational membership.

In the first, the qualifying criteria of recruitment are 'givens' such as parentage, age and position in the life course, gender, etc. Identifications of this kind are intersubjectively constructed – typically in terms of embodiment and folk notions of biology – as basic, natural or primordial. They are also typically collective: they identify the individual as a member of a group or category. They are understood as aspects of the individual for which she has little or no responsibility, and over which she has little or no control. Although in any specific situation the possibilities may exist of a renunciation of membership by a candidate, a refusal to recognise a candidate, or her subsequent expulsion, organisational membership of this kind is generally taken for granted, even if not inevitable. If my sister wants to join the Women's Institute, for example, her age and gender render her unproblematically eligible.

In the second trajectory, criteria of membership may be many and varied, but membership is not entailed in pre-existent characteristics. It is also much more a matter concerning the individual *as* an individual. Membership is, therefore, always to some degree uncertain and must typically be sought and endorsed: it is a matter of negotiation at the organisational boundary, and more or less competitive. However, in neither case is the presence or absence of self-determination and choice a defining feature. Both trajectories can involve involuntary or imposed organisational membership.

These two routes into organisational membership may be characterised thus: in the first an individual is a member or a prospective member by virtue of *who* she is, in the second by virtue of *what* she is. Often seen, erroneously, as a contrast between 'traditional' and 'modern' modes of identity, this has much in common with the distinction between *ascribed* and *achieved* statuses drawn by Linton (1936) in his original formulation of status and role.[2] Ascribed identification is constructed on the basis of the contingencies of birth. Achieved – or, to adopt Merton's subsequent, more accurate, terminology, *acquired* (1957: 382) – identifications are assumed during the subsequent life course, and are generally, although not necessarily, the outcome of a degree of self-direction. This general distinction between the ascribed and the acquired isn't specific to organisational identifications; it can in principle be applied to all identities.

The key distinction informing my model of identification, between the *internal* and *external* moments of the dialectic of identification, is heuristic, presented as an opposition for explanatory purposes. Much the same is true of ascription and achievement/acquisition. In everyday life the difference between them is likely to be at most a matter of emphasis. Organisational membership, no less than any other identity, is thus a particular combination of the acquired and the ascribed. The ins and outs of biography conspire to ensure that who I am and what I am are not easily disentangled.

This can be taken a little further. Primary identities such as gender, rooted in very early experience, are massively implicated in the embodied point of view of selfhood. Following Linton and Merton, they are ascribed identities and potentially criteria of organisational membership. But they are also – *qua* selfhood – important influences on the self-direction that is so influential in the acquisition of identities. However, the purposeful acquisition of achieved organisational identification depends upon more than unilateral self-determination. Most significantly, it involves negotiation and transaction with others – organisational gatekeepers of one kind or another – who are in a position to recruit individuals to the organisation or to exclude them, and to decide to which organisational positions individuals will be recruited. In making their choices, gatekeepers will frequently have recourse to (ascriptive) criteria such as gender or age.

Where acquired organisational identities are *imposed* on *non*-members – such as selection for conscription or imprisonment – ascriptive criteria are likely to be particularly influential. Imposition of this kind can have many consequences, including:

- no apparent reaction;
- internalisation;
- reluctant acceptance as legitimate;
- resentful endurance; and
- overt resistance.

However, as long as categorisation is recognised – seen, heard, understood – by those upon whom it is visited, or produces real consequences in their lives, it is never a question of imposition *only*. Whatever it might be, there is always a response: there is always the dialectic between internal and external identification.

Indeed, *all* the above scenarios can be understood with reference to an internal–external dialectic of identification, albeit with different emphases in each case. In each there is a relationship of mutual signification between the ascribed and the achieved or acquired. Even so, a loose analytical distinction between ascribed and acquired identities continues to make sense, particularly, perhaps, with respect to organisational identification. They differ – as Nadel, for example, seems to have appreciated (1957: 36–41) – in the manner in which individuals enter into them, or take them on.

With respect to organisations, this difference is largely, although not only, procedural. Recruitment to organisational identities where the emphasis falls upon ascription is a matter of *affirmation*. Although membership is immanent, it must be publicly confirmed, registered, solemnised, consecrated or whatever. Recruitment to organisational identities that are achieved or acquired is, however, a matter of *rationalisation* (cf. Collinson *et al.* 1990: 110ff.). Membership must be justified; reasons have to be offered. Affirmation and rationalisation reflect different sources or kinds of legitimate authority. In Weber's terms (1978: 212–41), affirmation is rooted in *traditional* understandings of legitimacy, and rationalisation – unsurprisingly – in *rational–legal* legitimacy.

AFFIRMATION

Affirmation takes many forms. The Christian ritual of confirmation or First Communion, in which the young person is received into full membership of the Church, is one example. The Jewish *Bar Mitzvah* and *Bat Mitzvah* rituals also come to mind (Mars 1990). And there are options other than the strictly religious: many societies around the world could be drawn upon to provide examples of life-course rituals in which young people are initiated into organised age-sets of one kind or another (Bernardi 1985; La Fontaine 1985). Coming of age ceremonies often touch upon more than the membership of specific organisations: 'These rites of initiation transform individuals by investing them with socialness' (Cohen 1994: 57). It may be nothing less than full membership of the collectivity in question that is at issue (see Richards [1956] for one of the classic anthropological accounts). Although the ritual dimensions of coming of age have atrophied in the industrialised societies of modernity, they can still be found, for example, in the notion of the 'key to the door', or in the informal humiliations that often attend the 'last night of freedom' of brides- and grooms-to-be.

More obviously organisational memberships can also depend primarily on the ascription of 'who you are'. In Northern Ireland, for example, membership of the Orange Lodge depends upon as many as three ascriptive criteria: being protestant, being male and, apropos *which* Lodge one joins, family (Bryan 2000: 105–11; Harris 1972: 163, 192–4). And if we recognise that the family is an informal organisation – or even, in the bureaucratised modern state, a formal organisation – then the rite of baptism, for example, is *inter alia* a public affirmation of the full organisational membership of a new infant.

Common to all the above is a transition from immanent membership to actual membership – literally, confirmation – and an element of ritualised initiation. These are important aspects of 'rites of passage', a general category of ritual first identified by van Gennep (1965) nearly a century ago. Building on his ideas, there is now a relatively settled consensus that humans experience life as a series of transitions from one identity to another, that these transitions are ritualised to a greater or lesser extent, and that the transitions have an *approximately* tripartite form (Leach 1976: 77–9; Morris 1987: 246–63). That form is not a structural universal, it simply makes sense logically and situationally: first *separation* from the present state or identity; then *transition* or *liminality* (a state of limbo which may draw upon a symbolic repertoire relating to death); then finally *incorporation* into, or *aggregation* with, the new state or identity (which may use birth as a metaphor). In ritual, these phases may be represented spatially; they always have a temporal sequence, one after the other. A processual structure of this broad kind appears in all explicit and organisationally marked identity transitions.

Rites of passage and the internal–external dialectic of identification have a bearing on each other. The enhancement of experience which ritual offers, cognitively and particularly emotionally, plays an important role in the internalisation of identification. To say this is, in most significant respects, to agree with Durkheim about the power of ritualised communion. Ritual can invest the symbols of organisational membership – flags, uniforms, logos, songs – with an affective weight that transcends occasion or ceremony. It is likely to be of particular moment in generating individual internal identification with the external collectivity: making the recruit *feel* that she belongs and is part of the greater organisational whole. It may also distance her from previous identities. Even the formal pattern of separation, transition and incorporation is amenable to interpretation in this light: separation weakens existing internal self-identification(s); during transition the new identity is introduced 'from outside' and dramatised; incorporation affirms and strengthens the new identification.

Victor Turner (1974: 119ff.), inspired by the theologian Martin Buber, understood that although the 'we' of collective identification is enormously powerful, it is always fragile and contingent, always vulnerable to subversion. In my terms, it is imagined but not imaginary. Among other things, this reflects a contradiction between the egalitarian inclusivity of 'us' and the internal hierarchical differentiation of an organisational division of labour. Similarity and difference play against rather than with each other within organisations. Hence the organisational importance of rituals of identification. While these are generally significant as occasions for acting out and practically participating in the symbolisation of identity, they are particularly momentous in combining an affirmation and reaffirmation of what Turner calls *communitas* – undifferentiated 'we-ness', if you like – with a recognition and legitimation of internal organisational structure.

Ritualised affirmation of ascriptive identity isn't only a matter of individual membership or affective affirmation, however, nor is it confined to initiation or recruitment. Ritual also plays an important part in the creation and communication of organisational common knowledge in the interests of coordination: 'A public ritual is not just about the transmission of meaning from a central source to each member of an audience; it is also about letting audience members know what other audience members know' (Chwe 2001: 4).

In addition to rites of passage, there are many other ritual occasions that organise, orchestrate and *re*affirm collective identifications. Public pageantry offers many obvious examples of rituals of communal affirmation. From the theatrical set pieces of modern state ceremonial (Handelman 1998: 191–233; Lane 1981), to the more modest ceremonial of 'traditional' states (Cannadine and Price 1987; Gluckman 1963: 110–36), to the parades of the 'marching season' in Northern Ireland (Bell 1990; Bryan

2000; Jarman 1997), the theme is similar: the public reaffirmation and consecration of ascriptive collective identification. Similar themes can be discerned in more secular rituals (Moore and Myerhoff 1977) such as carnivals (Cohen 1980) or beauty contests (Wilk 1993). Organised collective identities which claim to be more than merely 'socially constructed' are also likely – for both internal and external consumption – to use ritualised public ceremonial to affirm and symbolise their ahistorical essence. Examples of this include the characteristic and inevitable carnivals of national identity, and festivals such as the gay and lesbian Mardi Gras in Sydney, Australia.

As well as being an analytical category, class is an ascriptive identity of sorts. Class is equated in common sense with 'background', referring to family of origin, and often with 'breeding' too. A sophisticated version of this is the argument – with which the Eugenics movement, for example, identified itself – that class differences reflect differential genetic endowments; a view that probably persists more widely than we know. A mirror image of this, glorifying the essential nobility of working people, can be seen in Soviet socialist realist public art. Ceremonial or ritualised (re)affirmations of class identities are easy to exemplify: on the one hand, the sadly declining spectacles of May Day marches of international workers' solidarity and British Miners' Galas; on the other, Oxbridge May Balls and the numerous set pieces of upper-class 'Society'. It is no accident that the middle class(es) – often in upwardly mobile flight from their 'background', and generally thanks to achievement – appear less keen to affirm publicly the supposed essence of their identity.

So, with respect to ascriptive identifications such as family, age, ethnicity, gender and even class, ritual (re)affirmation is of considerable significance. It may actually be fundamental: identity – as a definitively interactional construct – can never be essential or primordial, so it has to be made to *seem* so. We have to be made to *feel* 'we'. And collectivities, as discussed in earlier chapters, are not embodied in quite the way that individuals are. In addition, the potential tension between ascriptive inclusion (similarity) and hierarchy (difference) should be born in mind. These difficulties are all addressed when the power of symbol and ritual is brought to bear. Organised collective identity is endowed, via collective ritual and 'communitas', with personal authenticity and experiential profundity. It is also given shape in common knowledge. Inasmuch as public ritual is performative, it is a powerful and visible embodiment of the abstraction of collective identity (cf. Connerton 1989: 41–71). Rituals gather together enough members for embodied collectivity to be 'socially real'. The individual – whether participating as an individual or as 'one of the crowd' – is included in the organised collectivity in the most potent fashion. Individual diversity finds a place within symbolised unity. The imagined ceases to be imaginary.

Ascription is, however, as much a principle of exclusion as inclusion; it encourages expulsion as well as recruitment. The refusal to admit women, Jews and black people – and these are only the most obvious cases – to membership of exclusive clubs is one such situation. More consequential are the less thoroughgoing but nonetheless significant discriminations that operate in the labour and education markets of a country such as Britain. At its most comprehensive, ascriptive exclusion can plumb the depths reached by regimes of slavery, by the Republic of South Africa during *apartheid* or by the racialised state created in Nazi Germany.

RATIONALISATION

The argument is now approaching situations in which important elements of rationalisation figure. The point that ascription and achievement/acquisition are not easy to disentangle in everyday life can be made in many ways. Ascriptive exclusion may, for example, define the arena within which the principle of competition comes into play in recruitment. A club may not admit women, Jews or black people, but that doesn't mean that *any* white male can join. The choice of which white males is a matter for rationalisation, even if only at the level of procedural correctness. Ascriptive inclusion – the organisational boundary – may delineate the space within which internal position and office are competitively achieved. And there are subtler possibilities. An employer who would rather not hire black employees is not committed to hiring whites regardless of their capacity to do the job in question. But nor, in the absence of a white person fitting the bill, is she totally constrained from hiring a black worker. Rationalisation permits both options.

These examples illustrate the interaction of selection criteria of 'acceptability' and 'suitability' (Jenkins 1983: 100–28; 1986: 46–79). In competitive organisational recruitment, ascriptive criteria – 'who you are' – are most likely to influence the identification of acceptability, which can be broadly defined as whether or not an individual will 'fit in' to the networks and relationships of the organisation, or be the right 'kind of person' in general. Suitability, however, emphasises achieved or acquired characteristics relating to 'what you are'. This is typically a matter of competence. It can also, however, in voluntary organisations for example, be a question of interests or attitudes. Suitability is more an issue when a particular organisational position, rather than just membership (or a broad category of membership), is at stake. Notions of suitability are definitively involved in employment recruitment, for example, but are less likely to influence recruitment to club membership. Where both criteria are influential, permutations are possible: individuals may be suitable but unacceptable, or *vice versa*.

The distinction between suitability and acceptability is rarely clear-cut. Being identified as the most suitable person for an organisational position doesn't guarantee your recruitment to it. 'Whether your face fits' may contribute to colleaguely relations and, hence, to fulfilling the organisational charter. So is it a kind of competence? Suitability can't always be easily specified; there may be a number of equally suitable candidates; the threshold of suitability may be low. In situations such as these, questions of acceptability – now concerning the individual and the idiosyncratic, rather than the categorical – may once again become influential. And both suitability and acceptability offer a basis for competitive recruitment. There is no straightforward equivalence between the ascribed and the acceptable, or the acquired and the suitable. It is possible to argue that gender, for example, is sometimes a legitimate criterion of suitability. And acceptability can depend on factors such as marital or domestic situation, or attitudes to abortion or nuclear disarmament (or whatever), which are unlikely to be a matter of ascription. And so on.

There may be no straightforward equivalences, but there is a modern discourse that emphasises opportunity, achievement and access, particularly with respect to economic activity and benefits. Or there are, rather, two related modern discourses: of meritocracy and of equality. The two do not always make happy partners – the idea of meritocracy, for example, owes a frequently unacknowledged debt to notions of 'liberty' which isn't readily compatible with equality – but they come together in the western democracies in the political project of equality of opportunity (Paul *et al*. 1987). This is relevant here because of its emphasis upon access for all to fair competitive organisational recruitment. From the point of view of the promotion of equality of opportunity, ascriptive criteria or criteria of acceptability require special justification.

And here we can begin to appreciate the sociological importance of the organisation of identification for the production and reproduction of large-scale patterns of differentiation and stratification. Ascriptive identities are not only collective; they are intersubjectively widely recognised. Significant numbers of people agree on the nominal boundaries of male and female, black and white, etc. The understandings of 'us' and 'them' across those boundaries – the virtual identifications – are less consensual; it depends on point of view. But the basic outlines, the scaffolding around which virtual identification – played out in the history of consequences – is constructed, will typically be relatively clear.

In this sense, ascription may be widely understood as the 'inevitable' result of 'natural differences': it isn't, however, innocent of self-interest or competition for collective advantage. It informs widespread processes of categorisation: the defining of others in the external moment of the dialectic of identification. Among those processes is recruitment into organisations. Organisational membership in any context is therefore likely to reflect local ascriptive categories of identification. We know that this is often the case. At least two, analytically distinct, organisational processes produce this situation.

In the first, people organise themselves in terms of ascription: this organisation is for 'us', with 'us' understood in a particular way. The organisational charter defines membership: Poppleton *Working Men's* Club, the Eastend *Punjabi Youth* Association, Old Sarum University *Women's* Society, Boyne Square *Protestant* Defenders Flute Band, and so on. Organisation along these ascriptive lines is a potent political and economic resource. Among its advantages are an ideology of natural or primordial community and loyalty, the symbolisation and valorisation of identity, comradeship and mutual support, pooled resources, the organisation of collective action and the creation of opportunities – jobs or whatever – for members.

In the second, the organisational charter does not define membership in ascriptive terms. It may in fact evince a commitment to competitive, achievement-based membership. However, those who are in a position to recruit or reject prospective members may draw upon ascriptive criteria in their decision-making. For example, a manager may refuse to employ men as production workers in a factory assembling electrical components, because he 'knows' that women are more dextrous and don't want to work full-time, and that men can't tolerate the boredom. As a result of this managerial categorisation, the factory employs only women in the majority of jobs. If there is consistency in the common knowledge of managers in general – some participation in a shared symbolic universe – then their recruitment decisions will draw upon similar typifications and stereotypes, and will contribute to the production of a wider pattern in which women are disproportionately represented in part-time, semi-skilled assembly work.

Reflecting consistencies in *their* recruitment, careers and the constraints within which they work, managers *are* likely to have identification, experience and knowledge in common: class background, 'race', gender, politics, orientation towards business, organisational and professional socialisation, etc. That they should behave similarly in similar circumstances is not remarkable. The process may be even more avowedly exclusionary than the example given: racism and sexism, for example, remain potent forces in recruitment (Collinson *et al.* 1990; Jenkins 1986). Organisations – and although I have focused on employing organisations, discrimination operates in many other areas – may be nominally open to all but virtually closed to many categories of the population, excluded on the basis of ascription.

People join – or attempt to join – organisations for many reasons: to validate an existing self-identification, to change it, or for other reasons more idiosyncratic. This applies in employment and across the spectrum of politics, education and leisure activities. Distinctions between identity and other aspects of the person (whatever *that* means) are difficult to maintain. Does someone become a hunt saboteur because she is opposed to cruelty to foxes, because she likes the image of herself as a 'sab', because 'that'll really make my mother mad', because she can't stand 'upper-class pratts on horses', or because she fancies 'that bloke with the dreads'? It is not easy to know. But it all contributes to identification.

People also *form* organisations as vehicles for their identity projects. This has already been suggested in the case of ascription; it is no less true for acquired identities. The organisational charter may refer to facilitating and improving the wider public understanding of train-spotting, or sado-masochism, or whatever, but that cannot be divorced from the train-spotters or sado-masochists who are the members, and their cause(s). And many of the advantages that accrue in the case of organisations based on ascription – support, symbolisation, pooled resources, coordinated action – apply equally to organisations oriented around acquired identities.

Whether emphasising ascription or acquisition, membership in different organisations has different consequences for individual identification. Scarcity is an obvious factor. Joining the Mickey Mouse Club, where the only qualification for membership is a small fee sent through the mail, is clearly less significant than finally, the day after your ninth birthday, having made yourself a pain in the neck for the last few months, being initiated as only the fifth member of your big brother's gang. And exclusivity isn't just a matter of competitive scarcity: the membership criteria matter, too (hence the power of ascription). In ascriptive theory, at least, you can only be in or out. The boundary between 'in' and 'out', dramatised as it often is by ritual, may also be the threshold between the sacred and the profane. On one side purity, on the other danger (Douglas 1966). Certainly other factors contribute to the strength of particular organisational identifications – the effectiveness of initiation (and, indeed, its affectiveness), external pressures on the group, the penalties attached to leaving, and so on – but the importance of exclusivity shouldn't be underestimated.

Whatever the context, in competitive recruitment a degree of rationalisation is called for. This can be a matter of reasons, or a matter of procedure, or both. The question of reasons has already been discussed: Is someone acceptable? Are they suitable? These are reasons. Procedures may not be easily separable from reasons, however. Sometimes procedural correctness provides sufficient legitimation for the outcome. That the proper procedure has been followed is reason enough.

A good example here is the *ordeal*, a category of ritual which figures in a variety of organisational initiations: from the theatrical pretension of the Masonic rite, to the violence of a motorcycle gang, to the psychosexual emotional trials of some New Guinean peoples, to the torment often visited on new recruits to the military. In the ordeal, survival rationalises recruitment. As ritual, it dramatises and authenticates the achievement of membership, both for the recruit and for her new colleagues. In this sense it contributes to both internal and external identification. The other major context in which the ordeal figures historically – determination of guilt or innocence in the face of accusation[3] – also has serious implications for membership. An unfavourable outcome to a judgemental ordeal may result in expulsion from membership; recruitment may depend – and here we are back to initiation – upon satisfactory reputation or character.

More characteristic of modern organisational recruitment, however, is the *interview* and its associated screening procedures (which may also be experienced as an ordeal). Interviewing is rooted in the informally institutionalised or ritualised human world of Goffman's interaction order: one or more people talk to another person – this is a definitively oral interactional form – in order to find out sufficient about her to decide about her recruitment (or, indeed, whatever fate is in question). However, the organised interview has arguably become *the* generic form of bureaucratic interactional encounter. Its only rival is the committee (and the two are, of course, combined in the board or panel).

The bureaucratic interview has a number of characteristic features (see Jenkins 1986: 128–9, for more extended discussion):

- There are always two sides, interviewer(s) and interviewee(s).
- There is a situational hierarchy. One side – the interviewer – is typically in charge of the procedure and of the determination of outcomes. This hierarchy derives from the interviewer's organisational position (particularly her control over resources), and, although not always, from her possession of the legitimate competences to carry off interviewing authoritatively.

- The business of the interview is the allocation of resources or penalties to the interviewee. The legitimacy of that allocation is grounded in adherence to more or less formally constituted procedures and in the reasons which inform the decision-making.
- However, the interview is not necessarily about decision-making on the spot. It may, for example, be about the *ex post facto* justification or rationalisation of decision-making that has already taken place (Silverman and Jones 1976); alternatively, it may send recommendations on elsewhere.
- Finally, interviews are generally private. The protection of privacy is extended as much – indeed more – to interviewer(s) as to interviewee: decisions can be made without the scrutiny of an audience.

The ordeal, by contrast, is typically a public or semi-public event, which *requires* an audience for its legitimacy.

The ordeal and the interview are not the only forms of rationalisation: recruitment by *election*, by *nomination* or by *lottery* can be important too, drawing on legitimatory rhetorics of democracy, authority and chance. And rationalisation does not preclude affirmation. Once an individual's recruitment to an organisation has been rationalised, nothing prevents that decision being subsequently ceremonially affirmed. There is every reason for doing so, if the arguments about the affective power of ritual, and its role in organisational common knowledge, are correct. Rationalised membership needs authenticity too.

Existing members can also have their membership reaffirmed and re-authenticated. A good example is the 'team-building' which figures in staff development programmes in many employing organisations in industrial societies. One common model is the 'residential': staff are taken away from work and home to spend a few days 'out of time', engaging together in a range of activities – from outdoor pursuits, to intensive group work, to equally intense socialising – after which they return home, ideally somewhat transformed (otherwise what's the point?). Separation, limbo and (re)incorporation: the rite of passage analogy is irresistible.

These are some, but only some, of the ways in which organisations affect the identities of their members. Organisations are, first and foremost, groups. As we proceed through life, our organisational memberships make a significant contribution to the diversity of the expanding portfolios that are our individual identities: who we are. The internal–external dialectic of identification can be seen at work not only between members, but also between members and non-members. Organisations are constituted in the tension between solidary similarity, *vis-à-vis* outsiders, and the internal hierarchical differentiation of members from each other. Although the internal moment of group identification is a consistent and necessary thread of organisational identification, on balance categorisation – of outsiders by insiders, of members by other members – is the dominant theme of recruitment and initiation.

14

CATEGORISATION AND CONSEQUENCES

As argued in the previous chapter, every organisation is a group, with members who recognise it and their own membership of it. Organisations are also always networks of reciprocal identification: self-definition as a member depends upon recognition by other members. Specifically, membership must at least be registered by those who are authorised to do so (i.e. by 'the organisation'). Hierarchies of authority and control govern the reciprocity of identification within organisations, and group membership is always in part a matter of categorisation. Thus it is even, *in extremis*, possible to have organisational 'members' who are authoritatively registered as such, but are not themselves aware of their 'membership', or may not even exist.

Organisational membership can be a penalty *or* a resource or benefit. When the committee of an exclusive Country Club interviews a would-be member, none of the participants doubt that something scarce and attractive is at stake. A job selection interview is also allocating an organisational membership that is usually seen positively, as a resource. However, an interview assessing someone for a place in a psychiatric institution or residential care home is deciding something more ambiguous.

ORGANISATIONS AND OUTSIDERS

The examples immediately above prompt the question: When are the two sides to the transaction actual or potential co-members of the same organisation? The successful applicant and the Country Club committee are co-members. On the face of things, so are recruiters and recruits in an employing organisation. But that may not be straightforward. If one is a manager and the other an hourly paid worker, whose terms and conditions of membership – among which is security of membership – are dramatically different, in what sense are they co-members? Point of view is important here, as is the interplay of similarity and difference within organisations. Whether or not a psychiatric patient is a 'member' of the institution will depend upon institutional policy and style. And also upon point of view. Membership may be demanded of the patient by a therapeutic regime emphasising inclusion and participation; she, however, may refuse to connive in it, which in its turn may have consequences. Nominally she may be a member, but virtually? Virtually she is an inmate. Therapeutic rhetoric aside, she cannot enjoy membership of the same kind as her psychiatrist's.

To make a point which resonates with the arguments of Foucault and many others, although modern organisations produce engine parts, meals, telecommunication services, government information or whatever, they also contribute to the production of people, identified in particular ways. And just as other organisational product ranges are diverse, organisational membership is by definition heterogeneous and stratified. There is no such thing as an undifferentiated category of 'member'.

For some organisations 'people-production' is their core business. Schools, colleges and other organisations of formal education are perhaps the most obvious examples, but they aren't the only ones. The criminal courts, for example, impose penal membership and stigmatising identification. Instead of branding a felon on the forehead, modern criminal justice interrupts her official biography – her 'record' – with a prison sentence. This cancels or suspends most of her existing organisational memberships, locking her into a new one – convicted prisoner and inmate – which overrides practically all others. Branding iron and prison record are both effective stigmata. Both change her identity.

To take another example, institutional psychiatry, in addition to its provision of therapeutic benefits and care, is in the business of containment and, arguably, punishment.[1] Both involve the authoritative medical identification of individuals as patients of a particular type, and their location in appropriate niches within organisational hierarchies. 'Psychiatric patient' ('person with a serious mental health problem' or whatever) is another identification, its origins organisational, which overshadows most other aspects of individual identity. In Becker's terminology (1963: 32–3) – borrowed from Everett Hughes – it is a 'master status', to which most other identities are subordinate.

Identity of any kind is consequential (otherwise it wouldn't *be* identity). Organisational identification is consequential in particular ways. Membership may offer access to resources and it may have costs; it may be a benefit or a penalty. For example, organisations are generally something more than a symbolically constructed collective umbrella. Even if only in a modest way, they are often corporate groups, in which property and resources are vested and through which those resources are distributed. Furthermore, as hierarchical networks of authority and power, organisations entail the direction of the behaviour of members and at least minimal individual submission to collective routines (if not actual rule). Organisational membership closes some options as it opens others.

Members aside, organisations deal with a wide range of people – customers, competitors, victims, clients, and so on – on whose identifications they often have an impact. Take, for example, the inevitable, if perhaps unintended, consequences of organisational recruitment. An individual who applies unsuccessfully for organisational membership is affected by the experience. Recruitment is, after all, a labelling process: the rejected applicant's self-identification may change. She may find herself stigmatised and excluded from access to other organisations. Materially, the resources that she invested in the bid for membership may be lost. On the other hand, if successful, her recruitment may have consequences for the members of her network, and for her position within it (if she joins the police, for example, or if her working hours are altered). Joining one organisation may mean having to resign from another. And so on. A change of identity is a stick poked into a pond: ripples spread in all directions. Organisational recruitment – or rejection – touches the lives and identities of more people than those immediately involved.

Typically, organisations are also substantial and visible in the human world: in buildings, artefacts and public symbols, in the organisation of time (timetables, the working day, the prison sentence, visiting time, opening hours, etc.), and in the wearing of uniforms or other visible identifications by members. Interactionally, an individual's organisational identification may be framed at least as much by that organisation's public image as by her presentation of self. This doesn't necessarily mean that, in the case of a railway employee, for example, passengers 'see' the organisational identity rather than the individual. But they certainly *do* see that, and to them it may be the most important thing about her in *that* situation.

The public presence of organisations is an important dimension of their impact on non-members. From the dawning of our experience of the human world – during the processes of primary identification – our environment is organised and signified by organisations of which we are not members. Space is defined in terms of its ownership or control by organisations. The skyline itself may be outlined by their buildings and monuments: think of the Eiffel Tower, the Sydney Opera House or the space left by the Twin Towers, the castles and cathedrals of medieval Europe or the great earth- and stoneworks of prehistory. Most organisations are visibly symbolised more modestly: a flag flies over the general's tent, the Post Office has a sign outside it, the removal company van is covered in the firm's name and logo, the local football club's fans wear its colours on match day, and so on. Individuals in public may be identified with this or that organisa- tion (which, as in the case of the football fans, needn't mean they're members in any formal sense). The human world is a highly visible world of organisations.

RESOURCES AND PENALTIES

It's not just a matter of visibility, however. For all sorts of reasons we all deal with organisations and their representatives. Many organisations are in the business of allocating resources or penalties to non-members, either as the theme of their organisational charter or a by-product of their main activities. In this way they organise the human world. The organised allocation of resources and penalties prompts questions. How do organ- isations classify collectivities in the abstract, and identify embodied individuals, in order to determine allocation? What are the consequences for the identification those people of that organised allocation (or denial)? What is the relationship between identification and the categorisation inherent in organisational allocation procedures?

In small-scale societies, without extensive markets or a state, the allocation of resources and penalties has, historically, been a matter for organisations of modest scale, with members typically recruited accord- ing to kinship or locality: family, lineage, village, etc. Here the criteria that inform allocation are implicit in the principles of organisation and predominantly bound up with group membership (which does not obviate the need for decision-making, or the competitive allocation of scarce resources: Plattner 1989; Sahlins 1974).

It is different in the large-scale urbanised and industrialised societies of the modern world. I shall concentrate on them for the purposes of illustration. Modernity, perhaps before anything else, differs from other eras in the extent to which everyday life is framed within and by complex organisations, and by the number and heterogeneity of those organisations. The existence in most modern states of a welfare system – even in countries, such as the United States, which are not usually identified as welfare states – means that all everyday life is entangled in organisations.

Organised and organisational allocation is a pervasive aspect of administrative systems. *Administrative allocation* (Batley 1981) takes place in many contexts; some have been touched upon in the discussion of labelling in Chapter 7, and in Chapter 13 with respect to organisational recruitment. A large literature discusses the topic in a range of organisational and cultural settings (Collmann and Handelman 1981; Hasenfeld *et al.* 1987). Administrative allocation procedures have some features in common. They are typically found in the organisations of the state and its licensees, although they also occur in market settings (particularly the most bureaucratised and regulated of markets, the labour market). They characterise agencies or enterprises (Weber 1978: 956), the main public spheres within and through which the large-scale allocation of resources and penalties occurs in modern, institutionally diverse societies.

Agencies and enterprises are bureaucracies, and the legitimacy of bureaucratic action is to a considerable extent grounded in procedural correctness. However, this doesn't necessarily mean that allocatory procedures are wholly, or even thoroughly, formalised. Formality and informality – much like control and deviance – are inescapably entailed in each other (Harding and Jenkins 1989: 133–8). The interview is at the heart of these procedures. As a ritualised encounter, between those-who-decide and those-about-whom-decisions-are-made, it requires the interviewee to engage in a presentation of self and the interviewer to categorise; each is involved in different identificatory work. The interview is an oral form, an organised encounter that blends the formal and the informal. Literate procedures, such as the written examination (Ong 1982: 55–6) or the diagnostic test (S. Cohen 1985: 183–96; Hanson 1993), are increasingly influential in some arenas of administrative allocation and do not depend upon the immediacy of interaction and situation. These are characteristically modern procedures; testing, in particular, exemplifies what Giddens describes as the increasing importance in the modern world of 'expert systems' (1990: 27–9). The test offers a vision of decision-making uncontaminated by its immediate context, 'objectivity' guaranteed by scientific method. With the IQ test as a basic model, a multitude of standardised tests – promoted by an expansionist academic discipline, psychology, and exploited in their professionalising strategies by personnel and training specialists – are now used to assess intelligence, motor skills, personality, aptitudes, etc. Formal testing adds apparent rigour and legitimate authority to bureaucratic classificatory processes. The relationship between testing and interviewing varies – either can rationalise decision-making – but testing, with its focus upon suitability rather than acceptability, is rarely determinate in itself.

Allocation is concerned, in large part, with rationing. Although scarcity is frequently exaggerated or constructed, if only to maximise organisational control over resources and increase their value, resources are always in finite supply. Penalties too, if they are to have meaning, must not be devalued by overuse. How to rationalise rationing is thus an important matter. Legitimate procedure is important, but so are reasons; these reasons are categorising judgements about whether or not recipients *qualify*. The politics framing administrative allocation mean that these judgements often derive from or reflect ideology and policy agendas.

Categorisation operates in two apparently contradictory, but actually complementary, modes: *discretion* and *stereotyping*. For a range of reasons, discretion is central to policy formulation and implementation in modern states (Hill 1997: 127–225; 2000: 85–108). Far from being a departure from bureaucratic niceties, without discretion bureaucratic organisations don't function well. Discretion permits a flexibility of response and decision-making that is appropriate to conditions of scarcity – whether real or imagined – and to the complexity of individual differentiation and situational variety. The interview has become so central to bureaucratic work because it creates the formally constituted space within which discretion can operate legitimately. Organisations are structured by rules, but rules only become meaningful in their operation and interpretation, and in the elaboration of exceptions.

The necessary simplification that facilitates judgement also encourages recourse to identificatory stereotypes. And discretionary exceptions aren't easily allowed without stereotypes from which to depart. Just as classification involves stereotyping – as argued in Chapter 11 – stereotyping is inherent in institutionalisation. In addition to its contributions to group identification (Pickering 2001; Tajfel 1981b), stereotyping is a routine feature of human attempts to enhance predictability – or at least a *sense* of predictability – in everyday situations of complexity and/or uncertainty. The maximisation of predictability is one respect in which bureaucratic organisations can claim what Weber called 'technical superiority' (1978: 973), so we should not be surprised to discover 'a close relationship between popular stereotypes and bureaucratic classification' (Herzfeld 1993: 71).

In everyday terms, what does all this mean? Some examples may help. Recruitment into employment was discussed in Chapter 13, and here the resource being allocated or denied is also an identification. As a competitive process, discrimination – defined neutrally as the evaluation of a number of options and selection between them – is inherent in employment recruitment. Apropos scarcity, however, the more vacancies there are, the more competition will favour the job seeker and the less discriminatory recruiters can be, the less discretion they can exercise (and, of course, *vice versa*). The recruitment process may be administrative, but market conditions are crucial, not least in determining the intensity of competition.

Stereotypes that are systematically related to situationally specific criteria of suitability and acceptability come into widespread play in employment selection (Jenkins 1983: 100–28; 1986: 46–79). The generality of the distinction between suitability and acceptability is suggested by the range of analogous concepts in the literature – 'functional' and 'extrafunctional' criteria (Offe 1976: 47–99), or 'quantitative efficiency' and 'qualitative efficiency' (Gordon 1976: 22–6), for example – and its subsequent use by other researchers (Collinson *et al.* 1990; Curran 1985). It is particularly significant because acceptability invokes perceived identity as an indicator of employability.

Examinations and diagnostic tests are most likely to feature in employment recruitment in the context of decisions about suitability. Even when 'personality' is tested, this is typically with respect to effectiveness in a particular post, rather than organisational 'fitting in' or general reliability. Acceptability is arguably less predictable than suitability, if only because it is difficult to define and highly context-specific. So we might expect recourse to stereotypes (and discretion) to be more common when acceptability is in question. Not only does this seem to be true, but some stereotypes are general enough to produce patterned outcomes across a range of unconnected recruitment occasions. There is ample evidence of the cumulative influence in employment recruitment of common stereotypes relating to 'race', ethnicity, gender, disability, class, and so on.

Take family responsibilities as an example. With respect to men, and particularly in secure, routine jobs, a stereotypical model of the ideal employee as 'a-married-man-with-two-kids-a-house-and-a-car' has been documented in British research (Blackburn and Mann 1979: 105; Jenkins 1986: 67–8; Nichols and Beynon 1977: 97, 199). It is strongly related to age-based notions of maturity. These are 'steadier' workers, recruiters believe, because the burden of their domestic responsibilities disciplines and habituates them to be so. If, as a consequence, men in this category stand a disproportionate chance of recruitment to secure manual jobs, then their perceived 'stability' will, at least in part, be a product of the stability of those jobs. In the process, a particular kind of worker is (re)produced: one who can afford a mortgage, a car, etc., who values a degree of predictable minor prosperity, who recognises the rewards attached to behaving in particular ways, who is tied in to consumerism.

Organisational recruitment decisions, and the criteria which inform them, are one of the processes whereby particular class identities – in this case, relatively affluent, 'respectable', politically conservative and working class – are constituted as distinct 'types'. In this case, the process is also predicated upon, and reproductive of, a set of gendered identifications. For a woman, employers may perceive the same domestic responsibilities as a disincentive to recruitment, because it is believed that they will weaken her commitment to a stable work pattern (Collinson *et al.* 1990: 192–213; Curran 1985: 26–9). The example further illustrates the power of routine and axiomatic ethnocentrism in the specification of the 'normal' family.

Administrative allocation is significant in other contexts and with respect to other resources: housing, for example. In the owner-occupier market and private-rented sector, decisions are conditioned by a variety of factors, particularly the contingencies of supply and demand at any particular moment. Looking at local relationships between identification and wealth, a great deal of the spatial materiality of identification – residential segregation – is generated in bilateral market transactions between private individuals, mediated by financial and brokerage organisations. In public housing,[2] however, demand – particularly for 'desirable' housing – typically exceeds supply, and scarcity is the norm. In the public housing sector – certainly in Britain, given its recent contraction – the scope for tenant choice is limited.

The organisation of public housing is more bureaucratised than in other housing sectors. This scarce public resource is allocated through assessment, involving the interviewing by officials of individuals and families. Assessment is conditioned by implicit or explicit stereotypes of eligibility and need, on the one hand, and of particular categories of people – 'blacks', 'single-parents', 'problem families', 'roughs', the 'homeless', or whatever – on the other. This may be reflected in local policy formulation (Gill 1977). More typically it operates in the immediacy and privacy of specific allocatory decisions (Flett 1979; Karn 1983), involving classificatory work such as the assessment and grading of housekeeping standards: here we have discretion and stereotyping combined once again. Desirable housing is a resource, undesirable housing a penalty, and they may be allocated as such. Access to public housing may be denied altogether. These tendencies may be encouraged by the politics of clientage to which local government is vulnerable. The end product is a spatial arrangement of public housing which identifies individuals as of greater or lesser worth according to where they live, and places them where they live on the basis of the identification of their worth. This is another way in which identification becomes mapped onto public space. It also illustrates the virtualities of identification. People are allocated a house in a 'good' area because they are judged to be worthy of it; because of where they live they are judged to be 'respectable'. And so on, and *vice versa*.

Administrative allocation is wide-ranging and pervasive. Discretion and stereotyping in allocatory decision-making can be seen at work in benefit allocation in social security offices in the United Kingdom (Dalley and Berthoud 1992; Howe 1990: 106–35). They have also been documented in 'street-level bureaucracy', social work encounters of one kind or another in the United States (Lipsky 1980; Prottas 1979). In Prottas's expression this is a business of 'people processing'. The 'gatekeeping encounters' of the interview room are concerned with 'social selection' as well as with alloca-tion (Erickson 1976). In fact, selection and allocation are one process, of authoritative classification: in contexts such as the administration of immigration rules this is particularly clear. Much policing work exhibits the same combinations of discretion and stereotyping, and can be under-stood as administrative allocation, in this case largely of penalties (Cicourel 1968; Turk 1969).

Reference to policing is a useful reminder that I am talking about labelling processes here. Although the labelling model originated in the study of deviance, as argued in Chapter 7 it can be applied to identification in general. Administrative allocation is a process of labelling, imbued with organisational and administrative authority, in which positive and negative stereotypes of particular categories are applied to individuals, systematically influencing the distribution to them of resources and penalties.

IDENTIFICATION AND MORALITY

Identificatory stereotypes are, therefore, consequential, affecting people's life-chances across a range of situations. But *which* stereotypes, and is there consistency in their mobilisation? Some are obvious: gender, sexual orien-tation, ethnicity, 'race', all the usual suspects. Among the more interesting are stereotypes of the 'deserving' and the 'undeserving'. These are typically concerned with attributes of lifestyle – cleanliness, thrift, sobriety, honesty – many of which are understood to be visibly embodied, encoded in appearance and demeanour. Allied to categorical distinctions such as 'rough/respectable' and 'reputable/disreputable' (Ball 1970; Matza 1967), these are particularly applied to working-class people. With their origins in nineteenth-century ideals of self-help and improvement, these ideas and categories are implicated in the ideologies of free-market capitalism, and still constitute an influential thread in the formulation and implementation of social policy in industrialised societies (Handler and Hasenfeld 1991; Katz 1989).

Stereotypes of the 'deserving' and the 'undeserving' are significant in a number of respects. The research cited in previous paragraphs (see also Hutson and Liddiard 1994; Jenkins 1983) suggests that in a variety of allotropes they inform policy and administrative allocation in Europe, North America and elsewhere. They are also conspicuous in everyday common sense. This is a cumulative and consistent classificatory process that is anything but trivial. Categorical boundaries are drawn that gloss morality and identity onto each other in a forthright manner.

It is this moral register, resonating as it does with underlying notions about fairness and justice, that makes these stereotypes so appropriate to allocatory decision-making. From its own point of view, the process appears, not as denial, but as a means of ensuring that the deserving are not deprived of scarce resources by the undeserving. What is more, stereotypical classifications such as these are sufficiently blunt to permit widespread application, yet sufficiently discriminating to allow their discretionary interpretation (and, as I have argued, the two things are not unconnected). They are general collective categories that can be applied to individuals. They are flexible, and adapt well to changing circumstances. They can be mapped onto other stereotypes – such as gender or 'race' – to produce cumulative and potent classifications of ineligibility and exclusion (Karn 1983: 170–3). They also resonate with homologous themes such as the discourse of moral responsibility informing the modern medical model of the patient (the 'sick role', as in Parsons 1951: 428–54).

However, stereotypical classification doesn't only affect the disadvantaged, and it isn't always disadvantageous. Nor do written examinations or other formally 'objective' assessment procedures guarantee immunity from the influence of stereotyping or discretion. Allocatory decision-making is enormously consequential in education (Cicourel and Kitsuse 1963), and here too we find stereotyping and discretion. Bourdieu (1988: 194–208) analyses the relationship of generally mutual reinforcement between the formal marks given to students' written work and the stereotypical professorial judgements of that work, as 'clumsy', 'vigorous', 'brash', 'cultivated' or whatever, and how this maps onto the cultural capital of the student, as indicated by class background. Bourdieu argues that 'social' inputs (class) are converted into educational outputs (marks, scholarships, university places) through the mediation of those stereotypical categories of judgement. Stereotypes also come into play in the careful descriptive qualification of formal results – the discretion – which the writing of references demands. Even if students have similar formal achievements, their work – and their worth – may be evaluated differently (another example of the difference between the nominal and the virtual). Stereotypes enable *class*ification to be euphemised as *academic* classification. This is analogous to the way in which the various distinctions between the 'deserving' and the 'undeserving' combine with procedurally correct allocations of resources to represent collective classification as the just satisfaction of legitimate individual 'need'.

Stereotypical categories of allocatory judgement do not arise wholly, or even mainly, within organisations. If they did they wouldn't be such common currency. Organisations aren't self-contained. The classifications that are evident in organisational categorisation are also mobilised and developed outside organisations. Indeed they feed *into* allocatory processes *from* the wider environment (which, of course, consists, in part, of other organisations). Officials, managers, teachers, whomsoever: they have histories, upbringings and backgrounds, they go home at the end of the day, they read newspapers and they talk to their friends. They live lives that are more than organisational. The mass communication media – television, cinema, the press, advertising – and the political institutions and arenas of the state, are significant frames of everyday life in the modern human world. The media and politics are not innocent with respect to each other: each feeds the other in the promotion and agitation of public discourses and campaigns focusing upon particular issues and particular categories of the population.

Some of these campaigns are familiar to us as 'moral panics', following Stanley Cohen's seminal account (1972) of the political demonisation of working-class youth culture – 'mods' and 'rockers' – in England in the 1960s (see also Goode and Ben-Yahuda 1994; Thompson 1998). However, the word 'panic' underplays the routine nature of many of these processes and overestimates their drama. Becker's notion of the 'moral crusade' (1963) is more downbeat, and has the virtue of emphasising organisation and direction. However we describe them, these campaigns are not new phenomena: the recurrent identification of working-class youth as a threat, for example, has a considerable history (Pearson 1983). Their volume, variety and pervasiveness have increased – and this is doubtless something other than a mere increase in magnitude – but there is a remarkable degree of historical continuity. These collective public discourses affect what individuals do – in administrative allocation, for example – and, in turn, they reflect individual behaviour. Hutson and Liddiard's account (1994) of the relationship between the construction of 'youth homelessness' as an issue and the bureaucratic processing of the young homeless illustrates this interplay between 'public issues' and 'personal troubles'.

Other categories which have been the recent subject and object of public agitation in this way include black youth (Hall *et al.* 1978; Solomos 1988: 121–45), welfare recipients (Golding and Middleton 1982), homosexuals and HIV-positive people in general (Cook and Colby 1992; Watney 1988), and young people organising and attending 'raves' (Critcher 2003: 48–63). Some public moral campaigns – dealing with child abuse and paedophilia (Jenkins 1992) or satanism (Richardson *et al.* 1991), for example – in addition to identifying deviant categories, whether real or imaginary, dramatise and normalise institutions and identities such as the family and Christianity. To re-emphasise that these campaigns are not distinctively modern, a parallel can be found with medieval and early modern anti-semitic public discourses, for example (Dundes 1991; Hsia 1988). Other, more routine collective public discourses – for example, the signification of conventional gender roles – dramatise and promote 'normal', positively valorised identities. Less likely to be crusades or panics, these are ubiquitous themes in advertising, cinema, literature, and so on (Goffman 1979; McRobbie 1991).

IDENTIFICATION AND NORMALITY

The identification and construction of the 'normal' has many facets. Returning to administrative allocation, the role of testing is important in this respect. Inspired in part by Foucault, Ian Hacking (1990) argues convincingly that the notion of 'normality' is in large part a modern artefact of the exponential growth of mathematics as a cultural discourse and a way of understanding of the world. The development of statistics transformed the imprecise everyday probability of chance and experience into a hard image of predictability, legitimated by science and suited to the needs of bureaucracy. This facilitated the imperialism of increasingly sophisticated and unforgivingly firm models of statistical 'normality'. Hand in glove with this went the elaboration of categories in general: 'many of the facts presented by the bureaucracies did not even exist ahead of time. Categories had to be invented into which people could conveniently fall in order to be counted' (Hacking 1990: 3).

The census of population – while it has antecedents in the empires of antiquity – is a distinctive product of the modern state's statistical governmentality that has had massive identificatory consequences (Kertzer and Arel 2002). From colonial Africa and India to the contemporary United States, census and other population classifications have interacted in complex ways with local collective identifications: reinforcing some, downgrading some and inventing yet others, inspiring responses ranging from cynical manipulation to resistance (Anderson and Fienburg 1999; Cohn 1988: 224–54; Lentz and Nugent 2000; Sundar 2000).

Censuses aside, the apparently aloof distance of statistical abstraction doesn't mean that mundane human life is unaffected. Hacking argues that the science of statistics has created a powerful *general* framework for everyday individual experience:

> The normal stands indifferently for what is typical, the unenthusiastic objective average, but it also stands for what has been, good health, and for what shall be, our chosen destiny. That is why the benign and sterile-sounding word 'normal' has become one of the most powerful ideological tools of the twentieth century.
>
> (Hacking 1990: 169)

One invented modern category – which definitively invokes 'normality' – is 'mental retardation' (in the United States) or 'learning difficulties' (in the United Kingdom). Where once some individuals were seen as 'idiots', 'half-witted' or whatever, a distinct population category has been created out of the diffuse individual diversity of intellectual (in)competences (Jenkins 1998). While its legitimacy is based in authoritative testing and psycho-medical diagnosis, such coherence as this category possesses derives largely from the treatment and services its members receive, rather than their 'intrinsic' collective characteristics (Trent 1994). Research in the United States by Mehan *et al.* (1986) and Mercer (1973) suggests that testing may be pre-eminently influential in the construction of individual institutional careers and identities as 'mentally retarded'. The symbolic power of the statistical model of normality is such that internal individual differentiation is submerged in a dominant classification of similarity, constituted in an external relationship of difference *vis-à-vis* the rest of the population (whose 'normality' it simultaneously confirms). In the process, the imagined has become anything but imaginary, and powerfully consequential in the lives of individuals.

Hanson (1993), also drawing on Foucault, offers a further perspective on testing. His concepts of *authenticity tests* and *qualifying tests* are broadly homologous with 'acceptability' and 'suitability'. Authenticity is concerned with commitment, attitude, faith, or whatever; qualification is largely a matter of competence or ability. Whereas the assessment of authenticity, through procedures such as the ordeal, is documented throughout history, Hanson, documenting the centrality of testing to much administrative allocation in the contemporary United States, argues that the quantitative assessment of qualification is distinctively modern.

Hacking and Hanson agree on the extent to which the categorising effects of normality-assessment procedures frame the identification of individuals and population categories. In the general contours of their argument and in their debt to Foucault, they are not alone. Rose (1989) argues, for example, that the twentieth century has seen the increasingly authoritative (and authoritarian) social construction, by practitioners of expert systems such as psychology, of a normalised model of responsible, autonomous and 'healthy' selfhood. More generally, Cohen talks about the 'classified society' (1985), Polsky about the 'therapeutic state' (1991) and de Swaan of the 'management of normality' (1990).

In the historical background, imperialistic normalisation has roots other than the statistical. The increasing centralisation of the nation-state, beginning in Europe in the late eighteenth century, was manifest in the codification of law, state education, language policies, public health reforms and public welfare (de Swaan 1988). The standardisation, centralisation and imposition of national identity (Calhoun 1997) went hand in hand with programmes of cultural homogenisation. It's not a coincidence that one of the chosen vehicles of French cultural integration and the modernisation of the state was called the *Ecole Normale* (E. Weber 1976: 303–38).

Finally, also with respect to historical background, it would be inappropriate to move on without pausing to remember the apotheosis – and the nadir – of the state categorisation of individuals and populations and the twentieth century's elaboration of normality. The genocide of Nazi Germany against Jews and Gypsies, and its assault upon those of its own citizens who were identified as 'unfit' in one sense or another, was rooted in scientific models of the 'normal' and in diagnostic procedures; it was, certainly in the first instance, in the hands of authoritative experts (Burleigh and Wippermann 1991; Müller-Hill 1988). The process was also thoroughly bureaucratised. It is chilling to recognise the continuity between allocation procedures that determined whether or not individuals should live, and our own mundane procedures of employment recruitment or educational assessment. As Bauman argues (1989), the Holocaust was a definitively modern phenomenon – with lessons for today – rather than an atavistic throwback to barbarism.

THE CONSEQUENCES OF IDENTIFICATION

Generally, organisations influence the identities of non-members through categorisation during the allocation of resources and penalties. A broad definition of resources, as something more than the common-sensically material or economic, is implied here. While I have focused on administrative allocation – the exercise of legitimate bureaucratic authority – resources and penalties can be allocated by other means. Typically involving force, they are no less consequential for identification. However achieved, the capacity of organisations to identify people – authoritatively or powerfully, as individuals or collectively – and to make those identifications 'stick' through the allocation of resources and penalties, should not be underestimated.

Identification and allocation are, in fact, mutually entailed in each other. Identity is consequential in terms of allocation: how you are identified may influence what, and how much, you get. Allocation is part of the process which generates identification: being deprived of or given access to particular resources is likely to colour the sense of what it means to be an X or a Y. A shared experience of being treated in particular ways may even generate a sense of collectivity where none existed before.

The significance of this lies in distinctions drawn in earlier chapters: between the *virtual* and the *nominal*, and between *groups* and *categories*. Identification is consequential in everyday life. It is in those consequences that what an identification means – whether individually or collectively – is generated. Consequences vary from place to place, and epoch to epoch, but in those consequences the virtualities of identification emerge. What it was to be Jewish in Germany in the late 1930s was utterly different, for example, from what it is to be Jewish in Israel in 2003. Nominally the same, virtually different. Same name, different identity?

The reciprocation between identification and its consequences is in large part established during the allocation of resources and penalties. Organisationally, this may be allocation to members (internal), or to non-members (external). It is, however, generally – perhaps necessarily – organised and coordinated. It is in the consistency over time and across organisations of (stereo)typifications of identification and patterns of allocation that 'structure' – an organised pattern of relationships between relatively stable collective identifications and the conditions of individual life – can be discerned in the human world.

Theoretical points about structure aside, the consequential nature of identification must be central to our understanding of it. Alongside internalisation – which in itself isn't enough – the weight of consequence is the main experience of identification. Coming back to groups and categories, this means that a collectivity or an individual can be categorised, and that categorisation produce major consequences for them, without their being fully aware of it (or aware at all). People with learning difficulties, who as individuals may be unaware of their categorisation (Davies and Jenkins 1996), are a case in point. Although there are *particular* groups of people with learning difficulties – clubs, residential units, and so on – in the largest sense they are a category, not a group. That category is a reality for the 'rest of society', however, and its consequences real for people with learning difficulties and their families.

Another possibility is that group members may know that they are nominally categorised by the Ys as Xs – indeed X may be what they call themselves – without understanding the consequences, the virtualities, of that categorisation. This is common in times of change. Many German Jews, for example, took a long time to realise the implications for them of National Socialist racial policies: that a census classification had become massively and fatally consequential. This example further illustrates how consequences can eventually feed into self-identification, through internalisation. The post-1945 history of Israel – and of Jewish people the world over – has been a painful working-through of the internalisation of the Holocaust, a reworking and historicisation of individual and collective experience in the construction of new Jewish identities (Hartman 1994; Kaplan 1994). That this process has also had consequences for how another group, the Palestinians, identify themselves and are identified by others is further support for the arguments of this chapter. Identification is never unilateral, never isolated and never without its consequences.

Organisational processes of identification take many forms, from the mundane to the terrible. The extent to which they shape our lives – who we are and our experience of being who we are – seems to be characteristic of the modern world. In the closing chapter I will return to some of the questions about modernity and identity that were raised in Chapter 2.

15

WHY IDENTITY MATTERS IN THE MODERN WORLD

In Chapters 1 and 2, I said that identity and identification are ubiquitous aspects of human life that we need to understand in order to do sociology, and strategic concepts for the sociological project of understanding better the relationship between individuality and collectivity. I went on to argue that:

- the human world as we know it would be an impossible creation without a sophisticated and extensive ability to know and communicate who's who and what's what;
- identification and identity are thus nothing new; and
- individual and collective concerns about identity and identification aren't definitively modern either: the increased volume of discourse about these aspects of what it is to be human are at least in part a reflection of increased global noise in general.

Throughout the rest of the book, there is a further consistent thread of argumentation to the effect that:

- individual and collective identity are as much an interactional product of 'external' identification by others, as they are of 'internal' self-identification; and
- identity is produced and reproduced both in discourse – narrative, rhetoric and representation – and in the practical, often very material, consequences of identification.

Putting all the above together, whichever way we look at it identification *matters*, in everyday life and to sociology.

The issue can't quite be left there, however. A number of recent contributors to the literature appear to doubt whether identity and identification matter as much as we sometimes appear to think they do. And they're right to do so, if only to prevent us taking the matter for granted. Martin, for example, insists that 'identity', despite its high profile in accounts of recent conflicts, 'fails to provide an explanation . . . [for] *why* actors are making certain utterances or *why* certain events are happening' (1995: 5). Similarly, while Brubaker and Cooper in their excellent assault on an overused and beleaguered term insist that they are solely concerned with 'identity' as an analytical concept, it's hard to resist the conclusion that they are somewhat sceptical about its worldly significance:

> People everywhere and always have had particular ties, self-understandings, stories, trajectories, histories, predicaments. And these inform the sorts of claims they make. To subsume such pervasive particularity under the flat, undifferentiated rubric of 'identity', however, does nearly as much violence to its unruly and multifarious forms as would an attempt to subsume it under 'universalist' categories such as 'interest'.
>
> (Brubaker and Cooper 2000: 34)

The issue comes to a head precisely with respect to the relationship between 'identity' and 'interests'. Which is the more important wellspring of human behaviour: the pursuit of individual and collective self-interest, or the imperative authenticity of individual and collective identity? This is a debate with a considerable history (Goldstein and Rayner 1994), which is unlikely to be resolved easily:

> in practice, interest and identity claims are closely intertwined. What I want is in some sense shaped by my sense of who I am. On the other hand, in clarifying my interests I may sometimes begin to redefine my sense of self. But there remains for me a fundamental distinction between my objectives that do not threaten my identity and those that do.
>
> (Goldstein and Rayner 1994: 367–8)

The alternatives appear in useful contrast if we compare Barth's anthropology (discussed in Chapter 9) and Tajfel's social psychology (Chapter 8). Despite the fundamentals in which their understandings of collective identification resemble each other, they differ sharply in this important respect. Barth argued that identification and collectivity are generated as emergent by-products of the transactions and negotiations of individuals pursuing, among other things, their interests. In this he was going against the grain of an axiomatic anthropological orthodoxy that at the time, in the 1960s, explained what people did by reference to their identity, their membership of corporate groups and 'cultural' collectivities.

Tajfel and his followers, by contrast, argued that membership of a group – even if it's only the result of being arbitrarily placed in a group by others – is sufficient *in itself* to generate identification with that group and to channel behaviour towards ingroup favouritism and discrimination against outgroup members. In this they were taking issue with social psychological accounts of identity that emphasised 'realistic competition' and conflicts of interest as the basis for cooperation and group formation (i.e. Sherif 1967).

To revisit the quotation from Goldstein and Rayner above, it isn't, however, clear that 'interests' and 'identity' are *really* alternatives. In both cases we are talking about individually internalised influences on behaviour: interests are motivational no less than the authentic voice of identification. We are also, no less necessarily, concerned with external factors: interests are frequently collectively defined, and can never be completely idiosyncratic or divorced from common sense and knowledge, while group identification is *definitively* sourced in the wider human world. Interests and identity are both definitively internal and external.

To approach the matter in another way, interests and identification are intimately bound up with each other, whether individually or collectively. Who I am has some bearing on what I see my interests to be, and what I see as being against my interests. How other people identify me has some bearing on what they perceive my – and, indeed, often *their* – interests to be. My pursuit of particular interests may cause me to be identified in particular ways by myself and by others. How I identify others may have a bearing on which interests I pursue. If my identities are consequential – as I argue – they are necessarily entangled with my interests. Even the single-minded calculative pursuit of material advantage, often taken to be the defining case of 'naked' unencumbered interest, cannot be understood outside a framework of organisational and other identifications – jobs, positions, reputations, and so on – summarised in a complex of common knowledge and sense. Capitalism, no less than any other human creation, is constituted in and generative of shared meanings and identification.

The quotation from Goldstein and Rayner leaves one more issue to address, however. Is a threat to one's identity *really* more serious than a threat to one's interests? Is it, indeed, easy to distinguish one from the other clearly? The answer, in both cases, has to be 'Only if you think or feel that it is', and there is no evidence that everyone does think or feel that. That a host of contemporary rhetoric, political and otherwise, sets a supreme price on identification doesn't mean we should accept that message at face value. As sociologists we are, in fact, obliged not to. Even in modern settings that are apparently characterised by intense individual or collective 'identity politics' – among the intellectual elites of Europe and North America who can afford psychotherapy and personal growth, for example, or Hindu and Muslim politicians, fighters and villagers in Kashmir (who probably can't) – the extent to which interests are subordinated to the imperatives of identity is a matter for discovery.

Yes, identity matters. And individual or collective self-identification matters, as it always has, everywhere. But as to *how* it matters? And how *much*? Always and everywhere, those are local matters.

THE RATIONALITIES OF MODERNITY

Despite my consistent argument for a balanced understanding of identification as an internal–external dialectic, Chapter 14 emphasised the *external* moment of that dialectic. To revisit the distinction between interests and identity, that argument owed something to Foucault, and much to Weber's vision of the 'iron cage'[1] of modern life, in which the capitalist 'care for material goods' and the demands of rational conduct and bureaucratic organisation diminish the human spirit to a point beyond despair (Weber 1976: 181). Whereas in Chapter 2, criticising Giddens, I suggested that reflexive self-identification is a *universal* aspect of being human, the argument in Chapter 14 suggests that, if anything, it may be the power of categorisation – the subjugation of the internal moment of identification by the external – that characterises the modern human world.

This isn't the place to discuss comprehensively Weber's contribution to our understanding of rationality and modernity (see Brubaker 1984; Ray and Reed 1994; Schroeder 1992: 112–40; Whimster and Lash 1987). However, if we *do* find ourselves in an iron cage – and I don't for one moment believe that we do – it's clear that Weber intended us to understand that, in large part, *we* have manufactured the cage and imprisoned ourselves within it. The impositions of modern bureaucracy are both external and internal. To say this, however, begs two fundamental questions:

- How constraining and imposing is bureaucracy (and, by extension, modern government)?
- How rational is it?

There are a number of complementary grounds for scepticism about the existence, let alone the penal efficiency, of the bureaucratic cage.

The first can be found in the impressive body of social science research on formal organisations, from Alvin Gouldner (1954) onwards. Weber massively underestimated the capacity of individuals to subvert the formal rationalities – objectives *and* procedures – of bureaucracies. This applies as much to those who work in bureaucracies as to those who otherwise deal with them. The sources of this resistance include the 'rational' pursuit of other, non-organisational interests and objectives, the boredom and distress engendered by over-routinisation, and the self-expressive refusal to accept organisational categorisation (which can be put in other words as the expression of selfhood). Generations of managers have wrestled with these problems, and generations of management consultants and trainers have made a living offering solutions to them. None of them has been more than partially successful.

The second point is related. Formality and informality cannot be separated other than conceptually. Each is a presence and an absence in the other: each needs the other to make sense (Harding and Jenkins 1989: 133–8). Formal procedures *of necessity* bring the informal with them, for a number of reasons, of which the recurrent need to bypass bureaucratic formality simply in order to get things done, and the fact that not everything can be legislated for, are only the most obvious. Weber defined the 'formal rationality of economic action', which was for him at the heart of bureaucracy, as: 'the degree to which the provision for needs . . . is capable of being expressed in numerical, calculable terms, and is so expressed' (Weber 1978: 85). This is the realm of allocation and diagnostic testing, discussed in Chapter 14. However, not everything is amenable to quantification. Not everything is susceptible to formal rationalisation. Nor are efficiency and formal rationality necessarily the same thing (Ritzer 2000).

A further related point concerns organisational size and complexity: these are significant in the construction (or not) of the iron cage. Size is a function of number of employees, number of transactions, volume of business and spatial extension. Complexity relates to spatial patterning, relations with the external environment and specialisation of the division of labour. Size and complexity are interrelated. As size and/or complexity increase, the more irresistible one might imagine the impetus towards formal rationalisation. Paradoxically, however, the bigger and more complex the organisation, the more nooks and crannies are created in which its members can evade monitoring, the greater the potential and opportunity for the disruption of formal rationality, and the more difficult it becomes to rationalise and communicate procedures. Large, complex systems have their own special problems of coherence and consistency that are counter-vailing tendencies with respect to rationalisation.

Formal rationalisation is demanding of actors in terms of cognitive *and* interactional competences. Fortunately, however, *in*competence of both kinds is widespread and there are limits to the remedies and corrections that can be applied by training and education. Further, we must not forget one of the very few sociological laws of relatively universal application: Sod's Law, under and in a variety of different names and formulations, predicts that whatever can go wrong, will go wrong. I would, personally, want to add a codicil to the effect that *everything* can go wrong. The combination of everyday incompetence with Sod's Law is a powerful obstacle to successful rationalisation.

Comfort can also be taken from the fact that even within the most efficiently rationalised bureaucracy, many things other than organisational procedures and objectives influence what people do. The 'irrational' dimen-sions of everyday life – for example, symbolism, myth, notions of fate or luck, sexuality, religious or other ideologies, ethnic attachments, emotional ups and downs, and so on – are ubiquitous and significant, within organ-isations no less than in other walks of everyday life. Furthermore, as organisations with boundaries, memberships and recruitment processes, bureaucracies are themselves constitutive of all the devices and enchant-ments – rituals, symbols, *esprit de corps*, history, and so on – which, as we saw in Chapter 10, are implicated in collective identification. Upon close examination, rationalised bureaucracies are, in important respects, strikingly similar to the 'pre-modern' human worlds which anthropologists have in the past claimed as their special domains of expertise. Although the use of a term such as 'pre-modern' is problematic – it is potentially, if not downright, misleading – it serves to emphasise that formal bureaucratic organisations are no less under the sway of enchantments than other, less 'rationalised' areas of everyday life.

None of these arguments should distract us from acknowledging the harsh organisational facts of life, or the realities of inequality and stratification in the modern world. The inefficiencies of organisational procedure can be as much a burden as a liberation. Not everyone is equally well placed to resist the compulsion and degradation that many organisational hierarchies routinely inflict on their members, particu-larly those at the bottom of the heap. The capacity to exercise self-determination – whether individually or collectively – is systematically related to wealth, in terms of both material and other resources, and market position.

The power of formal rationality is thus no more to be underestimated than the power of enchantment. Be that as it may, however, the complexities of modern human life don't run smoothly, mechanically or predictably. Any organisational 'system' is so creaky, so partial and contingent upon so much else that there is always room for some manoeuvre, space for some self-determination and holes to slip through.

Good, but what has all this to do with identification? In the first place, it emphasises the 'built-in' constraints on the capacity of organisations – and governments – to impose their categorisations on their members or others. In the second, it suggests that humans, from their point of view of embodied reflexive selfhood and possessing the capacity to choose among alternatives, are likely to be persistently resistant to categorisation. If there is such a thing as 'human nature' (Jenkins 2002: 115–19), this is one area in which to look for it. This is something fundamentally important, of which Weber, for example, wasn't sufficiently aware. Individuals and groups will assert their own sense of who and what they are. They may not always be successful, but that's not the point. Nor does the fact that resistance often appears to be a *response* to categorisation undermine the point: if the notion of 'the internal–external dialectic' is an approximation of how identification works how could matters be otherwise?

It isn't just organisational categorisation that matters, either. Human beings are wont to resist categorisation in all sorts of ways, and whatever its source. Everyday life is the site of the most mundane and possibly the most important resistance. In terms of name and treatment, and in however modest a manner, human individuals assert themselves. Even the expression – asserting them*selves* – is telling. They may only do so 'in their heads', mindful of threat and constraint, waiting for a better day (even though that day may never come), but that is still something. This is not to present a naively idealised and utopian vision of the human spirit: it can be broken, and the body with it. But the point is not only that it *has* to be broken, *in extremis*, for complete domination, but that the costs of doing so generally frustrate the point of the exercise.

Collectively, spontaneous resistance can manifest itself in many different ways. Riot and protest, labour stoppages, uprising on the plantation, sullen minimal cooperation, the interactional refusal to recognise the oppressor: the possibilities are many and obvious. Organised resistance is also a multi-headed creature: neighbourhood groups and political movements and parties; persistent and delicate lobbying and non-violent mass civil disobedience; anonymous leaflets, newspapers and satellite television broadcasts; assassination, guerrilla tactics and full-scale armed mobilisation. And means and ends may be thoroughly implicated in each other.

Resistance, whether spontaneous or not, can be a potent affirmation of group identification; organising is necessarily so.

To resurrect the distinction between interests and identification one last time, struggles over the allocation of resources and resistance to categorisation are, by virtue of the fact that identification is consequential, one and the same thing. Weber ended *The Protestant Ethic* by enjoining us to avoid either one-sided materialism or equally one-sided idealism in our attempts to understand collective life and individual behaviour. That remains good advice today: human beings – blessed with sociable natures and dignified by a spirited embodiment – demand nothing less. Whether or not there is an explicit call to arms in these terms, something that can be called self-assertion – or 'human spirit' – is at the core of resistance to domination. It may ebb to the point of invisibility, but it remains a consistent thread in human life. It is as intrinsic, and as necessary, to that life as the socialising tyranny of categorisation. The internal and the external dance together in the unfolding of individual and collective identities. And although those identities are imagined, they are not imaginary.

NOTES

1 KNOWING WHO'S WHO

1 On the relationship between sociology, social anthropology and social psychology, and their contribution to a 'generic sociology', see Jenkins (2002: 22–7).

2 A SIGN OF THE TIMES?

1 See, in particular, Castells (1997).

3 UNDERSTANDING IDENTIFICATION

1 On 'everyday thinking' see Billig *et al.* (1988); on the relationship between sociology and 'common sense' see Jenkins (2002: 27–38); on 'common knowledge' see Chwe (2001).
2 'Intersubjectivity' is the subject of a specialised and complex literature in philosophy and social theory (e.g. Crossley 1996; Schutz 1967: 97–138; Williams 2000: 80–100). In this book I use the term as shorthand to remind us that, the philosophical problem of 'other minds' notwithstanding (see the discussion in Chapter 4), meanings and understandings are to some extent shared, and can to some extent be communicated, between people in the everyday human world. This doesn't imply agreement or consensus or perfect cognitive equivalence, but without *some* sharing there wouldn't even be minimal mutual intelligibility.
3 See Connerton (1989), Fentress and Wickham (1992), Hobsbawm and Ranger (1983) and Samuel and Thompson (1990).

4 SELFHOOD AND MIND

1 The following are all worth a look: Breakwell (1992), Burkitt (1991), Carrithers *et al.* (1985), Carruthers (1986), Erikson (1968), Finkelstein

(1991), Freeman (1993), Heelas and Lock (1981), Morris (1991; 1994), Rorty (1976), Shoemaker and Swinburne (1984), Woodward (1997) and a thematic issue of *History of the Human Sciences* (vol. 7, no. 2, May 1994) dedicated to 'Identity, Self and Subject'.

2 This may put the ontological questions into quarantine, but it doesn't deport them from my argument. However, I had to start somewhere and this seemed to be the most modest position to adopt.

3 Such a framework would be a more general version of the model of identification which I develop here.

4 For social anthropology from a mutualist viewpoint, see Carrithers (1992).

5 Joas (1985) is an intellectual biography of Mead which discusses his relationship to Cooley and other pragmatist thinkers.

6 On the affinities between Marx and Mead, see Goff (1980).

5 EMBODIED SELVES

1 Although I suspect that Ryle would have dismissed Mead's model as an example of the absurd notion of the person as 'some sort of committee' (Ryle 1963: 181).

2 An idea that runs from Dewey all the way to Habermas (Thompson 1982).

3 This point is *very* obvious and not original (e.g. Parsons 1963: 34).

4 I'm not ignoring the ubiquity of 'mental health problems' here. The acute/serious personality disorders to which I refer are, however, *relatively* uncommon, and are on a continuum, towards the other end of which are 'most people, most of the time'.

5 I am grateful to John Parker, my former colleague at Swansea, for the insights and some of the phrasing of this paragraph.

6 ENTERING THE HUMAN WORLD

1 The bibliography in Poole's article is indispensable for anyone interested in the matters which are being discussed here.

2 One – regrettably unrealistic – assumption that I make here is the routine availability of adequate nutrition for the infant.

3 See Goodman 1964; Heskin 1980: 132–4; Milner 1983; Phinney and Rotherham 1987; Troyna and Hatcher 1992; van Ausdale and Feagin 2001.

7 SELF-IMAGE AND PUBLIC IMAGE

1 Also known as the 'social reaction' perspective.

2 And Becker's concept of the 'secret deviant' (1963: 20) is, even within the labelling perspective's own terms, a contradiction.

8 GROUPS AND CATEGORIES

1 The author of this encyclopedia entry is Michael Banton.

2 I could at this point have mentioned, for example, the classificatory schemes of medicine. These, however, are, by definition, intervention-oriented, and generally consequential for those on the receiving end.

3 Both examples cited are historically associated with administration and government. African 'tribal' identities were *at least in part* the product of colonial government (e.g. Lentz and Nugent 2000), while social class has been a conceptual tool of government in industrial societies since the nineteenth century. Both are important in population monitoring and censuses.

4 Although this is how Marx's idea is generally referred to, I haven't been able to find, in the major texts by Marx (or Engels) which I have to hand, this exact form of words. The closest is a passage in *The Poverty of Philosophy* (1847) discussing the English working class: 'Economic conditions had first transformed the mass of the people of the country into workers. The domination of capital has created for this mass a common situation, common interests. This mass is thus already a class as against capital, but not yet for itself. In the struggle, of which we have pointed out only a few phases, this mass becomes united and constitutes itself as a class for itself' (Marx 1975: 159–60).

5 Useful summaries can be found in Hewstone *et al.* (2002), Hogg and Abrams (1988: 1–30), Skevington and Baker (1989) and Turner (1996). For an important alternative view see Billig (1996).

6 Although it is probably unfair to single out anyone from the field in respect of this criticism, see Hogg (1996) for an example of what I mean.

9 BEYOND BOUNDARIES

1 Barth studied at Chicago during the late 1940s. His theoretical works, particularly *Models of Social Organisation* (1966) and *Ethnic Groups and Boundaries* (1969), acknowledge Goffman's influence. Hughes taught Goffman at Chicago; his essay 'The Study of Ethnic Relations', published in 1948 (Hughes 1994: 91–6), strikingly anticipates many of Barth's later arguments.

2 Although it could as easily be a reference to Merton (1957: 421), who calls W. I. Thomas's dictum about the relationship between social beliefs and social reality the 'self-fulfilling prophecy'.

3 Because of space constraints I have underplayed Barth's ethnographic stature: he has undertaken field research in Norway, Kurdistan, Pakistan, Iran, Sudan, New Guinea, Oman, Bali and Bhutan. Although he is among the most acutely theoretical of anthropologists, Barth's ideas have always

been hammered out on the anvil of empirical research, which is what he takes to be the core task of social science: 'What we . . . need is not a deductive theory of what these [social] systems will be but exploratory procedures to discover what they are: what degree of order and form they show in each particular situation in question. This needs to be discovered and described, not defined and assumed' (Barth 1992: 25).

10 SYMBOLISING BELONGING

1 No less interesting, Cohen seems recently to be moderating his 'excessive' opposition to the notion of negotiable boundaries; see, for example, Cohen 2000: 150–4.

2 And its analogues in other languages.

3 See Arlacchi 1983, 1986; Blok 1974; Gambetta 1993; Sabetti 1984; Schneider and Schneider 1976.

4 See Anderson 1978, 1993; Hannerz 1969; Liebow 1967; MacLeod 1987; Rainwater 1973.

5 One thing which Weber was attempting in his discussion of ideal types was to explicate the role in the analytical process of the point of view (including the value orientations) of the historian or the sociologist. He wasn't trying to banish values and points of view, in the futile pursuit of 'objectivity'; he was, rather, trying to make them more visible.

6 Although there is no space to deal with it here, Schutz also discusses our knowledge of our predecessors and our successors.

11 PREDICTABILITY

1 My use of Fortes here doesn't mean that I accept his arguments in the paper cited about altruism, or the centrality to the emergence of humans as 'cultured' beings of the development of the institution of fatherhood. Nor, however, should one reject these arguments out of hand.

12 INSTITUTIONALISING IDENTIFICATION

1 I have avoided the word 'culture' where possible throughout this book, because of the multiplicity of contested meanings attached to the word, because of its capacity for reifying everyday lived experience, and in a desire to avoid the culture/society dichotomy, which makes little sense and smuggles in further dichotomies – such as thinking/doing, or mind/body – which are at least as problematic (see Jenkins 2002: 51–4).

2 There is an analogous problem in Berger and Luckmann's work with respect to their neglect of embodiment as the site of the point of view of selfhood.

3 This is another way of putting things which I owe to to John Parker of the

Department of Sociology and Anthropology at the University of Wales Swansea (see note 5, Chapter 5).

4 Most of the literature addressing organisations from a broadly sociological point of view has only limited relevance here. Among the interesting exceptions are Blau and Scott (1963), Alvesson (1993), Herzfeld (1993) and Silverman (1970).

13 ORGANISING IDENTIFICATION

1 A third important contribution that organisations make to identification, which space constraints exclude from consideration here, is the process whereby positions and functions are produced (designed) as 'offices' – abstract positions in the network – before they are occupied by actual incumbents.

2 Much the same distinction is intended by Nadel, in contrasting the 'contingent' and the 'achieved', and 'recruitment roles' and 'achievement roles' (1957: 36). One could widen the net to suggest that anthropologically familiar distinctions between 'incorporation' and 'alliance' (Leach 1961: 21), or 'incorporation' and 'transaction' (Barth 1966: 4, 23–4), are addressing the same theme.

3 The ordeal has a long history (Bartlett 1986) as an arbiter of guilt and innocence, producing an identity transformation from 'suspect', to either 'innocent' or 'guilty'. Systematic torture may, at least in part, be interpreted as a relatively modern grafting onto *procedural* judgement of the organisational need for *reasons* that is manifest in the quest for confession (Peters 1985).

14 CATEGORISATION AND CONSEQUENCES

1 None of what I say here is a denial of the authenticity of 'mental health problems' (see note 4, Chapter 5).

2 For simplicity's sake I am ignoring here the publicly funded voluntary sector, and housing associations in particular.

15 WHY IDENTITY MATTERS IN THE MODERN WORLD

1 In deference to Weber's original language, see Chalcraft's discussion of the appropriateness of Parsons's translation (1994: 29–32).

BIBLIOGRAPHY

Abrams, D. (1996) 'Social identity, self as structure and self as process', in W. P. Robinson (ed.) *Social Groups and Identities: Developing the Theory of Henri Tajfel*, London: Butterworth Heinemann.

Althusser, L. (1971) *Lenin and Philosophy and Other Essays*, London: New Left Books.

Alvesson, M. (1993) *Cultural Perspectives on Organizations*, Cambridge: Cambridge University Press.

Amit, V. (ed.) (2002) *Realizing Community: Concepts, Social Relationships and Sentiments*, London: Routledge.

—— and Rapport, N. (2002) *The Trouble With Community: Anthropological Reflections on Movement, Identity and Collectivity*, London: Pluto Press.

Anderson, B. (1983) *Imagined Communities: Reflections on the Origins and Spread of Nationalism*, London: Verso.

Anderson, E. (1978) *A Place on the Corner*, Chicago, IL: University of Chicago Press.

—— (1993) *Streetwise: Race, Class and Change in an Urban Community*, Chicago, IL: University of Chicago Press.

Anderson, M. and Fienburg, S. E. (1999) *Who Counts? The Politics of Census Taking in Contemporary America*, New York: Russell Sage Foundation.

Antaki, C. and Widdicombe, S. (eds) (1998) *Identities in Talk*, London: Sage.

Anthias, F. (1998) 'Rethinking social divisions: some notes towards a theoretical framework', *Sociological Review*, vol. 46: 505–35.

Arlacchi, P. (1983) *Mafia, Peasants and Great Estates: Society in Traditional Calabria*, Cambridge: Cambridge University Press.

—— (1986) *Mafia Business: The Mafia Ethic and the Spirit of Capitalism*, London: Verso.

Aronson, E. (1991) *The Social Animal*, sixth edition, New York: W. H. Freeman.

Asad, T. (1972) 'Market model, class structure and consent: a reconsideration of Swat political organization', *Man* (n.s.), vol. 7: 74–94.

Baker, D. (1979) 'Social identity in the transition to motherhood', in S. Skevington and D. Baker (eds) *The Social Identity of Women*, London: Sage.

Ball, D. W. (1970) 'The problematics of respectability', in J. D. Douglas (ed.) *Deviance and Respectability: The Social Construction of Moral Meanings*, New York: Basic Books.

Barth, F. (1959) *Political Leadership Among Swat Pathans*, London: Athlone Press.

—— (1966) *Models of Social Organisation*, Occasional Paper no. 23, London: Royal Anthropological Institute.

—— (1969) 'Introduction', in F. Barth (ed.) *Ethnic Groups and Boundaries: The Social Organisation of Culture Difference*, Oslo: Universitetsforlaget.

—— (1981) *Process and Form in Social Life: Selected Essays of Fredrik Barth*, vol. 1, London: Routledge and Kegan Paul.

—— (1983) *Sohar: Culture and Society in an Omani Town*, Baltimore, MD: Johns Hopkins University Press.

—— (1984) 'Problems in conceptualizing cultural pluralism, with illustrations from Sohar, Oman', in D. Maybury-Lewis (ed.) *The Prospects for Plural Societies: 1982 Proceedings of the American Ethnological Society*, Washington, DC: American Ethnological Society.

—— (1987) *Cosmologies in the Making: A Generative Approach to Cultural Variation in Inner New Guinea*, Cambridge: Cambridge University Press.

—— (1989) 'The analysis of culture in complex societies', *Ethnos*, vol. 54, nos. 3–4: 120–42.

—— (1992) 'Towards greater naturalism in conceptualizing societies', in A. Kuper (ed.) *Conceptualizing Society*, London: Routledge.

—— (1994) 'Enduring and emerging issues in the analysis of ethnicity', in H. Vermeulen and C. Govers (eds) *The Anthropology of Ethnicity: Beyond 'Ethnic Groups and Boundaries'*, Amsterdam: Het Spinhuis.

—— (2000) 'Boundaries and connections', in A. P. Cohen (ed.) *Signifying Identities: Anthropological Perspectives on Boundaries and Contested Values*, London: Routledge.

Bartlett, R. (1986) *Trial by Fire and Water: The Medieval Judicial Ordeal*, Oxford: Clarendon Press

Bateson, G. (1972) *Steps to an Ecology of Mind*, New York: Ballantine.

—— (1991) *A Sacred Unity: Further Steps to an Ecology of Mind*, New York: HarperCollins.

Batley, R. (1981) 'The politics of administrative allocation', in R. Forrest, J. Henderson and P. Williams (eds) *Urban Political Economy and Social Theory*, Aldershot: Gower.

Bauman, Z. (1989) *Modernity and the Holocaust*, Cambridge: Polity Press.

—— (2001) *Community: Seeking Safety in an Insecure World*, Cambridge: Polity Press.

Becker, H. S. (1963) *Outsiders: Studies in the Sociology of Deviance*, New York: Free Press.

Bell, C. and Newby, H. (1971) *Community Studies*, London: George Allen and Unwin.

Bell, D. (1990) *Acts of Union: Youth Culture and Sectarianism in Northern Ireland*, London: Macmillan.

Bellah, R. N., Madsen, R., Sullivan, W. M., Swidler, A. and Tipton, S. M. (1991) *The Good Society*, New York: Knopf.

—— Madsen, R., Sullivan, W. M., Swidler, A. and Tipton, S. M. (1996) *Habits of the Heart: Individualism and Commitment in American Life*, updated edition, Berkeley, CA: University of California Press.

Bendle, M. F. (2002) 'The crisis of "identity" in high modernity', *British Journal of Sociology*, vol. 53: 1–18.

Benhabib, S. (1996) 'Introduction: the democratic moment and the problem of difference', in S. Benhabib (ed.) *Democracy and Difference: Contesting the Boundary of the Political*, Princeton, NJ: Princeton University Press.

Berger, P. L. and Luckmann, T. (1967), *The Social Construction of Reality*, London: Allen Lane.

Bernadi, B. (1985) *Age Class Systems*, Cambridge: Cambridge University Press.

Berne, E. (1968) *Games People Play: The Psychology of Human Relationships*, Harmondsworth: Penguin.

Billig, M. (1985) 'Prejudice, categorisation and particularisation: from a perceptual to a rhetorical approach', *European Journal of Social Psychology*, vol. 15: 79–103.

—— (1987) *Arguing and Thinking*, Cambridge: Cambridge University Press.

—— (1996) 'Remembering the particular background of social identity theory', in W. P. Robinson (ed.) *Social Groups and Identities: Developing the Theory of Henri Tajfel*, London: Butterworth Heinemann.

—— Condor, S., Edwards, D., Gane, M., Middleton, D. and Radley, A. (1988) *Ideological Dilemmas: A Social Psychology of Everyday Thinking*, London: Sage.

Blackburn, R. M. and Mann, M. (1979) *The Working Class in the Labour Market*, London: Macmillan.

Blau, P. M. and Scott, W. R. (1963) *Formal Organizations: A Comparative Approach*, London: Routledge and Kegan Paul.

Blok, A. (1974) *The Mafia of a Sicilian Village: A Study of Violent Peasant Entrepreneurs*, Oxford: Blackwell.

Blokland, T. (2003) *Urban Bonds*, Cambridge: Polity Press.

Blumer, H. (1986) *Symbolic Interactionism: Perspective and Method*, Berkeley, CA: University of California Press (first published 1969).

Boissevain, J. (1968) 'The place of non-groups in the social sciences', *Man* (n.s.), vol. 3: 542–56.

Boon, J. A. (1982) *Other Tribes, Other Scribes: Symbolic Anthropology in the Comparative Study of Cultures, Histories, Religions and Texts*, Cambridge: Cambridge University Press.

Bourdieu, P. (1977) *Outline of a Theory of Practice*, Cambridge: Cambridge University Press.

—— (1984) *Distinction: A Social Critique of the Judgement of Taste*, London: Routledge and Kegan Paul.

—— (1988) *Homo Academicus*, Cambridge: Polity Press.

—— (1990) *The Logic of Practice*, Cambridge: Polity Press.

—— (1991) *Language and Symbolic Power*, ed. J. B. Thompson, Cambridge: Polity Press.

—— and Passeron, J.-C. (1977) *Reproduction in Education, Society and Culture*, London: Sage.

Breakwell, G. M. (ed.) (1992) *The Social Psychology of Identity and the Self Concept*, London: Academic Press.

Brubaker, R. (1984) *The Limits to Rationality: An Essay on the Social and Moral Thought of Max Weber*, London: George Allen and Unwin.

—— and Cooper, F. (2000) 'Beyond "identity"', *Theory and Society*, vol. 29: 1–47.

Bryan, D. (2000) *Orange Parades: The Politics of Ritual, Tradition and Control*, London: Pluto Press.

Bulmer, M. (1987) *The Social Basis of Community Care*, London: George Allen and Unwin.

Burkitt, I. (1991) *Social Selves: Theories of the Social Formation of Personality*, London: Sage.

—— (1994) 'The shifting concept of the self', *History of the Human Sciences*, vol. 7, no. 2: 7–28.

Burleigh, M. (1994) *Death and Deliverance: 'Euthanasia' in Germany, 1900–1945*, Cambridge: Cambridge University Press.

—— and Wippermann, W. (1991) *The Racial State: Germany 1933–1945*, Cambridge: Cambridge University Press.

Burns, T. (1992) *Erving Goffman*, London: Routledge.

Burton, J. W. (1981) 'Ethnicity on the hoof: on the economics of Nuer Identity', *Ethnology*, vol. 20: 157–62.

Calhoun, C. (1997) *Nationalism*, Buckingham: Open University Press.

Campbell, J. (1994) *Past, Space and Self*, Cambridge, MA: MIT Press.

Cannadine, D. and Price, S. (eds) (1987) *Rituals of Royalty: Power and Ceremonial in Traditional Societies*, Cambridge: Cambridge University Press.

Capozza, D. and Brown, R. (eds) (2000) *Social Identity Processes*, London: Sage.

Carrithers, M. (1985) 'An alternative social history of the self', in M. Carrithers, S. Collins and S. Lukes (eds) *The Category of the Person*, Cambridge: Cambridge University Press.

—— (1992) *Why Humans Have Cultures: Explaining Anthropology and Social Diversity*, Oxford: Oxford University Press.

—— Collins, S. and Lukes, S. (eds) (1985) *The Category of the Person: Anthropology, Philosophy, History*, Cambridge: Cambridge University Press.

Carruthers, P. (1986) *Introducing Persons: Theories and Arguments in the Philosophy of Mind*, London: Croom Helm.

Castells, M. (1997) *The Power of Identity*, Oxford: Blackwell.

Chalcraft, D. (1994) 'Bringing the text back in: on ways of reading the iron cage metaphor in the two editions of *The Protestant Ethic*', in L. J. Ray and M. Reed (eds) *Organizing Modernity: New Weberian Perspectives on Work, Organization and Society*, London: Routledge.

Christensen, P. and James, A. (2000) 'Childhood diversity and commonality: some methodological insights', in P. Christensen and A. James (eds) *Research with Children: Perspectives and Practices*, London: Falmer.

Chwe, M. S.-Y. (2001) *Rational Ritual: Culture, Coordination and Common Knowledge*, Princeton, NJ: Princeton University Press.

Cicchetti, D. and Beeghly, M. (eds) (1990) *The Self in Transition: Infancy to Childhood*, Chicago, IL: University of Chicago Press.

Cicourel, A. V. (1968) *The Social Organization of Juvenile Justice*, New York: Wiley.

—— and Kitsuse, J. (1963) *The Educational Decision Makers*, Indianapolis: Bobbs Merrill.

Clark, G. (1992) *Space, Time and Man: A Prehistorian's View*, Cambridge: Cambridge University Press.

Cockburn, D. (ed.) (1991) *Human Beings*, Cambridge: Cambridge University Press.

Cohen, A. (1974) *Two-Dimensional Man: An Essay on the Anthropology of Power and Symbolism in Complex Society*, London: Routledge and Kegan Paul.

—— (1980) 'Drama and politics in the development of a London carnival', *Man* (n.s.), vol. 15: 65–87.

Cohen, A. P. (1982) 'Belonging: the experience of culture', in A. P. Cohen (ed.) *Belonging: Identity and Social Organisation in British Rural Cultures*, Manchester: Manchester University Press.

—— (1985) *The Symbolic Construction of Community*, London: Tavistock.

—— (1986) 'Of symbols and boundaries, or, does Ertie's greatcoat hold the key?', in A. P. Cohen (ed.) *Symbolising Boundaries: Identity and Diversity in British Cultures*, Manchester: Manchester University Press.

—— (1994) *Self Consciousness: An Alternative Anthropology of Identity*, London: Routledge.

—— (2000) 'Peripheral vision: nationalism, national identity and the objective correlate in Scotland', in A. P. Cohen (ed.) *Signifying Identities:*

Anthropological Perspectives on Boundaries and Contested Values, London: Routledge.

—— (2002) 'Epilogue', in V. Amit (ed.) *Realizing Community: Concepts, Social Relationships and Sentiments*. London: Routledge.

Cohen, R. (1978) 'Ethnicity: problem and focus in anthropology', *Annual Review of Anthropology*, vol. 7: 379–403.

Cohen, S. (1972) *Folk Devils and Moral Panics: The Creation of the Mods and Rockers*, London: MacGibbon and Kee.

—— (1985) *Visions of Social Control: Crime, Punishment and Classification*, Cambridge: Polity Press.

Cohen, Y. A. (1969) 'Social boundary systems', *Current Anthropology*, vol. 10: 103–26.

Cohn, B. (1988) *An Anthropologist among the Historians and Other Essays*, second edition, Delhi: Oxford University Press.

Collins, R. (1988) 'Theoretical continuities in Goffman's work', in P. Drew and A. Wooton (eds) *Erving Goffman: Exploring the Interaction Order*, Cambridge: Polity Press.

—— (1989) 'Towards a neo-Meadian sociology of mind', *Symbolic Interaction*, vol. 12: 1–32.

Collinson, D. L., Knights, D. and Collinson, M. (1990) *Managing to Discriminate*, London: Routledge.

Collmann, J. and Handelman, D. (eds) (1981) *Administrative Frameworks and Clients*, thematic issue of *Social Analysis*, no. 9.

Condor, S. (1996) 'Social identity and time', in W. P. Robinson (ed.) *Social Groups and Identities: Developing the Theory of Henri Tajfel*, London: Butterworth Heinemann.

Connerton, P. (1989) *How Societies Remember*, Cambridge: Cambridge University Press.

Cook, T. E. and Colby, D. C. (1992) 'The mass-mediated epidemic: the politics of AIDS on the nightly network news', in E. Fee and D. M. Fox (eds) *AIDS: The Making of a Chronic Disease*, Berkeley, CA: University of California Press.

Cooley, C. H. (1962) *Social Organization: A Study of the Larger Mind*, New York: Schocken (first published 1909).

—— (1964) *Human Nature and the Social Order*, New York: Schocken (first published 1902).

Corsaro, W. A. (1997) *The Sociology of Childhood*, Thousand Oaks, CA: Pine Forge Press.

Costa, J. and Bamossy, G. (eds) (1995) *Marketing in a Multicultural World*, London: Sage.

Coulson, M. (1972) 'Role: a redundant concept in sociology? Some educational considerations', in J. A. Jackson (ed.) *Role*, Cambridge: Cambridge University Press.

Craib, I. (1998) *Experiencing Identity*, London: Sage.

Crisp, R. J. and Hewstone, M. (1999) 'Differential evaluation of crossed category groups: patterns, processes and reducing intergroup bias', *Groups, Processes and Intergroup Relations*, vol. 2: 307–33.

Critcher, C. (2003) *Moral Panics and the Media*, Buckingham: Open University Press.

Crossley, N. (1996) *Intersubjectivity: The Fabric of Social Becoming*, London: Sage.

Crow, G. and Allan, G. (1994) *Community Life: An Introduction to Local Social Relations*, London: Harvester Wheatsheaf.

Curran, M. M. (1985) *Stereotypes and Selection: Gender and Family in the Recruitment Process*, London: HMSO.

Dalley, G. and Berthoud, R. (1992) *Challenging Discretion: The Social Fund Review Procedure*, London: Policy Studies Institute.

Damon, W. and Hart, D. (1988) *Self-Understanding in Childhood and Adolescence*, Cambridge: Cambridge University Press.

Davies, C. A. and Jenkins, R. (1995) 'Lives in context: the transition to adulthood of young people with learning difficulties', Swansea: unpublished report to the Joseph Rowntree Foundation.

—— and Jenkins (1996), '"She has different fits to me": how people with learning disabilities see themselves', *Disability and Society*, vol. 12: 95–109.

Davies, N. and Moorhouse, R. (2002) *Microcosm: Portrait of a Central European City*, London: Jonathan Cape.

Deaux, K. (2000) 'Models, meanings and motivations', in D. Capozza and R. Brown (eds) *Social Identity Processes*, London: Sage.

Delanty, G. (2003) *Community*, London: Routledge.

Deschamps, J.-C. and Devos, T. (1998) 'Regarding the relationship between social identity and personal identity', in S. Worchel, J. F. Morales, D. Páez and J.-C. Deschamps (eds) *Social Identity: International Perspectives*, London: Sage.

de Swaan, A. (1988) *In Care of the State: Health Care, Education and Welfare in Europe and the USA in the Modern Era*, Cambridge: Polity Press.

—— (1990) *The Management of Normality: Critical Essays in Health and Welfare*, London: Routledge.

—— (2001) *Human Societies: An Introduction*, Cambridge: Polity Press.

Donzelot, J. (1980) *The Policing of Families: Welfare versus the State*, London: Hutchinson.

Douglas, M. (1966) *Purity and Danger: An Analysis of Concepts of Pollution and Taboo*, London: Routledge and Kegan Paul.

—— (1973) *Natural Symbols: Explorations in Cosmology*, Harmondsworth: Pelican.

Doyal, L. and Gough, I. (1991) *A Theory of Human Need*, Basingstoke: Macmillan.

Dundes, A. (ed.) (1991) *The Blood Libel Legend: A Casebook in Anti-Semitic Folklore*, Madison, WI: University of Wisconsin Press.

Dunn, J. (1988) *The Beginnings of Social Understanding*, Oxford: Basil Blackwell.

Eiser, J. R. (1990) *Social Judgment*, Buckingham: Open University Press.

Epstein, A. L. (1978) *Ethos and Identity: Three Studies in Ethnicity*, London: Tavistock.

Erickson, F. (1976) 'Gatekeeping encounters: a social selection process', in P. R. Sanday (ed.) *Anthropology and the Public Interest*, New York: Academic Press.

Eriksen, T. H. (1993) *Ethnicity and Nationalism: Anthropological Perspectives*, London: Pluto Press.

Erikson, E. H. (1968) *Identity: Youth and Crisis*, London: Faber.

Erikson, R. and Goldthorpe, J. H. (1993) *The Constant Flux: A Study of Class Mobility in Industrial Societies*, Oxford: Clarendon Press.

Etzioni, A. (1993) *The Spirit of Community: Rights, Responsibilities and the Communitarian Agenda*, New York: Crown.

Evens, T. M. S. (1977) 'The predication of the individual in anthropological interactionism', *American Ethnologist*, vol. 79: 579–97.

Fentress, J. and Wickham, C. (1992) *Social Memory*, Oxford: Blackwell.

Finkelstein, J. (1991) *The Fashioned Self*, Cambridge: Polity Press.

Flett, H. (1979) 'Bureaucracy and ethnicity: notions of eligibility in public housing', in S. Wallman (ed.) *Ethnicity at Work*, London: Macmillan.

Fortes, M. (1983) *Rules and the Emergence of Society*, Occasional Paper no. 39, London: Royal Anthropological Institute.

Foucault, M. (1970) *The Order of Things: An Archaeology of the Human Sciences*, London: Tavistock.

—— (1980) *Power/Knowledge: Selected Interviews and Other Writings 1972–1977*, ed. C. Gordon, Brighton: Harvester.

Freeman, M. (1993) *Rewriting the Self: History, Memory, Narrative*, London: Routledge.

Freud, S. (1984) *On Metapsychology: The Theory of Psychoanalysis* (Penguin Freud Library no. 11), ed. A. Richards, Harmondsworth: Pelican.

Gambetta, D. (1993) *The Sicilian Mafia: The Business of Private Protection*, Cambridge: Harvard University Press.

Geertz, C. (1973) *The Interpretation of Cultures*, New York: Basic Books.

—— (1983) *Local Knowledge: Further Essays in Interpretive Anthropology*, New York: Basic Books.

Gibson, J. J. (1979) *The Ecological Approach to Visual Perception*, Boston, MA: Houghton Mifflin.

Giddens, A. (1984) *The Constitution of Society*, Cambridge: Polity Press.

—— (1990) *The Consequences of Modernity*, Cambridge: Polity Press.

—— (1991) *Modernity and Self-Identity: Self and Society in the Late Modern Age*, Cambridge: Polity Press.

Gill, O. (1977) *Luke Street: Housing Policy, Conflict and the Creation of the Delinquent Area*, London: Macmillan.

Gledhill, J. (1994) *Power and its Disguises: Anthropological Perspectives on Politics*, London: Pluto Press.

Gluckman, M. (1956) *Custom and Conflict in Africa*, Oxford: Basil Blackwell.

—— (1963) *Order and Rebellion in Tribal Africa*, London: Cohen and West.

Goff, T. W. (1980) *Marx and Mead: Contributions to a Sociology of Knowledge*, London: Routledge and Kegan Paul.

Goffman, E. (1961) *Encounters: Two Studies in the Sociology of Interaction*, Indianapolis, IN: Bobbs Merrill.

—— (1968a) *Stigma: Notes on the Management of Spoiled Identity*, Harmondsworth: Pelican.

—— (1968b) *Asylums: Essays on the Social Situation of Mental Patients and Other Inmates*, Harmondsworth: Pelican.

—— (1969) *The Presentation of Self in Everyday Life*, London: Allen Lane (first published 1959).

—— (1970) *Strategic Interaction*, Oxford: Basil Blackwell.

—— (1971) *Relations in Public: Microstudies of the Public Order*, London: Allen Lane.

—— (1975) *Frame Analysis: An Essay on the Organization of Experience*, Harmondsworth: Peregrine.

—— (1979) *Gender Advertisements*, Cambridge: Harvard University Press.

—— (1983) 'The interaction order', *American Sociological Review*, vol. 48: 1–17.

Golding, P. and Middleton, S. (1982) *Images of Welfare: Press and Public Attitudes to Poverty*, Oxford: Basil Blackwell.

Goldstein, J. and Rayner, J. (1994) 'The politics of identity in late modern society', *Theory and Society*, vol. 23: 367–84.

Goldthorpe, J. H. and Hope, K. (1974) *The Social Grading of Occupations*, Oxford: Clarendon Press.

Goode, R. and Ben-Yahuda, N. (1994) *Moral Panics: The Social Construction of Deviance*, Cambridge, MA: Blackwell.

Goodman, M. E. (1964) *Race Awareness in Young Children*, revised edition, New York: Collier.

Gordon, D. M. (1976) 'Capitalist efficiency and socialist efficiency', *Monthly Review*, vol. 28, no. 3: 19–39.

Gouldner, A. W. (1954) *Patterns of Industrial Bureaucracy*, New York: Free Press.

Gove, W. R. (ed.) (1980) *The Labelling of Deviance: Evaluating a Perspective*, second edition, Beverley Hills, CA: Sage.

Gumperz, J. J. (ed.) (1982) *Language and Social Identity*, Cambridge: Cambridge University Press.

Haaland, G. (1969) 'Economic determinants in ethnic processes', in F. Barth (ed.) *Ethnic Groups and Boundaries*, Oslo: Universitetsforlaget.

Hacking, I. (1990) *The Taming of Chance*, Cambridge: Cambridge University Press.

Hakken, D. (1999) *Cyborgs@Cyberspace: An Ethnographer Looks to the Future*, New York: Routledge.

Hall, S. (1992) 'Our mongrel selves', *New Statesman and Society*, supplement, 19 June 1992: 6–8.

—— (1996) 'Introduction: who needs identity?', in S. Hall and P. du Gay (eds) *Questions of Cultural Identity*, London: Sage.

—— Critcher, C., Jefferson, T., Clarke, J. and Roberts, B. (1978) *Policing the Crisis: Mugging, the State and Law and Order*, London: Macmillan.

Handelman, D. (1998) *Models and Mirrors: Towards an Anthropology of Public Events*, New York: Bergahn.

Handler, J. F. and Hasenfeld, Y. (1991) *The Moral Construction of Poverty: Welfare Reform in America*, Newbury Park, CA: Sage.

Hannerz, U. (1969) *Soulside: Inquiries into Ghetto Culture and Community*, New York: Columbia University Press.

Hanson, F. A. (1993) *Testing Testing: Social Consequences of the Examined Life*, Berkeley, CA: University of California Press.

Harding, P. and Jenkins, R. (1989) *The Myth of the Hidden Economy: Towards a New Understanding of Informal Economic Activity*, Milton Keynes: Open University Press.

Harré, R. (1979) *Social Being: A Theory for Social Psychology*, Oxford: Basil Blackwell.

—— (1981) 'Psychological variety', in P. Heelas and A. Lock (eds) *Indigenous Psychologies: The Anthropology of the Self*, London: Academic Press.

—— (1983) *Personal Being: A Theory for Individual Psychology*, Oxford: Basil Blackwell.

—— (ed.) (1986) *The Social Construction of Emotions*, Oxford: Basil Blackwell.

—— (1998) *The Singular Self: An Introduction to the Psychology of Personhood*, London: Sage.

—— (2000) *One Thousand Years of Philosophy*, Oxford: Blackwell.

—— and Gillett, G. (1994) *The Discursive Mind*, Thousand Oaks, CA: Sage.

Harris, C. C. (1990) *Kinship*, Milton Keynes: Open University Press.

Harris, R. (1972) *Prejudice and Tolerance in Ulster: Neighbours and 'Strangers' in a Border Community*, Manchester: Manchester University Press.

Hartman, G. (ed.) (1994) *Holocaust Remembrance: The Shapes of Memory*, Oxford: Basil Blackwell.

Hasenfeld, Y., Rafferty, J. A. and Zald, M. N. (1987) 'The Welfare State, citizenship, and bureaucratic encounters', *Annual Review of Sociology*, vol. 13: 387–415.

Heelas, P. and Lock, A. (eds) (1981) *Indigenous Psychologies: The Anthropology of the Self*, London: Academic Press.

Herzfeld, M. (1993) *The Social Production of Indifference: Exploring the Symbolic Roots of Western Bureaucracy*, Chicago, IL: University of Chicago Press.

Heskin, K. (1980) *Northern Ireland: A Psychological Analysis*, Dublin: Gill and Macmillan.

Hewstone, M., Rubin, M. and Willis, H. (2002) 'Intergroup bias', *Annual Review of Psychology*, vol. 53: 575–604.

Hill, M. (1997) *The Policy Process in the Modern State*, third edition, London: Prentice Hall.

—— (2000) *Understanding Social Policy*, sixth edition, Oxford: Blackwell.

Hobsbawm, E. and Ranger, T. (eds) (1983) *The Invention of Tradition*, Cambridge: Cambridge University Press.

Hirst, P. and Woolley, P. (1982) *Social Relations and Human Attributes*, London: Tavistock.

Hockey, J. and James, A. (2003) *Social Identities across the Life Course*, Basingstoke: Palgrave Macmillan.

Hogg, M. A. (1996) 'Intergroup processes, group structure and social identity', in W. P. Robinson (ed.) *Social Groups and Identities: Developing the Theory of Henri Tajfel*, London: Butterworth Heinemann.

—— and Abrams, D. (1988) *Social Identifications: A Social Psychology of Intergroup Relations and Group Processes*, London: Routledge.

Hollis, M. (1977) *Models of Man: Philosophical Thoughts on Social Action*, Cambridge: Cambridge University Press.

—— (1985) 'Of masks and men', in M. Carrithers, S. Collins and S. Lukes (eds) *The Category of the Person*, Cambridge: Cambridge University Press.

Holy, L. and Stuchlik, M. (1983) *Actions, Norms and Representations: Foundations of Anthropological Inquiry*, Cambridge: Cambridge University Press.

Honneth, A. and Joas, H. (1988) *Social Action and Human Nature*, Cambridge: Cambridge University Press.

Howe, L. E. A. (1990) *Being Unemployed in Northern Ireland: An Ethnographic Study*, Cambridge: Cambridge University Press.

Howell, S. (2002) 'Community beyond place', in V. Amit (ed.) *Realizing Community: Concepts, Social Relationships and Sentiments*, London: Routledge.

Hsia, R. P. (1988) *The Myth of Ritual Murder: Jews and Magic in Reformation Germany*, New Haven, CT: Yale University Press.

Hughes, E. C. (1994) *On Work, Race, and the Sociological Imagination*, ed. L. A. Coser, Chicago, IL: University of Chicago Press.

Hutchinson, S. (1995) *Nuer Dilemmas: Coping with Money, War and the State*, Berkeley, CA: University of California Press.

Hutson, S. and Liddiard, M. (1994) *Youth Homelessness: The Construction of a Social Issue*, London: Macmillan.

Ignatieff, M. (1984) *The Needs of Strangers*, London: Chatto and Windus.

Jackson, J. A. (1972) 'Role – editorial introduction', in J. A. Jackson (ed.) *Role*, Cambridge: Cambridge University Press.

James, A. (1993) *Childhood Identities: Self and Social Relationships in the Experience of the Child*, Edinburgh: Edinburgh University Press.

—— Jenks, C. and Prout, A. (1998) *Theorizing Childhood*, Cambridge: Polity Press.

Jameson, F. (1991) *Postmodernism, or The Cultural Logic of Late Capitalism*, London: Verso.

Jarman, N. (1997) *Material Conflicts: Parades and Visual Displays in Northern Ireland*, Oxford: Berg.

Jenkins, P. (1992) *Intimate Enemies: Moral Panics in Contemporary Great Britain*, New York: Aldine de Gruyter.

Jenkins, R. (1981) 'Thinking and doing: towards a model of cognitive practice', in L. Holy and M. Stuchlik (eds) *The Structure of Folk Models*, London: Academic Press.

—— (1983) *Lads, Citizens and Ordinary Kids: Working-class Youth Lifestyles in Belfast*, London: Routledge and Kegan Paul.

—— (1986) *Racism and Recruitment: Managers, Organisations and Equal Opportunity in the Labour Market*, Cambridge: Cambridge University Press.

—— (1990) 'Dimensions of adulthood in Britain: long-term unemployment and mental handicap', in P. Spencer (ed.) *Anthropology and the Riddle of the Sphinx: Paradoxes of Change in the Life Course*, London: Routledge.

—— (1994) 'Rethinking ethnicity: identity, categorization and power', *Ethnic and Racial Studies*, vol. 17: 197–223.

—— (1997) *Rethinking Ethnicity: Arguments and Explorations*, London: Sage.

—— (1998) 'Culture, classification and (in)competence', in R. Jenkins (ed.) *Questions of Competence: Culture, Classification and Intellectual Disability*, Cambridge: Cambridge University Press.

—— (2001) 'Categorization: identity, social process and epistemology', *Current Sociology*, vol. 84, no. 3: 7–25.

—— (2002) *Foundations of Sociology: Towards a Better Understanding of the Human World*, Basingstoke: Palgrave Macmillan.

—— (2003) *Pierre Bourdieu*, second edition, London: Routledge.

Jenks, C. (1996) *Childhood*, London: Routledge.

Joas, H. (1985) *G. H. Mead: A Contemporary Re-examination of his Thought*, Cambridge: Polity Press.

Kagan, J. and Lamb, S. (eds) (1987) *The Emergence of Morality in Young Children*, Chicago, IL: University of Chicago Press.

Kapferer, B. (ed.) (1976) *Transaction and Meaning*, Philadelphia: ISHI.

Kaplan, H. (1994) *Conscience and Memory: Meditations in a Museum of the Holocaust*, Chicago, IL: University of Chicago Press.

Karn, V. (1983) 'Race and housing in Britain: the role of the major institutions', in N. Glazer and K. Young (eds) *Ethnic Pluralism and Public Policy: Achieving Equality in the United States and Britain*, London: Heinemann.

Katz, M. B. (1989) *The Undeserving Poor: From the War on Poverty to the War on Welfare*, New York: Pantheon.

Kaye, K. (1982) *The Mental and Social Life of Babies: How Parents Create Persons*, Brighton: Harvester.

Keesing, R. M. (1975) *Kin Groups and Social Structure*, New York: Holt, Rhinehart and Winston.

Keller, S. (2003) *Community: Pursuing the Dream, Living the Reality*, Princeton, NJ: Princeton University Press.

Kertzer, D. I. and Arel, D. (ed.) (2002) *Census and Identity: The Politics of Race, Ethnicity and Language in National Censuses*, Cambridge: Cambridge University Press.

Kuhse, H. and Singer, P. (1985) *Should the Baby Live? The Problem of Handicapped Infants*, Oxford: Oxford University Press.

Lacan, J. (1977) *Écrits: A Selection*, London: Tavistock.

La Fontaine, J. (1985) *Initiation*, Harmondsworth: Penguin.

Laing, R. D. (1971) *Self and Others*, Harmondsworth: Pelican.

Lakoff, G. and Johnson, M. (1999) *Philosophy in the Flesh: The Embodied Mind and its Challenge to Western Thought*, New York: Basic Books.

Lamont, M. and Fournier, M. (eds) (1992) *Cultivating Differences: Symbolic Boundaries and the Making of Inequality*, Chicago, IL: University of Chicago Press.

Lane, C. (1981) *The Rites of Rulers: Ritual in Industrial Society – The Soviet Case*, Cambridge: Cambridge University Press.

Leach, E. R. (1954) *Political Systems of Highland Burma: A Study of Kachin Social Structure*, London: Athlone Press.

—— (1961) *Rethinking Anthropology*, London: Athlone Press.

—— (1976) *Culture and Communication: The Logic by which Symbols are Connected*, Cambridge: Cambridge University Press.

Lee, R. and Morgan, D. (eds) (1989) *Birthrights: Law and the Beginning of Life*, London: Routledge.

Lemert, E. M. (1972) *Human Deviance, Social Problems and Social Control*, second edition, Englewood Cliffs, NJ: Prentice Hall.

Lentz, C. and Nugent, P. (eds) (2000) *Ethnicity in Ghana: The Limits of Invention*, Basingstoke: Macmillan.

Liebow, E. (1967) *Tally's Corner*, Boston: Little, Brown.

Lindesmith, A. R., Strauss, A. L. and Denzin, N. K. (1999) *Social Psychology*, eighth edition, Thousand Oaks, CA: Sage.

Linton, R. (1936) *The Study of Man: An Introduction*, student edition, New York: Appleton Century.

Lipsky, M. (1980) *Street-Level Bureaucracy: Dilemmas of the Individual in Public Services*, New York: Russell Sage Foundation.

Maass, M., Castelli, L. and Arcuri, L. (2000) 'Measuring prejudice: implicit versus explicit techniques', in D. Capozza and R. Brown (eds) *Social Identity Processes*, London: Sage.

McDonald, M. (1993) 'The construction of difference: an anthropological approach to stereotypes', in S. MacDonald (ed.) *Inside European Identities: Ethnography in Western Europe*, Oxford: Berg.

McGarty, C. (1999) *Categorization in Social Psychology*, London: Sage.

MacIntyre, A. (1985) *After Virtue: A Study in Moral Theory*, London: Duckworth.

MacLeod, J. (1987) *Ain't No Makin' It: Leveled Aspirations in a Low Income Neighbourhood*, London: Tavistock.

McRobbie, A. (1991) *Feminism and Youth Culture: From 'Jackie' to 'Just Seventeen'*, London: Macmillan.

Mann, M. (ed.) (1983) *The Macmillan Student Encyclopedia of Sociology*, London: Macmillan.

Mars, L. (1990) 'Coming of age among Jews: Bar Mitzvah and Bat Mitzvah ceremonies', in P. Spencer (ed.) *Anthropology and the Riddle of the Sphinx: Paradoxes of Change in the Life Course*, London: Routledge.

Marshall, G., Rose, D., Newby, H. and Vogler, C. (1988) *Social Class in Modern Britain*, London: Unwin Hyman.

Martin, D.-C. (1995) 'The choices of identity', *Social Identities*, vol 1: 5–20.

Marx, K. (1975) *The Poverty of Philosophy*, Moscow: Progress Publishers.

—— and Engels, F. (1974) *The German Ideology, Part One*, ed. C. J. Arthur, London: Lawrence and Wishart.

Matza, D. (1967) 'The disreputable poor', in R. Bendix and S. M. Lipset (eds) *Class, Status and Power: Social Stratification in Comparitive Perspective*, second edition, London: Routledge and Kegan Paul.

—— (1969) *Becoming Deviant*, Englewood Cliffs, NJ: Prentice Hall.

Mauss, M. (1985) 'A category of the human mind: the notion of person; the notion of self', in M. Carrithers, S. Collins and S. Lukes (eds) *The Category of the Person: Anthropology, Philosophy, History*, Cambridge: Cambridge University Press (first published 1938).

Mayer, A. C. (1966) 'The significance of quasi-groups in the study of complex societies', in M. Banton (ed.) *The Social Anthropology of Complex Societies*, London: Tavistock.

Mead, G. H. (1934) *Mind, Self and Society from the Standpoint of a Social Behaviorist*, ed. C. W. Morris, Chicago, IL: University of Chicago Press.

Mehan, H., Hertweck, A. and Meihls, J. L. (1986) *Handicapping the Handicapped: Decision Making in Students' Educational Careers*, Stanford, CA: Stanford University Press.

Mehler, J. (1994) *What Infants Know: The New Cognitive Science of Development*, Cambridge, MA: Blackwell.

Memmi, A. (1990) *The Colonizer and the Colonized*, London: Earthscan (first published 1957).

Mercer, J. R. (1973) *Labeling the Mentally Retarded: Clinical and Social System Perspectives on Mental Retardation*, Berkeley, CA: University of California Press.

Merton, R. K. (1957) *Social Theory and Social Structure*, second edition, Glencoe, IL: Free Press.

Meyer, P. (1983) *The Child and the State: The Intervention of the State in Family Life*, Cambridge: Cambridge University Press and Paris: Editions de la Maison des Sciences de l'Homme.

Migdal, M. J., Hewstone, M. and Mullen, B. (1998) 'The effects of crossed categorization on intergroup evaluations: a meta analysis', *British Journal of Social Psychology*, vol. 37: 303–24.

Mills, C. W. (1959) *The Sociological Imagination*, New York: Oxford University Press.

Milner, D. (1983) *Children and Race: Ten Years On*, London: Ward Lock.

Moerman, M. (1965) 'Ethnic identification in a complex civilization: who are the Lue?', *American Anthropologist*, vol. 67: 1215–30.

Molnár, V. and Lamont, M. (2002) 'Social categorization and group identification: how African-Americans shape their collective identity through consumption', in A. McMeekin, M. Tomlinson, K. Green and V. Walsh (eds) *Innovation by Demand*, Manchester: Manchester University Press.

Moore, R. I. (1987) *The Formation of a Persecuting Society: Power and Deviance in Western Europe, 950–1250*, Oxford: Basil Blackwell.

Moore, S. F. and Myerhoff, B. G. (eds) (1977) *Secular Ritual*, Assen: van Gorcum.

Morris, B. (1987) *Anthropological Studies of Religion: An Introductory Text*, Cambridge: Cambridge University Press.

—— (1991) *Western Conceptions of the Individual*, New York: Berg.

—— (1994) *Anthropology of the Self: The Individual in Cultural Perspective*, London: Pluto Press.

Müller-Hill, B. (1988) *Murderous Science: Elimination by Scientific Selection of Jews, Gypsies, and Others, Germany 1933–1945*, Oxford: Oxford University Press.

Murphy, R. F. (1990) *The Body Silent*, New York: Norton.

Nadel, S. F. (1951) *The Foundations of Social Anthropology*, London: Cohen and West.

—— (1957) *The Theory of Social Structure*, London: Cohen and West.

Newcomer, P. J. (1972) 'The Nuer are Dinka: an essay on origins and environmental determinism', *Man* (n.s.), vol. 7: 5–11.

Nichols, T. and Beynon, H. (1977) *Living With Capitalism: Class Relations and the Modern Factory*, London: Routledge and Kegan Paul.

Oakes, P. (1996) 'The categorization process: cognition and the group in the social psychology of stereotyping', in W. P. Robinson (ed.) *Social Groups and Identities: Developing the Theory of Henri Tajfel*, London: Butterworth Heinemann.

Offe, C. (1976) *Industry and Inequality*, London: Edward Arnold.

Ong, W. J. (1982) *Orality and Literacy: The Technologizing of the Word*, London: Methuen.

Paine, R. (1974) *Second Thoughts about Barth's Models*, Occasional Paper no. 32, London: Royal Anthropological Institute.

Parker, J. (2000) *Structuration*, Buckingham: Open University Press.

Parsons, T. (1951) *The Social System*, London: Routledge and Kegan Paul.

—— (1963) 'The interpenetration of two levels. Social structure and the development of personality: Freud's contribution to the integration of psychology and sociology', in N. J. Smelser and W. T. Smelser (eds) *Personality and Social Systems*, New York: Wiley.

—— (1968) 'Cooley and the problem of internalisation', in A. J. Reiss (ed.) *Cooley and Sociological Analysis*, Ann Arbor: University of Michigan Press.

Paul, E. F., Miller, F. D., Paul, J. and Ahrens, J. (eds) (1987) *Equal Opportunity*, Oxford: Blackwell.

Pearson, G. (1983) *Hooligan: A History of Respectable Fears*, London: Macmillan.

Peters, E. (1985) *Torture*, Oxford: Basil Blackwell.

Phinney, J. S. and Rotherham, M. J. (eds) (1987) *Children's Ethnic Socialization: Pluralism and Development*, Newbury Park, CA: Sage.

Pickering, M. (2001) *Stereotyping: The Politics of Representation*, Basingstoke: Palgrave.

Plattner, S. (ed.) (1989) *Economic Anthropology*, Stanford, CA: Stanford University Press.

Plummer, K. (1979) 'Misunderstanding labelling perspectives', in D. Downes and P. Rock (eds) *Deviant Interpretations: Problems in Criminological Theory*, London: Martin Robertson.

Polsky, A. J. (1991) *The Rise of the Therapeutic State*, Princeton, NJ: Princeton University Press.

Poole, F. J. P. (1994) 'Socialization, enculturation and the development of personal identity', in T. Ingold (ed.) *Companion Encyclopedia of Anthropology*, London: Routledge.

Potter, J. (1996) *Representing Reality: Discourse, Rhetoric and Social Construction*, London: Sage.

—— and Wetherell, M. (1987) *Discourse and Social Psychology*, London: Sage.

Prottas, J. M. (1979) *People Processing: The Street-Level Bureaucrat in Public Service Bureaucracies*, Lexington, MA: Lexington Books.

Putnam, R. D. (2000) *Bowling Alone: The Collapse and Revival of American Community*, New York: Simon and Schuster.

Raban, J. (1989) *God, Man and Mrs Thatcher: A Critique of Mrs Thatcher's Address to the General Assembly of the Church of Scotland*, London: Chatto and Windus.

Rainwater, L. (1973) *Behind Ghetto Walls: Black Families in a Federal Slum*, Harmondsworth: Pelican.

Ray, L. J. and Reed, M. (eds) (1994) *Organizing Modernity: New Weberian Perspectives on Work, Organization and Society*, London: Routledge.

Richards, A. I. (1956) *Chisungu: A Girl's Initiation Ceremony in Northern Rhodesia*, London: Faber.

Richards, M. P. M. (ed.) (1974) *The Integration of a Child into a Social World*, Cambridge: Cambridge University Press.

Richardson, J. T., Best, J. and Bromley, D. G. (eds) (1991) *The Satanism Scare*, New York: Aldine de Gruyter.

Ritzer, G. (2000) *The McDonaldization of Society: An Investigation into the Changing Character of Contemporary Social Life*, second edition, Thousand Oaks, CA: Pine Forge.

Robinson, W. P. (ed.) (1996) *Social Groups and Identities: Developing the Theory of Henri Tajfel*, London: Butterworth Heinemann.

Rorty, A. (ed.) (1976) *Identities of Persons*, Berkeley, CA: University of California Press.

Rose, N. (1989) *Governing the Soul: The Shaping of the Private Self*, London: Routledge.

Rosenthal, R. and Jacobsen, L. (1968) *Pygmalion in the Classroom*, New York: Holt, Rinehart and Winston.

Rubin, M. and Hewstone, M. (1998) 'Social identity theory's self-esteem hypothesis: a review and some suggestions for clarification', *Personality and Social Psychology Review*, vo. 2: 40–62.

Ryle, G. (1963) *The Concept of Mind*, Harmondsworth: Peregrine (first published 1949).

Sabetti, F. (1984) *Political Authority in a Sicilian Village*, New Brunswick, NJ: Rutgers University Press.

Sahlins, M. (1974) *Stone Age Economics*, London: Tavistock.

Samuel, R. and Thompson, P. (eds) (1990) *The Myths We Live By*, London: Routledge.

Schneider, J. and Schneider, P. (1976) *Culture and Political Economy in Western Sicily*, New York: Academic Press.

Schutz, A. (1967) *The Phenomenology of the Social World*, Evanston: Northwestern University Press (first published 1932).

—— and Luckmann, T. (1973) *The Structures of the Life-World*, Evanston, IL: Northwestern University Press.

Schroeder, R. (1992) *Max Weber and the Sociology of Culture*, London: Sage.

Seidman, S. (1997) *Difference Troubles: Queering Social Theory and Sexual Politics*, Cambridge: Cambridge University Press.

Sennett, R. (1998) *The Corrosion of Character: The Personal Consequences of Work in the New Capitalism*, New York: Norton.

Sherif, M. (1967) *Group Conflict and Co-operation: Their Social Psychology*, London: Routledge and Kegan Paul.

Shoemaker, S. and Swinburne, R. (1984) *Personal Identity*, Oxford: Blackwell.

Shotter, J. (1974) 'The development of personal powers', in M. P. M. Richards (ed.) *The Integration of a Child into a Social World*, Cambridge: Cambridge University Press.

Silverman, D. (1970) *The Theory of Organisations*, London: Heinemann.

—— and Jones, J. (1976) *Organizational Work: The Language of Grading/The Grading of Language*, London: Collier-Macmillan.

Simmel, G. (1950) *The Sociology of Georg Simmel*, ed. K. H. Wolff, New York: Free Press.

Singer, P. (1994) *Rethinking Life and Death: The Collapse of our Traditional Ethics*, Oxford: Oxford University Press.

Skevington, S. and Baker, D. (1989) 'Introduction', in S. Skevington and D. Baker (eds) *The Social Identity of Women*, London: Sage.

Smith, J. (1991) 'Conceiving selves: a case study of changing identities during the transition to motherhood', *Journal of Language and Social Psychology*, vol. 10: 225–43.

—— (1994) 'Reconstructing selves: an analysis of discrepancies between women's contemporaneous accounts and retrospective accounts of the transition to motherhood', *British Journal of Psychology*, vol. 85: 371–92.

Smith, M. G. (1960) *Government in Zazzau 1800–1950*, London: Oxford University Press for the International African Institute.

Solomos, J. (1988) *Black Youth, Racism and the State: The Politics of Ideology and Policy*, Cambridge: Cambridge University Press.

Southall, A. (1976) 'Nuer and Dinka are people: ecology, economy and logical possibility', *Man* (n.s.), vol. 11: 463–91.

Sperber, D. (1975) *Rethinking Symbolism*, Cambridge: Cambridge University Press.

Stein, M. R. (1960) *The Eclipse of Community: An Interpretation of American Studies*, Princeton, NJ: Princeton University Press.

Stewart, A., Prandy. K. and Blackburn, R. M. (1980), *Social Stratification and Occupations*, London: Macmillan.

Still, A. and Good, J. M. M. (1991), 'Mutualism in the human sciences: towards the implementation of a theory', *Journal for the Theory of Social Behaviour*, vol. 22: 105–28.

Sundar, N. (2000) 'Caste as census category: implications for sociology', *Current Sociology*, vol. 84, no. 3: 111–26.

Tajfel, H. (1970) 'Experiments in intergroup discrimination', *Scientific American*, no. 223: 96–102.

—— (ed.) (1978) *Differentiation Between Social Groups: Studies in the Social Psychology of Intergroup Relations*, London: Academic Press.

—— (1981a) *Human Groups and Social Categories*, Cambridge: Cambridge University Press.

—— (1981b) 'Social stereotypes and social groups', in J. C. Turner and H. Giles (eds) *Intergroup Behaviour*, Oxford: Blackwell.

—— (ed.) (1982) *Social Identity and Intergroup Relations*, Cambridge: Cambridge University Press and Paris: Editions de la Maison des Sciences de l'Homme.

—— and Turner, J. C. (1979) 'An integrative theory of intergroup conflict', in W. G. Austin and S. Worchel (eds) *The Social Psychology of Intergroup Relations*, Monterey: Brooks Cole.

—— Flament, C., Billig, M. G. and Bundy, R. P. (1971) 'Social categorization and intergroup behaviour', *European Journal of Social Psychology*, vol. 5: 245–53.

Tannenbaum, F. (1938) *Crime and Community*, New York: Columbia University Press.

Taylor, D. (1998) 'Identity and social policy: engagements with postmodern theory', *Journal of Social Policy*, vol. 27: 329–50.

Taylor, I., Walton, P. and Young, J. (1973) *The New Criminology: For a Social Theory of Deviance*, London: Routledge and Kegan Paul.

Thompson, J. B. (1982) 'Universal pragmatics', in J. B. Thompson and D. Held (eds) *Habermas: Critical Debates*, London: Macmillan.

Thompson, K. (1998) *Moral Panics*, London: Routledge.

Trevarthen, C. (1987) 'Infancy, mind in', in R. L. Gregory (ed.) *The Oxford Companion to the Mind*, Oxford: Oxford University Press.

Troyna, B. and Hatcher, R. (1992) *Racism in Children's Lives: A Study of Mainly-White Primary Schools*, London: Routledge.

Trent, J. W. (1994) *Inventing the Feeble Mind: A History of Mental Retardation in the United States*, Berkeley, CA: University of California Press.

Turk, A. (1969) *Criminality and the Legal Order*, Chicago, IL: Rand-MacNally.

Turner, B. S. (1988) *Status*, Milton Keynes: Open University Press.

Turner, J. C. (1985) 'Social categorization and the self-concept: a social cognitive theory of group behaviour', *Advances in Group Processes: Theory and Research*, vol. 2: 77–122.

—— (1996) 'Henri Tajfel: an introduction', in W. P. Robinson (ed.) *Social Groups and Identities: Developing the Theory of Henri Tajfel*, London: Butterworth Heinemann.

—— and Bourhis, R. Y. (1996) 'Social identity, interdependence and the social group: a reply to Rabbie et al.', in W. P. Robinson (ed.) *Social Groups and Identities: Developing the Theory of Henri Tajfel*, London: Butterworth Heinemann.

—— Hogg, M. A., Oakes, P. J., Reicher, S. D. and Wetherall, M. S. (1987)

Rediscovering the Social Group: A Self Categorization Theory, Oxford: Blackwell.

Turner, V. W. (1967) *The Forest of Symbols*, Ithaca, NY: Cornell University Press.

—— (1974) *The Ritual Process: Structure and Anti-Structure*, Harmondsworth: Pelican.

van Ausdale, D. and Feagin, J. R. (2001) *The First R: How Children Learn Race and Racism*, New York: Rowman and Littlefield.

van Gennep, A. (1965) *The Rites of Passage*, London: Routledge and Kegan Paul (first published 1908).

Vogler, C. (2000) 'Social identity and emotion: the meeting of psychoanalysis and sociology', *Sociological Review*, vol. 48: 19–42.

Wallace, A. F. C. (1970) *Culture and Personality*, second edition, New York: Random House.

Wallman, S. (1986) 'Ethnicity and the boundary process in context', in J. Rex and D. Mason (eds) *Theories of Race and Ethnic Relations*, Cambridge: Cambridge University Press.

Watney, S. (1988) 'AIDS, "moral panic" theory and homophobia', in P. Aggleton and H. Homans (eds) *Social Aspects of AIDS*, Brighton: Falmer.

Weber, E. (1976) *Peasants into Frenchmen:The Modernisation of Rural France, 1870–1914*, Stanford, CA: Stanford University Press.

Weber, M. (1949) *The Methodology of the Social Sciences*, eds. E. A. Shils and H. A. Finch, New York: Free Press.

—— (1976) *The Protestant Ethic and the Spirit of Capitalism*, London: George Allen and Unwin.

—— (1978) *Economy and Society: An Outline of Interpretive Sociology*, eds. G. Roth and C. Wittich, Berkeley, CA: University of California Press.

Wellman, B. (ed.) (1999) *Networks in the Global Village: Life in Contemporary Communities*, Boulder, CO: Westview Press.

Wenger, E. (1998) *Communities of Practice: Learning, Meaning, Identity*, Cambridge: Cambridge University Press.

Wetherell, M. (1996) 'Constructing social identities: the individual/social binary in Henri Tajfel's social psychology', in W. P. Robinson (ed.) *Social Groups and Identities: Developing the Theory of Henri Tajfel*, London: Butterworth Heinemann.

Whimster, S. and Lash, S. (eds) (1987) *Max Weber, Rationality and Modernity*, London: George Allen and Unwin.

Wikan, U. (1977) 'Man becomes woman: transsexualism in Oman as a key to gender roles', *Man* (n.s.), vol. 12: 304–19.

Wilk, R. R. (1993) 'Beauty and the feast: official and visceral nationalism in Belize', *Ethnos*, vol. 58: 294–316.

Williams, R. (2000) *Making Identity Matter: Identity, Society and Social Interaction*, Durham: sociologypress.

Williamson, L. (1978) 'Infanticide: an anthropological analysis', in M. Kohl (ed.) *Infanticide and the Value of Life*, Buffalo, NY: Prometheus.

Winnicott, D. W. (1965) *The Maturational Processes and the Facilitating Environment: Studies in the Theory of Emotional Development*, London: Hogarth Press

Wisdom, J. (1952) *Other Minds*, Oxford: Basil Blackwell.

Wittgenstein, L. (1974) *On Certainty-Über Gewissheit*, ed. G. E. M. Anscombe, Oxford: Basil Blackwell.

Wollheim, R. (1984) *The Thread of Life*, Cambridge: Cambridge University Press.

Woodward, K. (1997) 'Introduction', in K. Woodward (ed.) *Identity and Difference*, London: Sage.

Worchel, S., Morales, J. F., Páez, D. and Deschamps, J.-C. (eds) (1998) *Social Identity: International Perspectives*, London: Sage.

Wright, E. O. (1985) *Classes*, London: Verso.

—— (ed.) (1989) *The Debate on Classes*, London: Verso.

Wrong, D. H. (1961) 'The oversocialized conception of man', *American Sociological Review*, vol. 26: 184–93.

Zerubavel, E. (1997) *Social Mindscapes*, Cambridge, MA: Harvard University Press.

INDEX

eBooks – at www.eBookstore.tandf.co.uk

A library at your fingertips!

eBooks are electronic versions of printed books. You can store them on your PC/laptop or browse them online.

They have advantages for anyone needing rapid access to a wide variety of published, copyright information.

eBooks can help your research by enabling you to bookmark chapters, annotate text and use instant searches to find specific words or phrases. Several eBook files would fit on even a small laptop or PDA.

NEW: Save money by eSubscribing: cheap, online access to any eBook for as long as you need it.

Annual subscription packages

We now offer special low-cost bulk subscriptions to packages of eBooks in certain subject areas. These are available to libraries or to individuals.

For more information please contact webmaster.ebooks@tandf.co.uk

We're continually developing the eBook concept, so keep up to date by visiting the website.

www.eBookstore.tandf.co.uk